TOUGH TIMES FOR THE PRESIDENT

TOUGH TIMES FOR THE PRESIDENT

Political Adversity and the Sources of Presidential Power

Ryan J. Barilleaux and Jewerl Maxwell

Politics, Institutions, and Public Policy in America series
Series editors: Scott A. Frisch and Sean Q Kelly

CAMBRIA
PRESS

Amherst, New York

Requests for permission should be directed to:
permissions@cambriapress.com, or mailed to:
Cambria Press
University Corporate Center, 100 Corporate Parkway, Suite 128
Amherst, NY 14226

Library of Congress Cataloging-in-Publication Data

Barilleaux, Ryan J.
Tough times for the president : political adversity and the sources
of presidential power / Ryan J. Barilleaux & Jewerl Maxwell.
p. cm.
Includes bibliographical references and index
ISBN 978-1-60497-817-9 (alk. paper)
1. Presidents—United States--History. I. Maxwell, Jewerl. II. Title.

JF255.B375 2012
352.23'50973—dc23

2012032871

For Betsy Burger, Cheryl Chafin, and Opal Crist
in gratitude and friendship—RJB

To my daughter Makayla
A Gift from Above (James 1:17)—JM

TABLE OF CONTENTS

List of Figures

LIST OF TABLES

ACKNOWLEDGMENTS

An author owes many debts, and I hope to acknowledge those who assisted with this project. In addition to my coauthor, who has made this collaboration an easy one, I want to thank a number of people who have given me help in ways both big and small.

This book grew from a conference paper that I wrote along with my coauthor and Marc Bacharach. Their enthusiasm for the project stimulated my own interest even when other responsibilities got in the way. Marc has left the academic life for service in the federal government; our loss is the nation's gain.

Many colleagues and friends have helped by answering questions, making suggestions, responding to ideas, and making it possible for me to concentrate on this project. These good people include Steven DeLue, Christopher Kelley, Melanie Marlowe, Brett Pendleton, Gary Gregg, and students in my class on the American presidency at Miami University.

Thanks go as well to several scholars who commented on various stages of this project, from discussants at professional meetings to the anonymous reviewers for Cambria Press. Their comments have helped us to improve this work considerably; any flaws that remain in it are our own.

Thanks also Sean Kelly and Scott Frisch, the series editors for Cambria's series on *Politics, Institutions, and Public Policy in America*. They enthusiastically supported the project. Toni Tan, Michelle Wright, and the rest of the incredible staff of Cambria Press have made the publication process—from our original contact to the finished book—pleasant and productive. We are very impressed with their professional skill and assistance.

I also want to thank my family, especially my wife, Marilyn. She has put up with this and other projects that have distracted me from other responsibilities. Her support over thirty-one years has been vital to anything I have been able to accomplish.

I have dedicated this book to three colleagues who have made my professional life successful. Over the time that I worked on this project, I leaned heavily on Betsy Burger, Cheryl Chafin, and Opal Crist—administrative professionals in my department—to make it possible to focus on research and writing. I owe them much, and the dedication is a tribute to their professionalism and good humor.

This book received generous assistance from the Paul Rejai Professorship of Political Science. I am grateful to my late colleague Dr. Paul Rejai for establishing this endowment and his generosity and foresight in supporting high-quality scholarship and teaching in political science.

—Ryan J. Barilleaux

Because this is my first academic publication, there are many people I would like to recognize and honestly not enough space to give credit where credit is due. To me, this project is really a culmination of people and events that have significantly influenced me over the years. It began of course with my parents, Gary and Sharon Maxwell. Their support, guidance, continual desire to see me grow spiritually, mentally, physically, and emotionally—and most importantly, their sacrificial love—helped mold me into the individual I am today. I will never be able to repay them for all that they have done and continue to do in my life.

I was also blessed to have several wonderful teachers growing up, but two were particularly important for my development; Gary Anderson and Geoffrey Kovacik. Mr. Anderson was my seventh-grade American history teacher. Mr. Anderson made the subject matter come alive. But it was more than his entertaining and informative classes that meant so much to me; it was his professional example that later made me decide that I too wanted to pursue a career in education. Mr. Kovacik was my eleventh-grade AP American history teacher. Simply put, Mr. Kovacik expected excellence from his students. As a result, I had to work harder in his course than I did in many of my undergraduate courses. In many ways, his course made my transition to college much smoother than that of many of my colleagues.

After graduating from high school, I attended Muskingum University. Once again there are many people to acknowledge from my four years there, but with limited space, I would like to recognize Brian King, Walter Huber, and Anne Steele. Dr. King was my advisor and mentor. It was also in one of his lectures during my sophomore year that for the first time I heard that graduate schools offered assistantships. I had envisioned myself as a high school teacher who would one day go back to school when I could afford it and become a college professor later in life. After class I immediately went to Dr. King's office, where he explained the graduate school process, and from that day forward I was determined to enroll in graduate school immediately after graduating from Muskingum, so that I could begin my career as a professor as soon as possible. Dr. Huber was particularly influential because of his leadership within the political science department, and it was Dr. Huber who encouraged me to consider attending Miami University. I will forever be grateful for that advice. Lastly, Dr. Steele, the college president, encouraged all students to become leaders; but more influential than her encouragement was her willingness to follow through and make this happen.

At Miami, in addition to my coauthor, there are four individuals who deserve special recognition: John Rothgeb, Phil Russo, Gus Jones, and Betsy Burger. Shortly before I arrived, Dr. Rothgeb established a unique graduate program that successfully allowed me and many of my colleagues to immediately enter into academia upon our completion of the program. Words cannot explain my appreciation for his leadership. Dr. Russo demanded professional growth in students. Had I not taken his course my first semester at Miami, I would not have been as successful in my time there. Dr. Jones took a special interest in me as a graduate student and allowed me to coauthor two conference papers with him. Finally, Betsy Burger was the graduate secretary. She was always a personal encouragement to me, and she made sure the program ran smoothly. In addition, she played a vital role in my job searches.

Professionally, six people stand out. Christopher Qualls and Joseph Lane of Emory & Henry College gave me my first opportunity in higher education when they allowed me to fill a visiting position while I was still completing my dissertation. Dr. Lane really became a mentor to me, and I could not have asked for a better colleague during my first year of teaching. Likewise, Robert Wells of Thiel College provided me with an additional opportunity to continue to grow as a young teacher. Finally, there are an inordinate number of individuals whom I could thank at Cedarville University, but I will limit it to David Rich, Steve Winteregg, and Tom Mach. Dr. Rich and Dr. Winteregg played integral roles in the hiring process and provided me with an opportunity to teach at *the* university at which I had hoped to establish a career. Since being here, Dr. Mach has served as a mentor, friend, and leader in the department and provided much-needed encouragement throughout the research process.

Lastly, I will forever be indebted to my coauthor, Ryan Barilleaux. He was one of the top reasons why Dr. Huber encouraged me to attend Miami University for graduate studies. I knew I wanted to study the presidency, and Dr. Huber recognized Dr. Barilleaux as a special teacher/scholar in this field. To me, Dr. Barilleaux exemplifies what it means to be a teacher/scholar. His classes are engaging, challenging, and rewarding. But more than that, he takes a personal interest in his students. For me, this became especially important when, in my third year in the program, he invited me to work on a conference paper with him and another student on the topic of "presidential adversity." That was the birth of this current project. And when I left Miami, even though he continued for a time in his role as department chair, continued to chair several dissertation committees, and continued his pursuit of other research avenues, he never gave up on this research project. As a young scholar, I cannot thank him enough for allowing me to be a part of this venture.

—Jewerl Maxwell

TOUGH TIMES FOR THE PRESIDENT

CHAPTER 1

PRESIDENTS IN TOUGH TIMES

As Barack Obama celebrated the second anniversary of his election as president, he faced a political situation that called into question what he had done for the past two years and his political future. His job approval ratings—which had been nearly 66% shortly after he took office early in 2009—hovered near or below 50% throughout 2010, with a correspondingly high disapproval rating. On the day of the congressional midterm elections (November 2, 2010), the Gallup survey reported that a higher percentage of respondents (49%) disapproved of his performance as president than approved of it (44%).[1] In the 2010 congressional midterm elections, voters across the nation elected Republican candidates, giving the opposition party a sizable majority in the House (242 Republicans to 193 Democrats) and narrowing the Democrats' majority in the Senate (53 Democrats to 47 Republicans). Independent voters, who had been so important to Obama's victory in 2008, had abandoned the president and Democratic candidates. Political observers and party officials were speculating about whether the president could win reelection in 2012. Unemployment remained high, the economy was still weak, and the president's conduct of the wars in Iraq and Afghanistan seemed to satisfy neither his antiwar base nor his conservative critics. The euphoria of Election Night

2008 was gone; 2010 was, in the words of elections scholar James Ceaser, "the great repudiation" of Barack Obama.[2]

The president's political situation following the 2010 midterm elections may have been a disappointment for him and his supporters, but it is not so unusual for American presidents. Even a cursory glance at the history of the office in modern times reveals that presidents rarely enjoy the sort of strong support and solid political foundation that Americans associate with "heroic" presidents. As the historical record demonstrates, even the "heroic" presidents of the twentieth century—such as FDR and Reagan —encountered difficulties along the way. Roosevelt encountered setbacks and a low period after the 1938 midterm congressional elections, when Southern Democrats overcame the president's attempts to purge them from the party and went on to forge a coalition with Republicans and block further domestic policy changes. Reagan encountered pressure in 1982 and 1983 as a recession drove up the unemployment rate and Republicans lost twenty-six seats in the House in the 1982 midterms, then another low period when the Iran-Contra affair (1987–1988) rocked his administration. All presidents encounter difficulties along the way, although some suffer from more setbacks or adverse situations than others.

Nevertheless, the way Americans think about the presidency tends to focus on great expectations of what presidents can accomplish, not the more workaday political challenges that most presidents face. As a number of scholars have pointed out, the public tends to have high expectations of what the chief executive can achieve, but even expert observers continue to direct their attention to presidential "greatness,"[3] "heroic" presidents,[4] and various interpretations of presidential leadership.[5] Observers pay much less attention to those situations in which presidents encounter political adversity that make all efforts at governing difficult, even if any person occupying the Oval Office is more likely to experience tough times rather than grand achievements.

What difficulties do presidents face? How do episodes of presidential adversity reveal aspects of the office not seen when times are good? How do presidents respond to such situations, and how can adversity both limit incumbents and stimulate them to be innovative in their actions? This book will explore presidents in "tough times," a situation that is all too familiar to the White House but that has been generally overlooked by students of the presidency fascinated with heroic presidents and strong leadership in the White House. Examining cases of tough times for the president can broaden our understanding of presidential power as well as both the limits and opportunities chief executives face as they govern from the Oval Office.

THE BEST OF TIMES, THE WORST OF TIMES

The focus on presidential leadership and greatness has had significant consequences for the chief executive and the way Americans understand the presidency. It has led to unrealistic expectations of what presidents can achieve and has contributed (at least in part) to what Gene Healy called the "cult of the presidency"[6] (i.e., support for sweeping presidential power and a tendency to regard the chief executive as having unlimited responsibility—and power—for delivering national well-being). Another consequence has been to make times of political adversity—tough times for the president—appear unusual or even prima facie evidence of failure. History shows, however, that adversity is certainly not unusual.

All presidents experience stressful situations. Even in times of apparent tranquility, presidents have faced difficulties. The Eisenhower era, remembered as one of prosperity and somnolence, was also a period of Cold War confrontations that conjured up images of nuclear holocaust. The Coolidge years were not only the "Roaring Twenties" but also a time of agricultural problems, organized crime (spurring the creation of Eliot Ness's elite band the "Untouchables"), and international instability (which would lead to the rise of fascism and Nazism). Even James Monroe's "Era of Good Feelings" was marked by disputes over the extension of slavery (leading to the Missouri Compromise) and European designs on the Western Hemisphere (which resulted in proclamation of the Monroe Doctrine). Each president has experienced difficulties, although some have certainly faced more than others.

Difficult problems are challenging but not necessarily crippling. Backed by strong support, the chief executive can take on great threats: Franklin Roosevelt enjoyed strong support in Congress and the nation as World War II loomed, thus giving him much freedom of action; Dwight Eisenhower faced the Soviet Union with high public approval ratings and a bipartisan consensus on foreign policy; and even John Kennedy faced the Cuban Missile Crisis with congressional and public deference to presidential leadership in nuclear politics.

Presidents who govern from a position of political strength, as was the case in the examples just cited, have a much easier time living up to the great expectations that Americans have of their chief executives. Figure 1 summarizes the key factors that make up ideal political circumstances for the president. First, the president has come to office with an electoral victory sufficient to claim a "mandate" to implement policy changes.[7] The president's party controls both houses of Congress, so the executive's priorities are reflected on Capitol Hill. The president enjoys high public approval ratings, and no scandal looms to weaken the chief's reputation. Under such circumstances, conditions are favorable for presidential leadership (although students of American politics know that the multiple "veto points" in our system make sweeping policy changes difficult to achieve even under the best conditions).

Presidents do not always govern under such favorable conditions. They are often forced to govern under adverse circumstances rather than ideal ones. The president may have come to office by succession, with a plurality of popular votes, or even (as did George W. Bush in 2001) with a minority of popular votes.

Figure 1. Ideal Circumstances for Presidential Governance

- Electoral victory sufficient to claim a "mandate" to govern
- Unified government—the president's party controls both houses of Congress
- High public approval ratings for president
- The president's reputation is undamaged by scandal

If the president's party is in the minority in both chambers of Congress, divided government makes it harder for the chief executive to prevail on Capitol Hill. Low public approval ratings and/or scandal also undercut support for the president, whereas sharp divisions over policy (e.g., division over the Vietnam War) can sap much of the president's political support. *Political adversity* refers to circumstances that present the president with the fewest opportunities for persuasive influence; they are situations in which presidents lack what are considered the normal building blocks of political power (see figure 2).

Figure 2. Adverse Circumstances for the President

- Absent or weak electoral mandate—successor and minority presidents, as well as presidents with very narrow margins of victory
- Divided government, especially "unmandates" (when President's party loses control of one or both houses of Congress in an election)
- Low public approval ratings
- Scandal/impeachment
- Sharp divisions in the nation over significant policy issue(s) on president's agenda

Consider these situations in which chief executives faced conditions of political adversity:

- Harry Truman, after Democrats lost control of Congress in the 1946 elections;
- Lyndon Johnson, as the Vietnam War divided the nation and damaged his career;
- Richard Nixon, whose landslide reelection in 1972 turned to ashes over the next two years as the Watergate scandal loomed ever larger;
- Gerald Ford, who lacked any kind of electoral base and whose September 1974 pardon of Nixon robbed him of popular support;
- Jimmy Carter, whose presidency appeared paralyzed in the face of national and international problems;
- Ronald Reagan, as the Iran-Contra affair (1987–1988) threatened his presidency;
- Bill Clinton, at two points: after his party lost its forty-year majorities in Congress in 1994 and when the Monica Lewinsky scandal led to his impeachment (1998–1999);
- George W. Bush, after setbacks and problems in his second term cost Republicans their congressional majorities in 2006 and the president's unpopularity grew.

Even under such trying circumstances, several presidents have lived to fight another day—they have even been able to recover their political fortunes in ways that are fairly dramatic. Despite the setbacks he faced in the 1946 election and its aftermath, Harry Truman worked his way back to victory in the 1948 election (which everyone but Truman himself expected him to lose). Even in the face of the Iran-Contra affair, Ronald Reagan was able to salvage his presidency. Bill Clinton, despite being assigned much of the blame for the 1994 defeat of congressional Democrats and facing a highly motivated Republican majority in Congress, managed to revive his political fortunes, break the momentum of Newt Gingrich's "Contract with America," and win reelection in 1996.

Despite facing significant political disadvantages, presidents have been able to succeed. While not all presidents who have encountered adversity have been able to overcome it, the record shows that some have done so.

What is to account for this fact? The answer, we contend, lies in moving away from the prevailing understanding of presidential power—as influence obtained through the "power to persuade"—and examining unilateral strategies that presidents have employed to shape policy and revive their political fortunes.

EXPLORING THE NATURE AND SOURCES OF PRESIDENTIAL POWER

In the single most influential book written on the American presidency, *Presidential Power*, Richard Neustadt declared, "Presidential power is the power to persuade."[8] Neustadt saw the institutional power of the presidency as weak, characterizing the office as a "clerkship," but tended to see the personal power of the incumbent as strong. That personal power rested on bargaining and persuasion, which presuppose a combination of political skills and political capital necessary for the president to be compelling in bringing other political actors to see things as the White House sees them. Neustadt disdained unilateral assertions of presidential power—such as Truman's firing of General Douglas MacArthur in 1952, Eisenhower's dispatch of federal troops to Little Rock, Arkansas, in 1957 to enforce desegregation of public schools, and Truman's 1951 seizure of the steel mills because he thought a strike by steelworkers threatened the credibility of America's commitment in the Korean War—because these cases of "command" were signs of failure at persuasion and were ultimately self-defeating exercises.

Neustadt's characterization of presidential power highlights the fact that presidents do not exercise these powers in a vacuum. It is not enough to say that the chief executive has the power to veto, to command the armed forces, to propose legislation, or to direct the executive branch. What also matters is how those powers are used and how that use affects the goals and political standing of the nation's highest officer. Neustadt wisely taught that presidential power is embedded in a political context, but more problematic is his claim that this power is no more or less than the "power to persuade."

Is Presidential Power Only the "Power to Persuade"?

An elaborate body of literature on the presidency has grown up since Neustadt's book appeared in 1960, and there has also been significant attention by scholars to the book itself.[9] Now that *Presidential Power* is fifty years old, a range of admirers and critics have focused their attention on the book's central claim—that the presidency is a weak office and that its power is but the "power to persuade"—as well as on Neustadt's evidence and other aspects of his argument. The analysis of *Presidential Power* has been challenged on a variety of fronts—it is overstated, it is time-bound to the late 1950s, it focuses too much on personal power, it is Machiavellian in its outlook—but certain problems in Neustadt's presentation are most relevant to our consideration of presidents acting in adverse circumstances.

Most fundamentally, power as persuasion leaves us unable to explain how presidents operate in those tough times that many chief executives have had to confront—and which several have managed to overcome. If presidential power *is* nothing more or less than bargaining and persuasion, then how can that view account for presidents reviving their fortunes in the face of political adversity? How can it account for the fact that presidents have engaged in actions other than persuasion to shape policy and have been effective and successful in doing so? Consider, for example, Franklin Roosevelt (who used the veto extensively, issued many executive orders, and undertook other unilateral actions), the "hero" of Neustadt's book because of his success at persuasion. If Neustadt's idea of presidential power as coterminous with persuasion offers little help for understanding the complete record of presidential action, then his analysis is a problematic one. Indeed, we can identify four problems inherent in Neustadt's definition of presidential power as only the "power to persuade."

First, the "Power to Persuade" Is Overstated

Neustadt assumed, rather than demonstrated, that any use of what he called "command" is a sign of the president's failure and so politically costly as to be essentially self-defeating. But is that really the case? Consider the three "cases of command" that he used to demonstrate his thesis: Truman's firing of General Douglas MacArthur, Eisenhower's 1957 use of federal troops to carry out racial integration at Little Rock Central High School, and Truman's 1949 seizure of the steel mills. Not only did he mischaracterize these actions as "self-executing" (a peculiar designation, given that at least two of these cases required action beyond just the announcement of a presidential decision), but underlying each case study is the assumption that persuasion was a better option and that it would have worked.

Neustadt's account of Truman's dismissal of MacArthur is particularly problematic. His discussion of the case tends to emphasize that the general could and should have been fired sooner.[10] How would that have been persuasion? Why would firing the general a year earlier have been any less public or messy? Truman, like Lincoln with General McClellan, endured bad behavior from a senior military officer because that commander had a reputation for success (and, in MacArthur's case, some record of success). Given MacArthur's personality, there is no good evidence that any amount of persuasive effort would have changed his mind or that earlier dismissal would have been less politically costly to Truman. But dismissing MacArthur sent a message to all military personnel—even beyond Truman's day—about the power of the commander in chief and the control of the military by civilian authorities.

Consider now Eisenhower's dispatch of federal troops to Little Rock. Neustadt asserted that taking this action was costly to Eisenhower,[11] but he implied rather than demonstrated what that cost was. Nor did he show that Governor Orville Faubus of Arkansas was open to persuasion on the question of ending segregation. Given the subsequent violence that was employed by segregationists trying to stop implementation of desegregation court orders over the next decade, it is not clear how Eisenhower's action failed. Indeed, David A. Nichols argued persuasively that Eisenhower was resolute in dealing with the incident at Little Rock and that his dispatch of federal troops was a careful and constructive use of presidential power that was "smoothly executed" and contributed to the end of segregation in the South.[12] It made clear that the White House would be on the side of enforcing Supreme Court decisions. Had Eisenhower allowed Faubus to halt integration at the schoolhouse door, what good would that have done?

Finally, there is the case of Truman's seizure of the steel mills. This is the only one of the three cases in which Neustadt's argument that the president's action was mistaken and a failure holds up without alternative interpretations. Perhaps Truman did overreact to the steel strike, and seizing the steel mills did him little good. But one case—or even three—does not establish that presidential power is only the power to persuade. Neustadt proceeded from an assumption and read his evidence to support the assumption he had already made.

Second, Defining Presidential Power Only as Persuasion Is Self-Contradictory

Neustadt prescribed presidential influence by making reference to the "vantage points" that the president possesses. He implied the precise nature of these vantage points, but they consist of three key elements: formal constitutional and legal powers of the president, presidential prestige (public approval), and the president's professional reputation (among the political elites in Washington). The constitutional and legal powers of the president are precisely the sorts of "command" measures that Neustadt criticized: the veto, executive orders, military and emergency powers of the commander in chief, and so on. One might interpret Neustadt to say that some of these powers (such as the veto) can be used as instruments of persuasion when they remain as a threat rather than being explicitly used, but it is the willingness to actually use formal presidential powers when needed that makes them formidable.

Decisive uses of executive power have aided presidents in developing the professional reputation that Neustadt saw as important to a president's persuasiveness in Washington. Ronald Reagan's 1981 firing of striking air traffic controllers made his later threats to use presidential power more compelling. Clinton's willingness to shut down the government in 1995, when he and the 104th Congress reached an impasse over the budget, aided him in subsequent negotiations over spending priorities. In contrast, consider George W. Bush and the veto: Bush did not veto any bills until 2006, well into his second term. Although he did issue veto threats (141 up to that time, according to the White House[13]), the fact that he did not actually veto any legislation was taken by many observers as a sign of weakness in a president so willing to assert executive power.[14] Constitutional and legal powers, which are a key element of Neustadt's "vantage points," can be used skillfully to enhance the president's reputation rather than undercut executive influence. The professional reputation that Neustadt commended is enhanced by skillful use of the "command" powers that he claimed are self-defeating.

Third, the Reasoning Behind Power-as-Persuasion Is Faulty

At the outset of *Presidential Power*, Neustadt had already decided that "command" does not work and set out to prove that claim. His reading of three specific cases appears on the surface to be an exercise in generalizing the lessons of those cases, but his account of the cases is shaped by the conclusion he had already drawn. Therefore, all of his argument hangs on the validity of his premise, which is also his conclusion, thus making Neustadt's reasoning largely circular in nature. He told interesting stories and in the process succeeded in offering useful insights about the subtleties of power, but he did not construct an effective case for his argument.

Fourth, It Is Misleading to Claim that Power Is Only Persuasion

As Raymond Tatalovich and Thomas Engeman have pointed out, Neustadt's focus on bargaining and persuasion has resulted in "the nearly complete disregard of prerogative power in presidential scholarship."[15]

The influence of *Presidential Power* has been to teach several generations of scholars, journalists, citizens, White House staffers, and politicians[16] that the president needs "to be as big a man as he can"[17] and that this is to be accomplished through bargaining and persuasion. What matters are not formal powers of the president, but influence and personal power.

Certainly, some scholars, including Richard Pious,[18] Louis Fisher,[19] William Howell,[20] Kenneth Mayer,[21] and Robert Spitzer,[22] have examined aspects of presidential prerogative power, but they have tended to assume a context of broad political influence by the president. The historical record demonstrates that presidents have employed their unilateral powers (whether those explicitly granted in the Constitution or prerogative powers that reach beyond specific constitutional grants) to take action, to shape policy and events, and even to restore their political fortunes. Neustadt's definition of power as influence through persuasion helps one to understand some aspects of presidential power but far too little of it. Furthermore, it cannot really help to understand those incidents when presidents have managed to govern—and even to prevail (in a political sense)—when they have lost most of the political capital needed to be influential. These facts suggest that students of the presidency need a better understanding of unilateral presidential power and the role it plays in the work of the chief executive.

Presidential Unilateralism

Despite Neustadt's dictum that "[p]residential power is the power to persuade," all presidents rely on a mixture of persuasion and command in their conduct of office. Even Franklin Roosevelt, one of the nation's most persuasive chief executives, wielded unilateral power from the Oval Office. He employed the veto power extensively and was second only to Grover Cleveland in using the power to say "no."[23] He also issued more executive orders than any other president, including 286 orders related to World War II issued between July 1939 and June 1942.[24] As Peter Sperlich observed,[25] no president can operate on bargaining alone.

Over the decades of American history, presidents have employed several means for exercising unilateral power.[26] The veto is the most famous of these means. But others also exist, including the removal power, the power to make unilateral appointments to certain offices, the recognition power, pardon and clemency powers, and an array of military powers. Presidents make a variety of substantive decisions and issue executive orders, directives, proclamations, and—with growing frequency—signing statements.[27] To stifle attempts—usually from Congress—to inhibit unilateral or other executive actions, presidents also invoke executive privilege to withhold information[28] and usually meet with success. Indeed, the use of prerogative power has been a characteristic feature of the postmodern presidency (the period from Ronald Reagan forward),[29] and presidential unilateralism flows from several sources.

First, unilateralism is based in the president's constitutional roles: chief executive, commander in chief, chief diplomat, chief of state, and so on. These roles vest the president with some explicit powers and imply others, and incumbents from Washington through George W. Bush have often read those implications in favor of broader executive authority.

An important aspect of unilateralism is the president's powers and responsibilities in foreign affairs. Article II of the U.S. Constitution vests the president with the power to nominate ambassadors, recognize and communicate with foreign governments, and negotiate treaties, as well as to be commander in chief of the armed forces. Presidents have drawn on this foundation to expand those to include the power to conclude executive agreements, to exert broad control over the military (including deployment into combat without explicit congressional authorization), and to exercise sweeping powers in the name of national security.

Second, unilateralism is extended by "venture constitutionalism." When presidents find themselves caught between their need to take action, shape policy, or undertake other measures for which there is not a settled understanding of presidential power, they often engage in behavior that can be characterized as *venture constitutionalism*: actions that stretch the bounds of the chief executive's constitutional authority in order to promote national security, protect the institutional interests of the presidency, or enhance the president's ability to influence policy.[30] Over time, presidential power has been expanded through the accretion of precedents set by chief executives acting in this fashion, the cumulative effect of which is to constitute a kind of "common law" of presidential conduct. This "common law" includes unilateral actions that were acquiesced to by Congress, the courts, and/or the public. Examples of venture constitutionalism include Washington's Neutrality Proclamation, the Louisiana Purchase, Lincoln's conduct of the Civil War, Nixon's invasion of Cambodia, the creation and execution of regulatory review by the Office of Management and Budget, the internment of Japanese Americans during World War II, Clinton's proclamation setting aside millions of acres of wilderness as federally protected land, the creation of military tribunals to try suspects captured in the war on terror, the Bush administration's warrantless wiretap surveillance program, and the Obama administration's expansive interpretations of the "state secrets" privilege. Venture constitutionalism is what happens when the chief executive seeks to live up to the responsibilities of the highest office but encounters the constraints on executive power imposed by the American political system. (We will have more to say about venture constitutionalism and its role in the expansion of presidential power in chapter 6.)

Third, presidents resort to unilateralism when they believe that bargaining and persuasion will take too long or are likely to fail. This determination may come from the nature of the situation, the political environment, or the president's political resources. Bill Clinton could have asked Congress to set aside the Grand Staircase–Escalante National Monument, additional parts of the Florida Everglades, and Idaho's Craters of the Moon National Monument for special protection, but he did not expect the Republican-controlled legislature to accede to his request. So he acted unilaterally in 2000, believing his action to be vital to protecting these lands. Likewise, Jefferson thought it vital to the nation's interest to secure the Louisiana Territory (if only for Mardi Gras) and so overcame objections (including his own) about the constitutionality of the purchase. Several presidents, including Reagan, Clinton, both Bushes, and Obama, resorted to signing statements to shape the implementation or enforcement of laws passed by Congress, convinced in each case that his responsibility to "take care that the laws be faithfully executed" included the power to interpret the laws in the process of their execution.

Fourth, presidents employ public politics as a form of unilateralism. Faced with resistance from Congress or other elements of the political system, presidents have employed direct appeals for public support as a means of pressuring the legislature, the bureaucracy, or others to comply with the president's wishes.[31] The classic version of public politics is the nationwide televised address from the Oval Office in which the president calls on Americans to "tell your senators and representatives by phone, wire, and Mailgram that the future hangs in the balance" (as Ronald Reagan said in 1981 on the eve of a crucial House vote on his budget proposal). Samuel Kernell called this tactic "going public" and argued that it is more akin to Neustadt's notion of "command" than bargaining:[32]

*Public politics rarely includes the kinds of exchanges that bargaining requires—the president is calling on Congress (usually) to comply with his demands and the demands of his supporters, rather than offering to make a compromise;

*Appeals for public support for the president impose costs on those the president seeks to pressure and offer few benefits for compliance—instead of bargaining, the president seeks to force members of Congress to comply or face voters' displeasure but gives nothing in return when members do comply;

*Going public involves the president staking out a public position, thus making compromise more difficult; and,

*Public politics undermines the legitimacy of other politicians by insisting that the role of Congress is to go along with what the president

wants rather than playing its own legitimate role in the policy-making process.

As an effort to impose the president's will on Congress, going public is intended to avoid the compromises that are required by bargaining. To that extent, it is a strategy of unilateralism.

Adversity and Unilateralism

Unilateralism is a key strategy in the president's policy arsenal. To that extent, it is unsurprising that chief executives resort to unilateral actions and assert presidential prerogative when faced with adversity. In doing so, they draw on the wellsprings of the office's power. Of course, Neustadt would counsel that this strategy might be alluring but is ultimately self-defeating, because persuasion is more constructive than command and will lead to better results in the end. But the history of the presidency suggests that Neustadt's caution is wrongheaded. Would the nation have benefited if Lincoln had employed anything less than command in dealing with secession? How could Roosevelt have dealt with the presidency, either in his "Dr. New Deal" phase or as "Dr. Win the War," without reliance on a panoply of techniques that Neustadt would characterize as "command"? Reagan's use of command in the early months of his presidency—firing the air traffic controllers, for example—helped mark him as a formidable force in Washington and strengthened his bargaining position with Congress. Faced with the aggressive agenda of the 104th Congress, Clinton used the veto to shut down the government, which ultimately strengthened his position in Washington after the 1994 midterm elections, raised his approval ratings, and aided his reelection. Unilateral presidential power, used effectively, can promote the president's goals.

Prerogative power lies at the heart of the presidency, and it is available regardless of political circumstances. Granted, political conditions can affect how exercises of that power will be received, but even unpopular presidents can employ unilateralism to their own advantage. Clinton certainly did: in the 1994 midterm elections, most observers agreed that

Bill Clinton would have been removed from office if his name had been on the ballot (polls indicated that voters would have voted against Clinton if he had been up for reelection in 1994); by 1996, after struggling with the Republican congressional majority, he won by a margin of more than 8%. Persuasion may be important, but presidential power is not just the power to persuade.

Tough times for the president—situations of political adversity—are occasions when the chief executive is likely to take recourse to unilateralism. Moreover, because these times are characterized by the absence of those circumstances that tend to support and enhance presidential persuasion, they offer opportunities to illuminate the irreducible minimum of presidential power and how it forms a foundation for the grander sorts of influence that Neustadt and others saw as the epitome of presidential influence. Political adversity is a common experience for chief executives: since World War II, every president—except John F. Kennedy—has experienced at least one period of political adversity (see table 1).

As Tatalovich and Engeman have suggested, students of the presidency need a better understanding of prerogative power. There are many approaches that can be employed to examine prerogative, but all have their limitations: all must address the context in which power is exercised; some may be influenced by the substance of issues or the personality of the president; others may be rich in focusing on one type of unilateral power but lack breadth. None of these problems should deter scholars from conducting studies to develop a better understanding of executive power.

THE PLAN OF THIS BOOK

This book explores presidential responses to conditions of political adversity. Chief executives often find themselves in circumstances that are less than optimum, so we identify those times when conditions are especially unfavorable for presidential influence and leadership. We call these highly adverse situations "tough times for the president," and they can give us insights into the office and its powers.

We have suggested what kinds of circumstances (see figure 2) are least favorable for the president. But for purposes of identifying the cases we will study, we need more precision. Table 1 ("Presidents in Adverse Circumstances") summarizes several dimensions along which political adversity can be measured:

Unelected—Successor presidents lack the same electoral base as those elected in their own right (this condition is indicated by an *X*).

Margin—The president's margin of victory in the last election is a form of political capital; a president chosen by a narrow majority, plurality victory, or a minority of the popular vote finds this situation to be a political impediment.

Divided—If one or both chambers of Congress are controlled by the other party, the president will have a harder time influencing the agenda and outcomes of the legislature (a loss of control of one or both chambers by the president's party is indicated by **boldface**). Neustadt does not include party support in Congress among the "vantage points" that affect presidential influence, but the consensus among politicians, journalists, and scholars is that having the president's party in the majority in one or both chambers is an important form of political capital.

Seats gained or lost—The loss of seats in midterm congressional elections impedes presidential influence (Lyndon Johnson gave it as a reason that the president is weaker in the third year of a term), especially when the loss is large and most especially when the president's party loses control of one or both chambers (what Charles Jones refers to as an "unmandate"[33]).

Polls—Low presidential approval ratings (defined here as near or below 50%) impede the president and are taken by other politicians as a sign of trouble for the chief executive.

Scandal—Scandal weakens the president and serves as a distraction for the White House, the media, and all other actors in the political system; a presidential scandal is defined as an incident in which the media, the White House, and other political institutions focus on charges involving (1) sexual misbehavior by the president or another member of the administration; (2) financial misconduct by the president or others associated with the president; or (3) abuse of power by the president in a non-financial way for political ends.[34]

Those periods in which a president faces several factors that indicate political weakness and/or pressure are those we label as times of political adversity or tough times for the president. It is in these times that the presidency is stripped of those props—strong support in Congress, high public approval, and so forth—that are associated with strong leadership, broad persuasive influence, and other attributes of presidential greatness. Tough times are situations in which political and even institutional survival is the challenge confronting the president, and how chief executives have responded to this challenge illuminates much about the nature of the office and its powers.

Central Questions

We are concerned with not just the conditions of political adversity but how presidents respond to them. Even a cursory review of the historical record suggests that most presidents do not just wring their hands when times are tough. There is the rare case of James Buchanan, who faced the crisis of secession with a kind of fatalism and inaction, but one sees little of this in the history of the office. More typical are cases such as that of Harry Truman, who took on the "do nothing" 80th Congress in his 1948 reelection campaign, or Bill Clinton, who stared down the 104th Congress in a government shutdown and demonized Newt Gingrich in the process.

Table 1a. Presidents in Adverse Circumstances

President	Year	Unelected	Margin	Divided?	Seats lost (-) or gained (+)	Polls	Scandal
Truman	1945	X		N		82	
	1946	X		N		45	
	1947	X		HS	H -45/S -12	55	
	1948	X		HS		38	
	1949		4.9	N	H +75/S +9	59	
	1950			N		41	
	1951			N	H -29/S -6	28	X[1]
	1952			N		30	X[1]
Eisenhower	1953		10.7	N	H +22/S +1	69	
	1954			N		65	X[2]
	1955			HS	H -18/S -1	71	X[2]
	1956			HS		73	
	1957		15.4	HS	H -2/S-1	65	
	1958			HS		55	X[3]
	1959			HS	H -48/S -13	6	
	1960			HS		61	
Kennedy	1961		0.02	N	H -22/S +2	76	
	1962			N		72	
	1963			N	H -4/S +3	70	
Johnson	1963	X		N		79	
	1964	X		N		75	
	1965		22.6	N	H +37/S +1	66	
	1966			N		51	
	1967			N	H -47/S -4	44	
	1968			N		42	
Nixon	1969		0.7	HS	H +5/S +6	61	
	1970			HS		57	
	1971			HS	H -12/S +2	50	
	1972			HS		56	
	1973		23.2	HS	H +12/S -2	42	X[4]
	1974			HS		26	X[5]

Source. Truman-Bush (2007) from Vital Statistics on American Politics, various editions (figures rounded); Bush 2008 and Obama data from www.gallup.com.

Table 1b. Presidents in Adverse Circumstances

President	Year	Unelected	Margin	Divided?	Seats lost (-) or gained (+)	Polls	Scandal
Ford	1974	X		HS		54	X[6]
	1975	X		HS	H -48/S -5	43	
	1976	X		HS		48	
Carter	1977		2.1	N	H +1/S 0	63	
	1978			N		46	
	1979			N	H -15/S -3	38	
	1980			N		40	
Reagan	1981		9.7	H	H +34/S +12	58	
	1982			H		44	
	1983			H	H -26/S +1	44	
	1984			H		56	
	1985		18.2	H	H +14/S -2	61	
	1986			H		62	
	1987			HS	H -5/S -8	48	X[7]
	1988			HS		52	X[7]
GHW Bush	1989		7.8	HS	H -2/S 0	64	
	1990			HS		66	
	1991			HS	H -8/S -1	72	
	1992			HS		40	
Clinton	1993		4.6	N	H -10/S 0	49	
	1994			N		46	
	1995			**HS**	H -52/S -8	48	
	1996			HS		54	
	1997		8.5	HS	H -9/S -2	58	
	1998			HS		64	X[8]
	1999			HS	H +5/S 0	62	X[8]
	2000			HS		60	
GW Bush (I)	2001		-0.5	**S**	H -3/S -4	66	
	2002			S		72	
	2003			N	H +8/S +2	61	
	2004			N		51	X[9]

Source. Truman-Bush (2007) from Vital Statistics on American Politics, various editions (figures rounded); Bush 2008 and Obama data from www.gallup.com.

Table 1c. Presidents in Adverse Circumstances

President	Year	Unelected	Margin	Divided?	Seats lost (-) or gained (+)	Polls	Scandal
GW Bush (II)	2005		2.97	N	H +3/S +4	46	
	2006			N		38	
	2007			**HS**	H -30/S -6	35	
	2008			HS		34	
Obama	2009		5.2	N	H +23/S +8	57	
	2010			N		47	
	2011			**H**	H -63/S -6		

Key/Divided: N=not divided; H=House majority other party; S=Senate majority other party (**Boldface** means change in party control)

Notes for Scandal:

[1]Special inquiry into corruption in Executive Branch   [6]Nixon pardon
[2]Dixon-Yates (Energy) contract scandal   [7]Iran-contra affair
[3]Sherman Adams accepting gifts   [8]Lewinsky-impeachment
[4]Spiro Agnew corruption scandal & Watergate   [9]Abu Ghraib/Valerie Plame leak
[5]Watergate

Approval rating sources: Truman-Bush (2007) from *Vital Statistics on American Politics*, various editions (figures rounded); Bush 2008 and Obama data from www.gallup.com.

Source. Truman-Bush (2007) from Vital Statistics on American Politics, various editions (figures rounded); Bush 2008 and Obama data from www.gallup.com.

What have presidents done in the face of adversity, particularly in the matter of how they used and/or expanded the powers of their office, and how did they act in an innovative or unconventional fashion? To explore presidents in adverse circumstances, this book will focus on three central questions:

1) How do presidents respond to political adversity? What actions have chief executives taken to retain or increase their influence? Did their actions make any difference?

2) How does adversity limit the president, and how do chief executives look for different ways to assert their power and influence?

3) What powers does the president retain despite adverse circumstances, and how does the president exercise them?

To answer these questions, the remainder of the book will examine eleven case studies of presidents in situations of political adversity. The cases cover ten presidents—every president from Truman to George W. Bush (except John Kennedy) is included. These cases are selected from the record of the presidency since World War II, as identified in table 1.

A Common Format for the Case Studies

To enhance the clarity of the cases and our ability to draw lessons from them about the nature of the presidency and executive power, we will employ a common format for our case studies. Each case study will contain the following elements:

1. Prologue: This addresses the president's situation of political adversity. The prologue will examine how the president came to be in the situation, as well as providing a description and overview of the adverse circumstances facing the president (such as approval rating, loss of seats in Congress, etc.). The prologue presents the challenge facing the president.

2. The president's response to adversity: What did the president do in response to the challenge? Each case study will examine the possible dimensions of presidential response, including efforts at persuasion, executive actions, foreign policy initiatives and actions, and the use of public politics. In addition, each case study will look for unconventional actions by the president in an effort to see how chief executives may take innovative actions in response to the challenges of political adversity.

   a. Bargaining and persuasion—Is there evidence of presidential engagement in bargaining and persuasion to meet the challenge of adversity? Were these efforts successful?

   b. Executive actions

      i. Use of constitutional powers—How did the president employ the constitutional powers of the office in response to adversity?

      ii. Other unilateral actions—What actions did the chief executive undertake to expand presidential power?

    c. Foreign policy initiatives and actions—Did the president engage in foreign policy initiatives and actions that circumvented the constraints of political adversity?

    d. Organizational changes—Did the president make any changes in the structure of the White House and the administration, including personnel changes, reorganization of the staff or decision-making processes, or the use of special or innovative organizational actions?

    e. Going public—To what extent did the president employ public politics, even in the context of a political campaign, to seek a stronger political position?

    f. Unconventional actions—Did the president employ any unconventional actions to seek a stronger political position or to advance a goal?

3. Outcome and assessment

    a. Did the president's actions make any difference (such as election outcome, significant shift in polls, etc.)? If so, how? If not, why not?

    b. How did adversity limit what the president could do or accomplish?

    c. Did adversity open opportunities in any way (including unconventional action)?

    d. What powers did the president retain despite adversity, and how did the president exercise them in a relevant way?

The Case Studies

The chapters that follow present case studies of presidents facing situations of political adversity. The eleven cases were selected using the dimensions in tables 1a–1c.

Chapter 2 examines four cases in which presidents faced unmandates in midterm congressional elections that is, occasions in which the president's party lost control of one or both legislative chambers. These midterm setbacks were followed by periods in which the chief executive faced an opposition Congress: Truman (1947–1948), Eisenhower (1955–1956), Clinton (1995–1996), and George W. Bush (2007–2008). (Ronald Reagan lost the Senate in the 1986 midterm elections, but 1987–1988 was also the period of the Iran-Contra affair and will be explored in chapter 3.) Among these examples, only Eisenhower maintained strong public approval ratings; the others faced weak public support or even outright unpopularity in addition to the unmandate.

Chapter 3 focuses on presidents attempting to govern in the face of scandal. Three cases deserve attention: Nixon and Watergate (1973–1974), Reagan and the Iran-Contra affair (1987–1988), and Clinton and the Monica Lewinsky affair (1998–1999). These scandals placed enormous pressure on the White House, made it difficult for the president to govern, and led to major investigations. Watergate led to Nixon's resignation (August 1974) in the face of an impeachment threat, whereas Clinton was impeached in 1998 and tried in the Senate in 1999.

Chapter 4 examines presidents responding to circumstances of significant national political division and stress. In these cases, political and economic factors combine to place pressure on the president that makes governing more difficult, including Johnson in 1967–1968, under pressure because of the Vietnam War; Carter in 1979–1980, as the weak economy, international instability, and the Iranian Hostage Crisis weakened him; and Bush in 1992, as the recession and a backlash among conservatives within his own party undermined his leadership.

Chapter 5 examines the presidency of Gerald Ford, which in many respects constitutes a unique case of presidential adversity. Given the reasons why Ford became president and his pardon of Nixon within a few weeks of taking office, Ford faced a situation of political adversity unlike that of almost any other president. Not only had he not been elected to the presidency, but he had been appointed vice president in 1974 after Vice President Spiro Agnew resigned in the wake of a scandal involving his prior service as governor of Maryland. Ford faced a Congress controlled by the Democrats, and after his pardon of Nixon, his approval ratings plummeted and Republicans experienced significant losses in the midterm elections. Although Ford was personally unconnected to the Watergate scandal, his pardon of Nixon in September 1974 kept Watergate in the media and the public mind well after Ford assumed office. His time in office is a study in which the presidency seemed "on the ropes" and in danger of collapsing.

A PREVIEW OF RESULTS

The common format of the case studies enables us to compare the results of the cases and in chapter 6 to draw some general lessons from them. These cases illuminate how presidents have used the powers of the office and what constraints and opportunities they encountered in the face of political adversity. The situations enable the illustration of how both bargaining and unilateralism have affected the conduct of the presidency.

Certain discernible patterns emerge from the eleven case studies. First, in five cases (Truman, Eisenhower, Clinton/1995–1996, Reagan, and Clinton/Lewinsky) the president triumphed over adversity, and Gerald Ford recovered from the backlash to his pardon of Richard Nixon in 1974 to nearly win the 1976 election. In all of these recoveries, bargaining and persuasion played at best a mixed role in the outcome. More important were executive actions, foreign policy, going public, and (in some cases) unconventional presidential actions.

Three of the unmandate presidents won reelection. George W. Bush left office with low approval ratings but with his foreign policy largely intact. Because he was the only one of these presidents ineligible for reelection, his case raises the question of how a reelection bid might have affected his actions or his political fortunes. An unmandate delivered in a midterm election is not necessarily the final word on a presidency.

In the scandal cases, Reagan and Clinton survived, whereas Nixon resigned under the threat of impeachment. Reagan and Clinton both employed unilateral presidential powers to govern during these scandals. Three cases are too few from which to make significant generalizations, but it also true that scandal does not necessarily finish a presidency.

In contrast, the presidents facing national division (LBJ, Carter, and George H. W. Bush) did not recover. We consider some reasons why that was so—the nature of the division, the skills of the particular presidents, or other factors—and note that these results do not necessarily doom any future chief executive in a similar situation.

Gerald Ford's experience involved some of the most adverse circumstances any president has encountered. He lacked an electoral base, faced a backlash against the Nixon pardon, and then suffered significant Republican losses in the 1974. Nevertheless, Ford was able to direct foreign policy and to put his imprint on domestic policy. Ford engaged in bargaining and persuasion, but when that failed him, he employed unilateral presidential powers to advance his policy and political goals.

Although eleven cases do not represent the entire experience of the post–World War II presidency, they cover ten of the twelve chief executives in this period. These cases also offer examples of presidents reaching beyond bargaining and persuasion for power; they engaged in what Neustadt dismissed as "command" to revive their political fortunes and to advance their goals. In short, these cases suggest that students of the office need a better understanding of presidential power.

As we shall outline in chapter 6, our study of tough times leads to a new view of presidential power as *situational leverage*. We sketch an understanding of power as leverage that takes into account the resources a president is able to apply in a particular situation, weighed against the risks and obstacles that threaten to block or undermine presidential goals and the opportunities that help to motivate the president. This approach, we argue, presents a more accurate, realistic, and useful view of presidential power than the catchy but misleading "power to persuade." Moreover, viewing power as leverage helps us to account for why recent presidents have devoted time and attention to employing and expanding their capacity for unilateral action.

Many presidents face situations of political adversity. Some even face adversity on more than one occasion. The case studies will enhance our understanding not only of the power of the presidency but of how chief executives have been able to deal with adversity. Even the adverse circumstances faced by Barack Obama in 2011, or those that some future president will encounter, do not fall to the depths experienced by Gerald Ford, and examining this record will be instructive for chief executives and their advisors seeking a way to grapple with tough times for the president.

ENDNOTES

1. "Gallup Daily: Obama Job Approval," data for November 1–3, 2010, accessed January 13, 2011, http://www.gallup.com/poll/113980/gallup-daily-obama-job-approval.aspx. Gallup's daily presidential approval rating is based on a three-day rolling average.
2. James Ceaser, "The Great Repudiation," *Claremont Review of Books* 10 (Fall 2010): 6.
3. Marc Landy and Sidney M. Milkis, *Presidential Greatness* (Lawrence: University Press of Kansas, 2001).
4. Jon Roper, *The American Presidents: Heroic Leadership from Kennedy to Clinton* (New York: Routledge, 2000).
5. See, for example, Roper, *American Presidents*, but also such works as Walker Newell, *The Soul of a Leader* (New York: Harper, 2009); George C. Edwards and Stephen J. Wayne, *Presidential Leadership*, 8th ed. (New York: Wadsworth, 2009); Bert Rockman and Richard Waterman, *Presidential Leadership: The Vortex of Power* (New York: Oxford University Press, 2007); Dean Keith Simonton, *Why Presidents Succeed: A Psychology of Leadership* (New Haven, CT: Yale University Press, 1987); Stephen Skowronek, *Presidential Leadership in Political Time: Reprise and Reappraisal* (Lawrence: University Press of Kansas, 2008); Fred Greenstein, *The Presidential Difference: Leadership Style from FDR to George W. Bush* (Princeton, NJ: Princeton University Press, 2004); and James Macgregor Burns, *Running Alone: Presidential Leadership from JFK to Bush II* (New York: Basic Books, 2007). These authors do not all take the same view of what leadership means, but leadership is still a dominant concern of the scholarly literature on the presidency.
6. Gene Healy, *The Cult of the Presidency, Updated: America's Dangerous Devotion to Executive Power* (Washington, DC: Cato Institute, 2009).
7. On the meanings of the term *mandate*, see Charles O. Jones, *The Presidency in a Separated System*, 2nd ed. (Washington, DC: Brookings Institution, 2005).
8. Richard Neustadt, *Presidential Power and the Modern Presidents*, rev. ed. (New York: Free Press, 1991).
9. For a good introduction to the critical literature on Neustadt, see Michael Nelson, "Neustadt's 'Presidential Power' at 50," *Chronicle Review*, March 28, 2010, accessed September 9, 2010, http://chronicle.

com/article/Neustadts-Presidential/64816/; Erwin Hargrove, "Presidential Power and Political Science," *Presidential Studies Quarterly* 31 (June 2001): 245–261; David G. Wegge, "Neustadt's *Presidential Power*: The Test of Time and Empirical Research on the Presidency," *Presidential Studies Quarterly* 11 (Summer 1981): 342–347; Matthew Dickinson, "We All Want a Revolution: Neustadt, New Institutionalism, and the Future of Presidency Research," *Presidential Studies Quarterly* 39 (December 2009): 736–770; and Robert Y. Shapiro, Martha Joynt Kumar, and Lawrence R. Jacobs, eds., *Presidential Power: Forging the Presidency for the Twenty-first Century* (New York: Columbia University Press, 2000). See also David K. Nichols, *The Myth of the Modern Presidency* (State College: Pennsylvania State University Press, 1994). These references indicate places to begin studying the literature on Neustadt and point the way to further discussions and critiques.

10. Neustadt, *Presidential Power*, 24–25.

11. Ibid., 26–27.

12. David A. Nichols, *A Matter of Justice: Eisenhower and the Beginning of the Civil Rights Revolution* (New York: Simon & Schuster, 2007), 278–281.

13. Linda Feldman, "Bush Makes First Veto on Stem Cells," *Christian Science Monitor* [online], July 20, 2006, accessed November 13, 2009, http://www.csmonitor.com/2006/0720/p02s02-uspo.html.

14. See, for example, Kathleen Dunn Tempas, *The Veto-Free Presidency: George W. Bush (2001–Present)*, Brookings Governance Studies #4 (July 2006) (Washington, DC: Brookings Institution, 2006).

15. Raymond Tatalovich and Thomas S. Engeman, *The Presidency and Political Science* (Baltimore: Johns Hopkins University Press, 2003), 225–226.

16. The annual prize for the best book on the presidency, awarded by the American Political Science Association, is the Richard Neustadt Prize. David Broder of the *Washington Post* frequently cited Neustadt in his columns. In a major PBS documentary on the presidency that aired in the 1990s, the only expert to appear on camera was Neustadt. Also, Neustadt reported (see *Presidential Power*, xvi) that more than one Nixon aide told him *Presidential Power* was required reading among the White House staff. Neustadt advised JFK and Clinton in office and the Carter transition in 1976–1977. He was one of Vice President Al Gore's favorite professors at Harvard. His reputation has been tremendously widespread.

17. Neustadt, *Presidential Power*, 6.

18. Richard Pious, *The American Presidency* (New York: Basic Books, 1979).

19. Louis Fisher, *Constitutional Conflicts Between Congress and the President*, 5th rev. ed. (Lawrence: University Press of Kansas, 2007), and *Presidential War Power*, 2nd ed. (Lawrence: University Press of Kansas, 2004).

20. William Howell, *Power Without Persuasion: The Politics of Direct Presidential Action* (Princeton, NJ: Princeton University Press, 2003).

21. Kenneth Mayer, *With the Stroke of a Pen: Executive Orders and Presidential Power* (Princeton, NJ: Princeton University Press, 2002).

22. Robert Spitzer, "Presidential Prerogative Power: The Case of the Bush Administration and Legislative Power," *PS: Political Science and Politics* 24 (March 1991): 38–42.

23. Robert Spitzer, *The Presidential Veto* (Albany: SUNY Press, 1988), 74.

24. Mayer, *With the Stroke of a Pen*, 71.

25. Peter Sperlich, "Bargaining and Overload: An Essay on *Presidential Power*," in *Perspectives on the Presidency*, ed. Aaron Wildavsky (Boston: Little Brown, 1975).

26. Philip Cooper, *By Order of the President* (Lawrence: University Press of Kansas, 2002).

27. Christopher S. Kelley, "The Significance of the Presidential Signing Statement," in *Executing the Constitution: Putting the President Back into the Constitution*, ed. Christopher S. Kelley (Albany: SUNY Press, 2006).

28. Mark Rozell, *Executive Privilege: The Dilemma of Secrecy and Democratic Accountability* (Baltimore: Johns Hopkins University Press, 1994); and Louis Fisher, *The Politics of Executive Privilege* (Durham, NC: Carolina Academic Press, 2004).

29. Ryan J. Barilleaux, *The Post-Modern Presidency* (New York: Praeger, 1988); and Ryan J. Barilleaux, "The Presidency in the Twenty-first Century," in *Thinking About the Presidency*, ed. Gary L. Gregg II (Lanham, MD: Rowman & Littlefield, 2005).

30. Ryan J. Barilleaux, "Venture Constitutionalism and the Enlargement of the Presidency," in Kelley, *Executing the Constitution*.

31. This paragraph draws upon Samuel Kernell, *Going Public: New Strategies of Presidential Leadership*, 4th ed. (Washington, DC: CQ Press, 2007), 2–4.

32. Kernell makes this point explicitly; see ibid., 25.

33. C. O. Jones, *Presidency in a Separated System*.

34. On the definition of political scandal, see John B. Thompson, *Political Scandal: Power and Visibility in the Media Age* (Cambridge: Polity Press, 2000); Stephen C. Roeberds, "Sex, Money and Deceit: Incumbent Scandals in U.S. House and Senate Elections, 1974–1990" (PhD diss., Univer-

sity of Missouri–St. Louis, 1997); Jeffrey Schultz, *Presidential Scandals* (Washington, DC: CQ Press, 2000); and James T. Smith, "The Institution-alization of Politics by Scandal and the Effect on the American View of Government" (PhD diss. University of Nebraska, 2002).

Chapter 2

Governing in the Wake of an Unmandate

Presidents and their supporters like to claim that the chief executive has been given a mandate by voters to implement a policy agenda. This situation is especially apparent when the president has won election or reelection by a large margin, but even smaller margins have been claimed as the basis for change. John Kennedy famously remarked that even "one vote is still a mandate,"[1] a bit of presidential hyperbole that was contradicted by the difficulty JFK encountered in trying to push his legislative program through Congress. Charles Jones noted not only that plausible presidential claims to mandates are rare (and require certain specific conditions) but that chief executives also face situations that can only be characterized as "unmandates."[2]

What is an unmandate? The term applies to those situations in which voters repudiate the chief executive by punishing the president's party in a midterm election. Though it is usually the case that the president's party loses seats in a midterm election, in an unmandate the president's party suffers exceptionally high losses. The clearest case of an unmandate is when the president's party, holding a majority in both houses of

Congress, is reduced to minority status in the House and/or the Senate. In the period since World War II, this repudiation occurred five times: 1946, 1954, 1994, 2006, and 2010. The presidents affected by these unmandates faced congressional majorities eager to resist White House legislative initiatives and advance their own policy agendas. This chapter will examine the first four of these cases; owing to the recency of the last case, President Obama's interactions with the 111th Congress (2011–2012) will be considered in chapter 6.

HARRY TRUMAN, 1947–1948

When Harry S. Truman assumed the presidency in 1945, he faced a situation with few parallels. World War II was not yet complete, and he had to hold his own with the two political giants of the time, Winston Churchill and Joseph Stalin. However daunting it was to follow Franklin Roosevelt, some of Truman's most difficult times as president occurred after the war had ended. In November 1946, voters brought in a Republican Congress, wartime employment ended, and the nation experienced housing shortages and widespread labor strikes. As the historian David McCullough wrote about the president in 1946, "It was a bad time for Truman."[3] It would only get worse following the midterm elections.

By all objective measurements, the years 1946–1948 should have witnessed an unelected, unpopular, and minority president unable to command much influence. Despite a Republican Congress eager to reverse New Deal programs, mounting concerns about the growing strength of the Soviet Union, and a mere 32% approval rating, Truman would go on to win the presidential election in 1948. He staged a remarkable comeback and managed to exercise presidential power in important ways. His response to the situation he faced was instrumental in reversing his political fortunes.

Bargaining and Persuasion
Truman's friend Charlie Ross said that "the real Truman administration began the day after the elections."[4] After the Republicans took control of Congress, the president began making bold statements, proposed new legislation, and eventually managed to turn his political situation around. By the spring of 1947, newspapers across the country were reporting on the "new" Truman, a more confident and forceful president whose popularity rating had soared to 60%. This turn of events was certainly influenced by Truman's ability to direct the nation's foreign policy through the Truman Doctrine and the Marshall Plan, as well as by his dedication to domestic reform in the areas of civil rights and executive reorganization.

Legislative Successes/Compromises/Concessions
Truman's interactions with the 80th Congress present two very different stories. In domestic affairs, the Republican-dominated legislature wanted nothing to do with Truman's expansive "Fair Deal." Republicans were also eager to pass legislation, such as the Taft-Hartley Act, that Truman opposed. Yet in foreign affairs, the president and Congress cooperated to pass some of the most far-reaching legislation in American political history, and Truman presided over a broad bipartisan consensus on the appropriate role for the United States in a world divided by the Cold War.[5]

Following the end of World War II and the Republican landslide of 1946, there seemed to be every indication that the United States would retreat back to an isolationist policy.[6] Yet the president was able to rally support for an internationalist foreign policy with his appeal to the nation to stop the spread of communism. On March 12, 1947, Truman used a speech before a joint session of Congress to warn legislators that Greece, Turkey, and eventually the whole of the Middle East would soon fall to the Communists. The foreign policy of the United States, Truman declared, would be to "assist free people to work out their own destinies in their own way." If the United States did not stand up to communism now, he warned, "we may endanger the peace of the world and we shall surely endanger the welfare of our own nation."[7] The speech, which outlined what would become known as the Truman Doctrine, was greeted with a standing ovation and overall favorable news coverage in the following weeks.[8]

Beyond the Truman Doctrine, the administration also pursued an ambitious policy to promote capitalism and economic development throughout postwar Europe. When Secretary of State George Marshall delivered the commencement address at Harvard in June 1947, he proposed a new economic strategy in Europe. Rather than incremental changes in the amount and target of foreign aid, Marshall proposed that European aid be comprehensive, applying to virtually all of Europe, including Germany. Although the plan was Marshall's (the president rejected suggestions that he take the credit himself), Truman was ultimately responsible for selling the massive program to a public that had grown tired of deprivation, higher taxes, and curtailment of consumption.[9] Although the Marshall Plan would not be approved until April 1948, and with an overwhelming majority, Truman's strategy of pushing for the plan proved instrumental to the massive support it received.

In addition to the Truman Doctrine, Truman and Congress reorganized the government's structure for national security. The National Security Act of 1947 reorganized the federal government, unifying the armed forces under a new Department of Defense and establishing the Air Force as a separate military service. It also established a new national security council (which Truman did not want but decided to ignore rather than fight about) and formally authorized the Central Intelligence Agency (CIA). Overall, in foreign policy there was a high degree of cooperation between the president and Congress.

Failed Attempts at Legislative Bargaining/Compromise

The same cannot be said for domestic policy. Truman's Fair Deal proposals, which he saw as a necessary continuation of the New Deal (put on hold because of the war), were largely ignored or rejected by Congress. Moreover, Congress passed two key bills that Truman opposed and overrode his veto to do so. The first was the Taft-Hartley Act (June 1947), which limited the power of labor unions and gave the president authority to intervene in labor disputes (a power that Truman would later use). The other bill was a tax cut (April 1948) that Congress passed over Truman's veto.

Truman also failed to halt a congressional investigation into communist influence in the federal government. By Executive Order 9835, he instituted a loyalty program, with the clear intention of heading off an investigation by the House Committee on Un-American Activities.[10] He and his advisors did not think there was a significant problem of disloyal government employees, but the charge of disloyal officials in the government was creating a political challenge for the president.[11] All federal employees were made subject to loyalty investigations, and any employee could be dismissed on "reasonable grounds for belief that the person is disloyal."[12] (Only 212 employees were dismissed for questionable loyalty; none of these would be prosecuted for espionage or any other crime.) But the program did not stop Republican lawmakers from proceeding with their investigation, and years later Truman conceded that the program had been a "terrible" mistake.[13]

Executive Actions

Truman employed executive powers throughout this period. His vetoes of legislation were sustained 86% of the time, but as noted earlier, he was overridden on two key bills. He also employed executive orders as an instrument of presidential policy, not only in creating the federal employee loyalty program but in an innovative way in the area of civil rights.

Truman had created a Civil Rights Commission by executive order in 1946, and over the next two years he continued making initiatives. In particular, in July 1948, he issued two executive orders that would have long-lasting effects on civil rights. Executive Order 9980 mandated nondiscrimination in federal civilian employment, and Executive Order 9981 desegregated the armed forces. These actions were unpopular

(Gallup reported a mere 6% approving of armed forces desegregation),[14] but the president's authority was unchallenged.

He took other executive actions as well, including ordering the army to seize control of railroads in May 1948 when a strike halted rail traffic in the nation. This control would last until 1952. He also invoked executive privilege several times, including an announcement in August 1948 that no information obtained on federal employees from his loyalty program would be shared with the House Committee on Un-American Activities.[15]

Foreign Policy Initiatives and Actions

The years following World War II were marked by important developments in American foreign policy. These were the years of the Truman Doctrine, national security reorganization, and the Marshall Plan. But Truman also undertook a number of key initiatives in foreign affairs that were more unilateral in nature. He issued national security directives to shape American policy in the emerging Cold War, including directives to make the CIA responsible for "psychological warfare" (NSC-4) and clarify its responsibility for covert activities (NSC-10/2).[16] He also signed 376 executive agreements, including the 1947 protocol binding the United States to the General Agreement on Tariffs and Trade (GATT).

Truman undertook more significant actions the following year. In May 1948, he recognized the State of Israel shortly after it declared its independence. In June, when the Soviet Union blocked ground transportation crossing East German territory to bring supplies to the divided city of Berlin, he ordered American planes to deliver supplies by air. The Berlin Airlift, which involved hundreds of flights each day to bring food and other essential items into the city, lasted until September 1949.

Truman's entire presidency would be dominated by World War II, its aftermath, and the Cold War that followed. Despite the unmandate of 1946, the president was able to exercise broad authority—backed by a bipartisan consensus—as he laid the foundation for the nation's role in a bipolar world.

Going Public

Public politics was important to Truman in this period. He employed it to sell the Truman Doctrine and the Marshall Plan to Congress and the nation and also employed it in the cause of civil rights.

The Truman Doctrine speech of 1947 was the first time any president had publicly declared the Soviet Union to be an enemy whose totalitarian nature needed to be opposed by democratic governments. It began a new era of hostile rhetoric that Truman had not displayed in any of his prior speeches.[17] Truman's strategy of transforming the Soviet Union from a World War II ally into a menacing threat to freedom may have been the result of genuine concern over Soviet actions and noncooperation after the war's end. Nevertheless, the change in tone also had another purpose: only in an atmosphere of fear and concern could Truman have succeeded in selling his various policies to Congress and the American people. By presenting the Truman Doctrine as necessary for national security, he removed much of the skepticism that many Americans had about rebuilding its former enemies, something Truman would later boast was unique in world history.

Truman also knew how best to present his policies to the people and Congress. In selling the Marshall Plan, for example, Truman understood that the Republican Congress would be more receptive to the idea if he was not its chief advocate. He created two blue-ribbon commissions to study the impact of the Marshall Plan on American progress and instructed the Council of Economic Advisors to produce a report on the plan's economic impact. All of the reports, unsurprisingly, "extolled the manifest necessity of the plan and minimized any adverse effects on the country."[18] Truman also maintained the association of the plan with Secretary of State George Marshall, a man widely respected for his service as army chief of staff during World War II. The president also managed to marginalize the mostly grassroots pro-Soviet bloc within the Democratic Party who supported Henry Wallace for their candidate in 1948. Wallace's opposition to the Marshall Plan all but ensured Truman's nomination.

Truman also used public politics in support of his agenda for civil rights. In June 1947, he became the first president to address the National Association for the Advancement of Colored People (NAACP). On the steps of the Lincoln Memorial, he delivered "the strongest statement on civil rights heard in Washington since the time of Lincoln."[19] The speech outlined a series of legislative proposals that would form the basis of Truman's February 1948 message to Congress. It advocated a permanent Fair Employment Practices Committee, an anti-lynching law, the abolition of the poll tax, and an end to racial discrimination in interstate transportation facilities.[20] The political risk Truman faced from these proposals was best captured in a letter sent by a Southern minister, who warned that if Truman persisted in enacting these programs, "you won't be elected dog catcher in 1948."[21]

Unconventional Actions
In the period 1947–1948, Truman actively employed presidential power and both worked with and fought with the 80th Congress. As he headed toward the 1948 general election, he was determined to make the fall campaign a referendum on the right direction for the nation: his or that of the Republican Congress. To that end, he surprised his political allies and adversaries by invoking a rarely used presidential power. In his speech accepting the Democratic nomination on July 15, 1948, Truman invoked his constitutional authority and called an emergency session of Congress, the first special session in an election year since 1856. House Speaker Joseph Martin conceded that Truman had been a "devilishly astute" political strategist.[22] His move allowed him to set the political agenda, gain national and congressional attention, and challenge his Republican counterparts to act on the issues of the day. It also underscored one of the major elements of his campaign: his attack on the "do nothing" 80th Congress.

Epilogue
In 1948, Harry Truman defied every prediction and most editorial opinions by winning the presidential election. Democrats also regained majorities

both in the House and in the Senate. Truman's victory was one of the most impressive political comebacks in American history. His response to political adversity is summarized in table 2.

DWIGHT EISENHOWER, 1955–1956

When Dwight Eisenhower won the presidency in 1952, he brought into office slim Republican majorities in both the House and Senate. But by the 1952 midterm elections, public sentiment had turned against the Republican Congress. As Stephen Ambrose put the situation, Eisenhower "wanted his party to retain control of Congress, and despite his constant reiteration of his nonpartisanship, he exhorted his Cabinet members to do all they could to elect Republicans."[23] He thought that active campaigning on his own part was inappropriate, but he dispatched Vice President Richard Nixon to assist Republican candidates, and he ordered the Defense Department to do the "major portion of its buying" before the election to stimulate economic activity.[24] Nevertheless, Republicans lost seventeen seats in the House and two in the Senate, returning the Democrats to control in both chambers.[25]

In the face of this unmandate, Eisenhower—urged on by supporters who had encouraged him to run in 1952—began thinking of his own reelection. The next two years would involve governing with a Democratic Congress, facing dissension in his own party, and mounting a campaign for a second term. The period of 1955–1956 would be important for Eisenhower's foreign policy, for conflicts and successes with Congress, and for his landslide reelection.

Table 2a. Summarizing the President's Response to Adversity—Unmandate—
Truman 1947–1948

Type of response	Summary data & significant examples
1. Bargaining & persuasion	*Legislative successes/compromises/concessions:* • May 1947: Truman Doctrine • July 1947: National Security Act • Apr 1948: Marshall Plan *Failed attempts at legislative bargaining/compromise:* • June 1947: Taft-Hartley Act (over veto) • April 1948: tax reduction (over veto) *Other:* • Loyalty program not stop cong investigation into communists in federal govt
2. Executive actions constitutional	*Vetoes:* 42 regular (86% sustained), 33 pocket • June 1947: Income tax reduction bill • June 1947: Taft-Hartley Act (overridden) • July 1947: 2nd tax reduct bill • Apr 1948: 3rd tax reduct bill (overridden) *Pardons & clemency:* 516 *Proclamations:* 109 *Executive orders:* 217 • 9835—Fed loyalty program (Mar 1947) • 9980—Fed employ-no discrim (July 1948) • 9981—Deseg armed forces (July 1948) *Signing statements:* 37 (none significant) *Claims of executive privilege:* • Mar 1948: Aide not testify to House comm about conversations with president • Apr 1948: Refused to release FBI letter on loyalty of a government scientist • Aug 1948: No loyalty info on fed workers to be given to House Comm on Un-American Activities
Outcome of case: Truman won the 1948 presidential election, Democrats reclaimed majorities in House & Senate	

Table 2b. Summarizing the President's Response to Adversity—Unmandate—
Truman 1947–1948 (Continued)

Type of response	*Summary data & significant examples*
other actions	May 1948: Ordered Army to control railroads due to strike (lasted until 1952)
3. Foreign policy initiatives & actions	*National security directives:* • NSC-4: made CIA responsible for "psychological warfare" (Dec 1947) • NSC-10/2: clarified CIA responsibility for covert intelligence activities (June 1948) *Executive agreements:*376 • Oct 1947: Protocol binding US to GATT *Significant treaties:* • June 1947: Peace treaty with Italy *Uses of force:* • June 1948-Sept 1949: Berlin Airlift *Other:* • June 1947: Marshall Plan proposed • May 1948: recognition of State of Israel
4. Organizational changes	none significant
5. Going public	Jan1947: State of the Union Address Mar 1947: Truman Doctrine speech to Congress June 1947: Address to NAACP Jan 1948: State of the Union Address
6. Unconventional actions?	July 1948: Called Congress into special session on housing, civil rights, & price controls
Outcome of case: Truman won the 1948 presidential election, Democrats reclaimed majorities in House & Senate	

Table 2c. Comparing the President's Response to Non-Adverse Circumstances—Truman 1947–1948

Type of response	Comparison to non-adverse circumstances (1949-1952)
1. Bargaining & persuasion	*Legislative successes/compromises/concessions:* • Housing Act of 1949 (only part of "Fair Deal" to be enacted) • June 1950: Foreign Economic Assistance Act ("Point Four" program) *Failed attempts at legislative bargaining:* • Most of Truman's "Fair Deal" proposals (originally 1945, renewed 1949) were ignored or rejected
2. Executive actions constitutional	*Vetoes—total:* 180 reg (93% sustained), 70 pocket—None overridden until Taft-Hartley Act, 1947 *Pardons & clemency:* 2044 total *Proclamations:* 357 total *Executive orders:* 901 • 10340—directed Sec of Commerce to seize steel mills (Apr 1952) *Signing statements:* 107 (none challenges to laws) *Claims of executive privilege:* • May 1951: Gen. O Bradley not estify to Senate comm about conversation w/presid (Comm later conceded) • 1948 non-cooperation w/cong disloyalty investigations were basis for later non-cooperation w/investigation by Sen Jos McCarthy & others
other actions	Apr 1952: Army seized steel mills due to strike (led to defeat in case of *Youngstown Sheet & Tube v. Sawyer*, 1952) Several threats or actions to use Army and seizures to stop strikes throughout presidency, until *Youngstown* decision
Outcome of case: Truman won the 1948 presidential election, Democrats reclaimed majorities in House & Senate	

Table 2d. Comparing the President's Response to Non-Adverse Circumstances—Truman 1947–1948 (Continued)

Type of response	Comparison to non-adverse circumstances (1949-1952)
3. Foreign policy initiatives & actions	*National security directives:* • NSC-68 (1950)—"blueprint" for Containment *Executive agreements—total:* 1324 • several trade agreements, esp. with states in Latin America *Significant treaties:* (132 total) • Apr 1949: North Atlantic Treaty *Uses of force:* • June 1950: US enters Korean War • June 1950: 7th Fleet dispatched to protect Taiwan from attack by China *Other:* • Apr 1951: Truman fires Gen. MacArthur as commander in Korea and Japan
4. Organizational changes	National Security Council—became important during Korean War
5. Going public	Apr 1952: Address to nation of decision to seize steel mills due to strike
6. Unconventional actions?	N/A
Outcome of case: **Truman won the 1948 presidential election, Democrats reclaimed majorities in House & Senate**	

Bargaining and Persuasion

The interactions between Eisenhower and the 84th Congress are reminiscent of Truman's with the Republican 80th Congress, although without the same degree of rancor. That is so because a broad bipartisan consensus generally supported the president's foreign policy, whereas in domestic policy, discord between the parties inhibited legislative agreement. Some of the most important legislation of Ike's presidency was passed in this period, but there were also key defeats for the president.

In terms of House and Senate concurrence with the president, the midterm elections of 1954 highlight a shift in Eisenhower's success with Congress. According to Lyn Ragsdale, "Vote concurrence is measured by the number of times a majority of members of Congress vote with the president's position on roll call votes. Member concurrence is the percentage of members who agree with the president's position on a roll call vote."[26] As table 3 demonstrates, there was a distinct drop in congressional concurrence with the president after 1954; although the House and Senate would continue to agree with Ike most of the time, the unmandate of 1954 did have an effect on the president's success on Capitol Hill.

Table 3. Congressional Concurrence with the President, 1953–1956

Year	Total H&S Concurrence	House Concurrence	# of House Votes	Senate Concurrence	# of Senate Votes
1953	89.2	91.2	34	87.8	49
1954	82.8	78.9	38	77.9	77
Average	89.4	85.1		82.9	
Total			72		126
1955	75.3	63.4	41	84.6	52
1956	69.2	73.5	34	67.7	65
Average	72.3	68.9		76.2	
Total			75		117

Source. Compiled from data in *Vital Statistics on American Politics, 2009–2010* (p. 244) by Harold Stanley and Richard Niemi. Washington, DC: CQ Press, 2010.

Legislative Successes/Compromises/Concessions

The Cold War continued to dominate American foreign policy, and Eisenhower maintained the policy of containmbalent while trying to prevent a serious conflict with the Soviet Union or China. His major foreign-affairs request to Congress was passage of the Formosa Resolution. In 1954, the People's Republic of China (PRC) had put pressure on the Nationalist Chinese regime on Taiwan (called Formosa) by shelling the islands of Quemoy and Matsu in the Taiwan Strait.[27] This hostile act might have been the opening move in a plan to invade the islands and threaten Taiwan, which is less than 100 miles off the mainland of China. Eisenhower wanted to reassure Taiwan of American support and to signal the PRC that the United States would ensure Taiwan's security. To bolster his position, he asked Congress to pronounce a commitment to Taiwan's security and to authorize American intervention if the island was attacked. In January 1955, the House and Senate passed the Formosa Resolution by overwhelming majorities, and the crisis was brought to a successful conclusion.

In domestic affairs, however, the same broad consensus did not exist. Eisenhower was forced to make concessions on key proposals in order to see them passed into law, including a bill to extend the president's tariff reduction authority (passed in 1955 after a concession by the president) and the creation of the Interstate Highway System. The highway bill, which was the major domestic legislative accomplishment of Eisenhower's presidency, passed in 1956 only after the president compromised on highway funding. It had passed the Senate the previous year but had failed in the House. Only after Eisenhower accepted the Democrats' plan of user taxes to fund it (rather than his preferred method of toll roads) was Congress willing to support the plan.[28] Overall, the president's modest domestic legislative agenda and interparty competition meant that legislative activity was not the centerpiece of Eisenhower's governance during this period.

Failed Attempts at Legislative Bargaining/Compromise

Disagreement was the major characteristic of the domestic legislative arena during this time. As Ambrose put it, "Both parties were jockeying for position for the 1956 presidential election; neither party was willing to give the other credit for major legislation. The Democrats were unwilling to get behind Eisenhower's health reinsurance program, because they wanted a much broader approach to health care,"[29] and other disagreements meant that several administration proposals failed on Capitol Hill.

Some issues (e.g., health insurance) went unresolved, whereas others (e.g., a civil rights bill) had to wait until later (the 1957 Civil Rights Act passed after significant compromise). Eisenhower's determination to balance the federal budget also put him at odds with the Democratic majorities in Congress, which supported new federal spending programs and broad-based tax cuts.

Executive Actions

Executive actions were important to Eisenhower's conduct of the presidency, both in this period and throughout his two terms (see table 4). He exercised his veto several times, issuing eighteen regular vetoes (all sustained) and thirty-three pocket vetoes. He also issued forty-four signing statements during this period, including four that challenged a provision in a law. Although he employed careful language in signing statements to make his point, in these four cases Ike informed Congress that he would interpret objectionable provisions of laws in ways that would avoid unconstitutional mandates to the executive branch from the legislature. His most important actions came in foreign policy, which was consistent with his priorities and the ongoing Cold War.

Foreign Policy Initiatives and Actions

Eisenhower's presidency came during an important period for world affairs. The immediate aftermath of World War II was over, but there were still significant issues left over from the war to be settled. At the same time, the Cold War that had emerged while Truman was in office had solidified into a bipolar competition between the Western democracies and their allies (led by the United States) and the Communist states (the Soviet Union and China) and their allies. The central challenges of American foreign policy in this era focused on managing the delicate balance of international relations without a "shooting war" or significant political advantages for America's Communist adversaries.

Eisenhower made extensive use of executive power in this area, maintaining presidential control of foreign policy even as he requested Congress's support for his actions. He issued more than forty national security directives and endorsed the use of covert actions to further his foreign policy goals. In 1955, he signed 525 executive agreements (out of 1,705 total executive agreements signed during his presidency), the most in a single year. That same year, the Austrian peace treaty was finally signed, concluding one of the last remaining diplomatic issues outstanding from the war (not counting the East-West division of Europe that would continue until 1989). The U.S. occupation of Germany also ended in 1955.

One of the most significant episodes during this period was Eisenhower's management of the Taiwan Straits Crisis, which began in 1954. Not only did he obtain congressional support for the defense of Taiwan in the Formosa Resolution, but in March 1955, he delivered a not-so-veiled threat to employ nuclear weapons if military conflict over Taiwan erupted. On March 16, he responded to a reporter's question about the potential use of nuclear weapons by saying, "Now, in any combat where these things can be used on strictly military targets and for strictly military purposes, I see no reason why they shouldn't be used just exactly as you would use a bullet or anything else."[30] Within a few weeks, the PRC expressed interest in negotiations and ceased shelling the islands of Quemoy and Matsu.

The period of 1955–1956 was one of foreign policy activism for Eisenhower. In 1955, he unveiled his Open Skies proposal (to allow overflights of the United States and the Soviet Union by each other, to promote peace); it was rejected by the Soviet government. He also attended a summit meeting with Soviet leader Nikita Khrushchev in Geneva, attempting to reduce international tensions. The summit was, according to Ambrose, "a dramatic moment in the Cold War," and after it threats of a "shooting war"[31] between the superpowers were less common. The following year, Eisenhower refused to support the combined British-French-Israeli military action during the Suez Crisis (when Egypt nationalized the Suez

Canal) and endorsed action by the United Nations to reach a peaceful settlement of the crisis. The Suez Crisis occurred shortly before the 1956 election, and no doubt its peaceful resolution enhanced the president's reputation for calm and confident management of foreign policy in a difficult era. In 1956, Eisenhower also decided not to support the uprising by Hungarians against Soviet domination, a decision he believed would prevent a major war but that provoked much criticism.[32]

Going Public

Eisenhower's use of public politics in this period was divided between activities connected with presidential business and activities of his reelection campaign in 1956. He made an address to the nation in July 1955 at the Geneva Summit, as well as nineteen news conferences (many focusing on foreign policy). In February 1956, he made another major televised address announcing his decision to seek a second term in office, and that year he held twenty-four news conferences. From August through early November 1956, he made a series of appearances related to his campaign for reelection, including televised addresses, a heavy schedule of appearances, and television broadcasts with such titles as "The People Ask the President" and "The Women Ask the President" (both in October 1956).[33] Ike was the first president to make extensive use of television in this way.

Overall, Eisenhower's public politics reflected his general approach to the presidency: it was low-key but confident and upbeat. It conveyed the message that the president was warm and approachable but nevertheless an experienced and serious leader. The public responded enthusiastically, giving Eisenhower strong approval ratings throughout this period (mostly above 70% in 1955–1956 and ending 1956 with 79% job approval in the Gallup survey).[34]

Epilogue

The 1956 presidential election featured a rematch between Eisenhower and Governor Adlai Stevenson of Illinois, who had also been the Democratic nominee in 1952. Eisenhower won all but seven states and outpaced Stevenson by ten million votes, almost twice the margin of his earlier victory. Democrats maintained modest majorities in the House and Senate, but voters gave Ike the personal vote of confidence he had sought. He now turned his attention to his second term as president. His response to political adversity is summarized in table 4.

BILL CLINTON, 1995–1996

The midterm elections of 1994 delivered an almost-classic unmandate for the incumbent president. As the election drew closer that fall, polls indicated strong voter "dismay and disgust with Clinton,"[35] leading the president's own pollster to advise Democratic candidates to avoid identification with him.[36] The anti-Clinton mood led to a dramatic wave of defeats for Democratic candidates, sweeping away several incumbent governors, House Speaker Tom Foley, and majorities in both chambers of Congress. When the midterm results were tallied, Republicans controlled both the House and Senate for the first time since 1954; Clinton and his allies were in a state of shock.

In the new political reality of Washington, the center of political gravity shifted to Capitol Hill, and observers asked whether the president was even relevant. House Republicans were united behind their Speaker, Newt Gingrich of Georgia, and were eager to enact the "Contract with America" that had been their campaign manifesto.

Once he recovered from his shock, Clinton set himself on the task of reviving his political fortunes. He was determined to prepare for a successful reelection campaign in 1996; to that end, he adopted a deliberate comeback strategy aimed at occupying the broad middle ground in American politics.[37] The name given to this strategy by Dick Morris, a campaign consultant employed by Clinton, was "triangulation." It would guide Clinton's conduct as president for the next two years.

Table 4a. Summarizing the President's Response to Adversity—Unmandate—
Eisenhower 1955–1956

Type of response	*Summary data & significant examples*
1. Bargaining & persuasion	*House & Senate concurrence with president— average for 1955-1956*: 72.3% *Legislative successes/compromises/concessions:* • 1955: Formosa Resolution • 1955: Extension of tariff reduction authority (following concession by Eisenhower) • 1956: Soil Bank system • 1956: Interstate highway system (compromise after defeat in 1955) *Failed attempts at legislative bargaining/compromise:* • 1955: School construction bill failed • 1955: Health reinsurance bill failed • 1956: Ike calls for civil rights bill (not passed until 1957, after compromises)
2. Executive actions constitutional	*Vetoes:* 18 regular (100% sustained), 33 pocket *Pardons & clemency:* 330 *Proclamations:* 3 *Executive orders*: 109 • 10598—Operations Coord Board (to coordinate foreign policy implementation, esp psych warfare—1955) *Signing statements:* 44 (4 challenged part of a law) • 4 provisions to be interpreted so not be unconstitutional mandates to executive *Claims of executive privilege:* None
other actions	N/A
3. Foreign policy initiatives & actions	*National security directives:* 42 *Executive agreements:* 525 (1955: 300—most in one year for Eisenhower) *Significant treaties:* • 1955: Austrian peace treaty
Outcome of case: Eisenhower won 1956 election in landslide (57%-42%)	

Table 4b. Summarizing the President's Response to Adversity—Unmandate—
Eisenhower 1955–1956 (Cont.)

Type of response	Summary data & significant examples
Foreign policy initiatives & actions *continued*	*Uses of force:* • 1954-55: Tachen Islands • 1955: Cong okays force to defend Taiwan Straits; Ike implies nuclear threat • 1956: Suez crisis—evacuation of Americans *Other:* • 1955: End of US occupation of Germany • 1955: Open Skies proposal (USSR rejects) • 1955: Summit in Geneva • 1956: US opposes British-French-Israeli military action in Suez Crisis, endorses UN effort to seek peace • 1956: Ike decides not to support Hungarian uprising against Soviet domination
4. Organizational changes	N/A
5. Going public	*Major speeches:* 7 (1955-3; 1956-4) *News conferences:* 41 (1955-19; 1956-24) *Key events/activities:* • July 1955: Address & news conference following Geneva Conference • Feb 1956: Announced bid for reelection • Aug-Nov 1956: reelection campaigning, including acceptance speech to Republican Convention (Aug 23), natl address opening campaign (Sept 19), & heavy schedule of appearances (including TV broadcasts in Oct) • Oct 1956: Address to nation on events in Eastern Europe and the Middle East
6. Unconventional actions?	N/A
Outcome of case: Eisenhower won 1956 election in landslide (57%-42%)	

Table 4c. Comparing the President's Response to Non-Adverse Circumstances—Eisenhower 1955–1956

Type of response	Comparison to non-adverse circumstances (1953-54, 1957-60)
1. Bargaining & persuasion	*House & Senate concurrence with president— average for 1954-1954*: 89.4% *Legislative successes/compromises/concessions:* • 1954: St. Lawrence Seaway bill • 1954: Social Security expanded • 1957: Eisenhower Doctrine—aid Middle Eastern countries against communism • 1957: Civil Rights Act • Bricker Amendnt (limit exec agrements) defeated, Ike's opposition helped kill it *Failed attempts at legislative bargaining/compromise:* • 1957: FY 1958 budget—"a personal defeat" • 1960: Law of the Sea convention defeated
2. Executive actions constitutional	*Vetoes—total*: 73 reg (97% sustained), 108 pocket *Pardons & clemency:* 1157 total *Proclamations:* 23 total *Executive orders:* 478 • 10730—took control of Ark Natl Guard, Little Rock (1957) *Signing statements:* 145 (9 challenged part of a law) *Claims of executive privilege:* • 1954: Exec officials not testify in Army-McCarthy hearings
other actions	Sept 1957: sent troops to assist integration at Little Rock Central High School
3. Foreign policy initiatives & actions	*National security directives:* 187 • 1954: NSC 5412—on covert activities *Executive agreements—total:* 1834 *Significant treaties:* (89 total) • 1954: SEATO treaty • 1959: Antarctic treaty
Outcome of case: Eisenhower won 1956 election in landslide (57%-42%)	

Table 4d. Comparing the President's Response to Non-Adverse Circumstances—Eisenhower 1955–1956 (Cont.)

Type of response	Comparison to non-adverse circumstances (1953-54, 1957-60)
Foreign policy initiatives & actions *continued*	*Uses of force:* • 1957: Indonesia • 1957: Navy defends Quemoy • 1958: Indonesia • 1958: Lebanon—help support govt • 1959-60: Cuba—protect US citizens *Other:* • 1953: Korean armistice • 1953: Atoms for Peace proposal • 1953: US-backed coup in Iran • 1954: Eisenhower decides not to relieve French garrison at Dien Bien Phu (Vietnam) • 1954: "New Look" reshapes defense policy
4. Organizational changes	• 1958: Sherman Adams (chief of staff) fired because of scandal
5. Going public	*Major speeches:* 39 (total)—yr with most: 1957-10 *News conferences:* 193 (total)—yr with most: 1954-33 *Key events/activities:* • 1953: "Atoms for Peace" address to UN • 2nd term: Ike used speeches, appearances, meetings at White House with business & civic leaders, and advertising in support of admin's foreign • 1957: Eisenhower Doctrine address to Congress • Jan 1961: Farewell Address
6. Unconventional actions?	1957: tried to induce Congress to hold down spending by release of budget & public statement by Treasury Secy—backfired
Outcome of case: Eisenhower won 1956 election in landslide (57%-42%)	

Bargaining and Persuasion

Bill Clinton's relations with the 104th Congress were among the most
contentious in modern American political history. The new majorities in

Congress, especially in the House, were eager to put their stamp on policy and determined to alter the course of public policy. The results of the "showdown"[38] between Clinton and the 104th Congress were a partial shutdown of the federal government, record lows in congressional concurrence with the president, and various actions to assert Clinton's political relevance and autonomy from legislative constraints.

The House Republicans of the 104th Congress wanted to enact their "Contract with America," but they were also uninterested in advancing the president's policy goals. Congressional concurrence, which had been above 80% in the first two years of Clinton's presidency (despite their refusal to act on Clinton's health care reform plan), dropped to 36.2% in 1995. In fact, House concurrence with the president was lower in 1995 than in almost any other year since 1953 (the first year for which concurrence was calculated)—for either chamber of Congress (see table 5). Congress had agreed with Clinton 86.4% of the time in 1993 and 1994, but the 104th Congress agreed with him only 45.7% of the time. Moreover, the level of rancor between the branches was high—Speaker of the House Newt Gingrich openly attacked the values of Bill and Hillary Clinton, whereas Clinton portrayed Gingrich as an extremist more committed to an ideology than to the good of the nation.

Clinton's strategy of "triangulation" led him to engage in both compromise and conflict with Congress. On one hand, he endorsed the most popular Republican goals; the idea here was to "fast-forward the Gingrich agenda."[39] On the other hand, he would oppose those Republican objectives that he and his advisors believed the public would not support, such as cutting popular programs (e.g., Social Security and Medicare) or weakening environmental protections.

Table 5. Congressional Concurrence with the President, 1993–1996

Year	Total H&S Concurrence	House Concurrence	# of House Votes	Senate Concurrence	# of Senate Votes
1993	86.4	87.3	102	85.4	89
1994	86.4	87.2	78	85.5	62
Average	**86.4**	**87.25**		**84.45**	
Total			180		148
1995	36.2	26.3	133	49.0	102
1996	55.1	53.2	79	57.6	59
Average	**45.7**	**39.9**		**53.3**	
Total			212		161

Source. Compiled from data in *Vital Statistics on American Politics, 2009–2010* (p. 245) by Harold Stanley and Richard Niemi. Washington, DC: CQ Press, 2010.

As John Harris and others have explained it, this strategy would position Clinton as a centrist committed to reasonable change—but apart from the "extremist" ideas of Gingrich and his caucus:

> Once the electorate saw that Clinton and Gingrich agreed on these broad points…the Republicans would have played all their best cards. Public attention would then shift to the least popular parts of the GOP agenda…Only then, with the energy drained from the Republican advance, would the electorate who rejected Clinton so emphatically the previous autumn again be ready to listen to him talk about his own agenda.[40]

Clinton called for bipartisanship in addressing the nation's problems, but in 1995 the major focus of his relations with Congress became a stalemate over the federal budget. Clinton signed into law the parts of the Contract with America that did not conflict with his goals—reforms in Congress and a line-item veto for the president (later ruled unconstitutional by the Supreme Court)—but he wrangled with Congress over how to go about reducing the deficit and shrinking government.

Legislative Successes/Compromises/Concessions

To speak of legislative "successes" for Clinton during this period, at least in terms of administration proposals passed into law, is somewhat misleading. Most of the legislation passed into law in 1995 and 1996 was driven by the Republican agenda or represented compromises between Clinton and Congress—or even concessions by the president.

Much of 1995 was focused on the confrontation between the president and Congress over the budget (see the following section), but in 1996 Clinton signed several major acts. Many represented concessions by the White House and Clinton's positioning of himself in the ideological center; he signed the Telecommunications Act of 1996 (which included restrictions on pornographic material on the Internet), as well as the Helms-Burton Act (tightening the embargo against Cuba) and the Defense of Marriage Act (which defined marriage as between one man and one woman). One good example of concession was Clinton's signing of a welfare reform bill, the 1996 Personal Responsibility and Work Opportunity Act: on record supporting welfare reform and having already vetoed two earlier Republican bills, Clinton was reluctant to head into the 1996 election campaign without signing the bill, so he gave in and signed it.[41]

Clinton employed veto threats to induce Congress to modify or derail bills he found objectionable. Richard Conley found that the president threatened use of the veto forty-one times during the 104th Congress, which resulted in bills dying in committee or on the floor about 40% of the time.[42] The president relied on a veto strategy in large part because, as Conley put it, "his continuing domestic agenda [was] relegated to the sidelines of congressional and media attention"[43] as Congress focused on the Republican agenda. His situation was characterized more by attempts to block or moderate conservative legislation than by attempts to persuade Congress to promote his priorities. So it is no surprise that congressional concurrence with the president was very low during this period.

Failed Attempts at Legislative Bargaining/Compromise
The 104th Congress is remembered more for confrontation with the president than for anything else. The central issue was the budget because it was the key to most aspects of federal government policy, and a showdown between the branches loomed throughout 1995. The Republican Congress wanted to use the budget bill to begin a process of not only reducing the deficit but altering the size and power of the federal government itself. Clinton, as part of his triangulation strategy, endorsed the goal of a balanced budget and a leaner government but positioned himself as the defender of popular programs such as Medicare and Social Security.

The conflict came to a head late in the year. Because no budget had been passed by the beginning of the fiscal year (October 1), the federal government was operating on a continuing resolution[44] that was due to expire in November. Gingrich and the Republicans thought they could pressure Clinton to accept the cuts they wanted to make by threatening to shut down the federal government, believing that Clinton would not allow that to happen. Moreover, the Republicans thought that, if a shutdown did happen, the American public would blame Clinton for it and that it would cause the president to "break."[45]

Clinton endorsed the Republican goal of balancing the budget in seven years but rejected the GOP's insistence on using Congressional Budget Office (CBO) data to evaluate budget proposals. He also insisted that Medicare and other programs be protected while balancing the budget. Congress produced a new continuing resolution that included cuts in Medicare, as well as a bill to raise the federal debt limit that also contained provisions objectionable to Clinton. He vetoed both bills, and the result was a partial shutdown of the government for six days. Negotiations between the White House and Congress continued, and Clinton accepted a compromise continuing resolution that included balancing the budget in seven years and using CBO data. It would keep the government operating until December 15.

The shutdown began to turn the tide for Clinton. Newt Gingrich's popularity plummeted and Clinton's rose. The American public, unhappy with any disruption of government services, blamed Congress for the stalemate.[46] Nevertheless, the Republicans pressed on, passing a bill that contained sweeping cuts in the programs Clinton had promised to protect (Medicare, Medicaid, etc.) and making what Gingrich called "a fundamental change in the direction of government."[47] Clinton vetoed the bill, causing a second government shutdown that lasted twenty-one days (December 1995–January 1996).

With polls showing that the public was unhappy about the shutdown and that it blamed Congress—not the president—for what was happening, the two sides reached a compromise in January 1996. Newt Gingrich admitted to Leon Panetta, Clinton's chief of staff, that he had incorrectly assumed that Congress could impose enough pressure on Clinton to "break" him.[48] Clinton's approval rating was up—by the end of January 1996, it was back above 50%, and it did not go below that mark for the remainder of his presidency.[49]

Executive Actions
Clinton relied on executive actions to help sustain his presidency during this period. Most significant were his vetoes in the budget showdown, and his refusal to "break" under pressure from Congress was responsible for the turnaround of Clinton's presidency. He also issued ninety-three signing statements, of which thirteen challenged provisions in a law. His most important signing statements came in 1995, as Clinton sought to limit the restrictions that Congress could impose on the executive. In signing the Fisheries Act of 1995, for example, he objected to language that could be interpreted as directing foreign policy and instructed "all executive officials" to treat them as strictly advisory.[50] Likewise, in signing the Helms-Burton Act, which tightened the U.S. embargo against Cuba, Clinton pointed to provisions that might be read as limiting his discretion in foreign policy and warned Congress that he considered these to be "precatory."[51]

This period also marked the first time in his presidency that Bill Clinton invoked executive privilege, making at least four claims to withhold information from those investigating his administration. Privilege claims (successful and unsuccessful) would become even more important as he fought off investigations into his involvement with Paula Jones and Monica Lewinsky in his second term.

Foreign Policy Initiatives and Actions

Foreign policy was not one of Bill Clinton's central concerns during his first term, although like any post–World War II American president, he faced problems and issues that required his attention. Even with a primary focus on domestic and economic issues, Clinton followed the trend of his predecessors in asserting broad presidential control to direct American foreign policy.

Clinton sought to maintain presidential dominance of foreign policy by taking unilateral actions as much as possible. In 1995, learning of an impending collapse of the Mexican peso, he sought out congressional support for a loan to support Mexico; when told that Congress was not likely to approve it, the president issued a $20 million loan from emergency funds already under his control.[52] That same year, responding to continuing concerns about Iran being a "rogue state" (he had applied that term to Iran the year before), Clinton issued two executive orders (E.O. 12957 and 12959) that banned nearly all trade with that nation. The following year, he agreed to the Comprehensive Test Ban Treaty, although he did not submit it to the Senate until after his reelection (it was never approved by the Senate).

The most important issue in foreign policy during this period was the ongoing civil war in Bosnia and Herzegovina, which had declared its independence from Yugoslavia in 1992. The conflict pitted Bosnian Serbs, who wanted to remain in Yugoslavia, against the Bosnian Muslims and Croats. Clinton had failed to persuade NATO leaders to intervene in defense of the Muslims and Croats in 1994, and he also encountered public and congressional resistance to American involvement there. In 1995, however, the situation in the troubled country grew far worse. That summer, Serb forces slaughtered thousands of Bosnian Muslim men in Srebrenica (as part of a Serb campaign of "ethnic cleansing") and then shelled the capital city of Sarajevo. Clinton approved an escalation of military force against the Bosnian Serbs and convinced NATO allies to approve a bombing campaign in Bosnia and Herzegovina in response to Serb aggression.[53] He then dispatched Deputy Secretary of State Richard Holbrooke to convene a peace conference of the warring parties at Wright-Patterson Air Force Base in Dayton, Ohio. Holbrooke brokered a settlement, the Dayton Accords, which peacefully resolved the conflict and became a key diplomatic success for the administration. That fall, Clinton sent 20,000 U.S. troops to Bosnia as peacekeepers. Conflict in other parts of the Balkans would flare up in Clinton's second term, but by the end of 1995, the problem of Bosnia had been addressed.[54]

Although Clinton circumvented Congress on several fronts of foreign policy, he could not avoid all its constraints. He had used emergency funds to prop up the Mexican peso and managed to evade congressional limits on his freedom of maneuver in the Bosnia, but congressional resistance to the 1994 Agreed Framework with North Korea effectively derailed its implementation. The administration viewed that agreement, which was intended to halt North Korea's nuclear weapons program by providing it the technology needed to build nuclear power plants, as a significant diplomatic breakthrough. But the Agreed Framework required funding for long-term implementation (some emergency funds were used in the short run), and beginning in 1995 Congress refused to support the agreement. Eventually, the agreement failed, and in 2005 North Korea announced that it had manufactured nuclear weapons for its defense. As one official involved in the implementation of the agreement summarized the ill-fated deal, "The Agreed Framework was a political orphan within two weeks after its signature."[55]

Where he did not have to depend on Congress, Clinton was freer to act in international affairs. As shown in his signing statements, he also continued to assert broad presidential autonomy over foreign policy as a matter of constitutional principle.

Organizational Changes

Clinton did not undertake a shakeup of his administration in response to the unmandate of 1994, although two organizational changes occurred as consequences of the Republican victories. The first came only weeks after the November elections when Jocylen Elder, Clinton's surgeon general and a target of conservatives, was reported to have made controversial comments about sex education in a public forum. Incoming Speaker Newt Gingrich attacked Elder's comments as "destructive," and Clinton decided to dismiss her rather than provide the new Republican majority with a lightning rod and an opportunity to score political points against the president. She was fired in December 1994.[56]

More significant was the rise of Dick Morris as Clinton's political strategist. Clinton had consulted Morris in the past, but the devastating results of the 1994 midterms led the president to rely more heavily on the consultant. Morris was known then as a centrist campaign consultant (later he would be more conservative) who advised both Republican and Democratic candidates, and he developed and sold Clinton on the strategy of "triangulation." Beginning after the midterm elections, he became an influential advisor to the president and played a key role in plotting Clinton's actions during the government shutdown. For part of this time, Morris was unknown to others on the White House staff, and more liberal staff members (including Hillary Clinton and George Stephanopoulos) came to resent his influence. Eventually, Morris would be ousted in August 1996 when he was caught in a sex scandal. By that point, his influence had already begun to wane.[57]

Going Public

The period of 1995–1996 was marked not only by Clinton's use of unilat-eralism in a showdown with the 104th Congress but also by his use of public politics to remind the public that the president was still an important part of the political scene. Clinton embarked on two campaigns of going public to reestablish his presence in the national consciousness, then in the fall of 1996 engaged in literal campaigning as he appealed for a second term in office.

The first drive to ensure Clinton a place in the national political conver-sation involved developing a new technique for going public. Charles Jones described Clinton's approach:

> I call it "voice." Not satisfied in public debate simply to say no by vetoing congressional Republican initiatives, President Clinton developed a positive message in regard to lesser matters. Voice features constant monitoring of the interests and concerns of ordi-nary Americans, sympathetic exposure of these matters in a "family values" setting, exhortation for a community solution (typically but not always involving government), liberal use of executive orders and other presidential prerogatives that avoid congressional partic-ipation, and little deference to jurisdictional boundaries between public and private or levels of government. That an issue might be judged outside the president's usual domain is no barrier to his declarations.[58]

Using "voice," Clinton made statements on school uniforms, curfews for young people, the need for reading specialists in schools, V-chips for tele-visions, and the virtues of flexible time in the workplace. In his 1996 address accepting the Democratic nomination, he made forty separate proposals on a wide range of issues. As Jones summarized the advantages (for Clinton) of voice, "Properly done, there is reason almost every day to reinforce the president's presence in national, state, and local public affairs."[59]

Clinton's other endeavor to reclaim public attention and support in the face of the Republican revolution was an advertising campaign. Beginning in the summer of 1995, Dick Morris ran a barrage of TV ads highlighting Clinton's role in defending Medicare, Social Security, and public education, as well as his defense of the environment, all against the onslaught by Gingrich and Republican "extremists." This barrage eventually cost $85 million and, to the amazement of the Clinton camp, went largely unanswered by the Republicans. This advertising campaign, along with "voice" and the turnaround that resulted from the government shutdown, helped restore Clinton's standing with the public. Newt Gingrich later admitted that leaving the ad campaign unanswered was "our biggest mistake."[60]

With no opposition in the Democratic primaries in 1996, Clinton focused his public politics on building his own standing and undermining that of the Republicans. Beginning with his renomination by the Democratic convention in August, he began campaigning in earnest for reelection in November. These activities were ultimately successful.

Unconventional Actions
Clinton took a calculated risk in allowing a government shutdown late in 1995 because the move could have backfired. He did it because Dick Morris's polls suggested that the public would support him and in part because he needed to halt the Republican juggernaut. Gingrich and his caucus described their election and agenda as a revolution and in many ways had the (over)confidence of revolutionaries. In holding firm against Congress on the shutdown, Clinton forced the Republican majority to compromise with him and demonstrated that he—who had a reputation as a trimmer with no fixed convictions—stood for something no matter how strong the pressure placed on him. The public's reaction to Clinton's firmness in the showdown with Congress was to take another look at him and to help him reclaim much of the popular support he had lost in his first two years. It is arguable that standing firm on the shutdown made it possible for Bill Clinton to win a second term.

Epilogue

Following the unmandate of 1994, Bill Clinton was all but given up for dead politically. By the election of 1996, he commanded a nine-point lead over Republican Bob Dole, and Independent Ross Perot finished a distant third. He remained a dominant and controversial figure in American politics for the next four years. His response to political adversity is summarized in table 6.

GEORGE W. BUSH, 2007–2008

The George W. Bush presidency was "reset" after the attacks of September 11, 2001. Elected in 2000 as a result of the Supreme Court's decision in the disputed Florida recount, Bush had been a moderately conservative president focused on a modest domestic policy agenda. But in the fall of 2001, he became the commanding presence in American politics. As the nation rallied around its chief executive, he transformed himself into a war president who was "the decider" in issues of national security and the director of an aggressive war on terror. But Bush's wars—in Afghanistan, in Iraq, and one composed of antiterrorist activities including surveillance, detention of terror suspects, and other measures—became controversial and unpopular. By the midterm congressional elections in 2006, Bush and the Iraq war were in political trouble, and voters used the opportunity to punish Republican candidates and elect Democratic majorities in both the House and Senate. The main explanation for the midterm results, as Gary Jacobson put it, was "the electorate's unhappiness with the Iraq War and the president responsible for it."[61] Voters handed Bush an unmandate.

Table 6a. Summarizing the President's Response to Adversity—Unmandate—
Bill Clinton, 1995–1996

Type of response	Summary data & significant examples
1. Bargaining & persuasion	*House & Senate concurrence with president— average for 1995-1996: 45.7%* *Legislative successes/compromises/concessions:* • Jan 1996: compromise ends govt shutdown • Feb 1996: Telecommunications Act of 1996 • Mar 1996: Helms-Burton Act (Cuba embargo) • Aug 1996: Welfare reform bill (concession) • Sept 1996: Defense of Marriage Act *Failed attempts at legislative bargaining/compromise:* • Nov/ Dec 1995: budget impasse causes partial closure fed govt (Nov: 6 days; Dec: 21 days) • 1995-96: cong resistance limited implementing N. Korea agreement (see #3 below)
2. Executive actions constitutional	*Vetoes:* 17 regular (94% sustained), 0 pocket • Nov 1995: vetoes led to 1st govt shutdown • Dec 1995: veto led to 2nd govt shutdown *Pardons & clemency:* 12 pardons, 2 commutations *Proclamations:* 202 *Executive orders:* 89 *Signing statements:* 95 (13 significant) *Claims of executive privilege:* at least 4
other actions	N/A
3. Foreign policy initiatives & actions	*National security directives:* approximately 23 (unclear—many are classified and undated) *Executive agreements:* • 1995-96: cong resistance to 1994 Agreed Framework w/ North Korea limited implementation *Significant treaties:* • 1996: Comprehensive Test Ban Treaty (never approved by Senate)
	*Outcome of case: Clinton reelected with 49.2% of vote (9 percentage points ahead of Republican Bob Dole)*

Table 6b. Summarizing the President's Response to Adversity—Unmandate—
Bill Clinton, 1995–1996 (Cont.)

Type of response	Summary data & significant examples
Foreign policy initiatives & actions *continued*	*Uses of force:* • Aug 1995: Upped military force against Bosnian Serbs; NATO approved bombing • Oct 1995: US troops sent to Bosnia *Other:* • 1995: loan to Mexico from emergency funds • 1995: 2 exec orders halted most trade with Iran • 1995: Dayton Accords (Bosnian peace)
4. Organizational changes	Dec 1994: Jocylen Elders fired as Surgeon General (concession to Republicans) Jan 1995: Dick Morris becomes influential advisor (unknown to most of Clinton staff) Aug 1996: Dick Morris ousted in sex scandal
5. Going public	1995-1996: Clinton uses of "voice" to speak on school uniforms & other issues Jan 1995: Interview on NBC Nightly News Jan 1995: State of the Union Address Apr 1995: Memorial of Oklahoma City bombing Apr 1995: Interview on CBS "60 Minutes" Summer 1995: TV advertising to show Clinton as defender of popular govt programs Jun 1995: Town meeting w/Newt Gingrich in NH Jun 1995: Address to nation on budget Nov 1995: Address to nation on Bosnia Jan 1996: State of the Union Address Aug 1996: Acceptance speech, Democ Natl Conv Fall 1996: Campaigning for reelection Oct 1996: Pres debates with Senator Bob Dole Nov 1996: Victory remarks after reelection
6. Unconventional actions?	Nov & Dec 1995: Vetoes lead to partial shutdown of fed govt
Outcome of case: Clinton reelected with 49.2% of vote (9 percentage points ahead of Republican Bob Dole)	

Table 6c. Comparing the President's Response to Non-Adverse Circumstances—Bill Clinton, 1995–1996

Type of response	Comparison to non-adverse circumstances (1993-94)
1. Bargaining & persuasion	*House & Senate concurrence with pres—average for 1993-1994:* 86.4% *Legislative successes/compromises/concessions:* • Aug 1993 — Omnibus Budget Reconciliation Act of 1993 • Nov 1993 — Brady Handgun Violence Prevention Act • Nov 1993 — Don't ask, don't tell (concession) • Dec 1993 — North Amer Free Trade Agreement Implementation Act *Failed attempts at legislative bargaining/compromise:* • 1994: Health care reform plan dies in Congress without a vote
2. Executive actions constitutional	*Vetoes—total:* 36 reg (94% sustained), 1 pocket *Pardons & clemency:* Total—396 pardons, 61 commutations, 2 remissions (none controversial) *Proclamations:* 878 total • 6641 – Implementation of NAFTA *Executive orders:* 364 total • 12866—regulatory planning & review *Signing statements:* 381 (70 challenged part of law) *Claims of executive privilege:* none
other actions	Apr 1993: Clinton authorizes assault on Branch Davidian sect, Waco, TX
3. Foreign policy initiatives & actions	*National security directives:* 75 *Executive agreements—total:* 2048 • 1994: Agreed Framework to halt N. Korean nuclear weapons program
Outcome of case: Clinton reelected with 49.2% of vote (9 percentage points ahead of Republican Bob Dole)	

Table 6d . Comparing the President's Response to Non-Adverse Circumstances—Bill Clinton, 1995–1996

Type of response	Comparison to non-adverse circumstances (1993-94)
Foreign policy initiatives & actions *continued*	*Significant treaties:* (209 total) • 1993: N. Amer Free Trade Agreement • 1993: Strategic Arms Reduction, II • 1993: Chemical Weapons Convention *Uses of force:* • June 1993: missile attack on Iraq—to retaliate for trying to kill former Pres George HW Bush • 1993: Somalia • July 1994: Rwanda—relief supplies, but no action to halt genocide • Sept 1994: Haiti—support democracy *Other:* 1993: Oslo Accords (Israel & PLO) brokered by US
4. Organizational changes	Jul 1994: Leon Panetta replaces Thos "Mack" McLarty as chief of staff in face of media reports of a White House in chaos
5. Going public	Jan 1993: Inaugural Address Feb 1993: Economic program Feb 1993: Administration goals Aug 1993: Economic program Sept 1993: Health care reform Jan 1994: State of the Union Address Sept 1994: Haiti Oct 1994: Iraq Dec 1994: Middle Class Bill of Rights
6. Unconventional actions?	N/A
Outcome of case: Clinton reelected with 49.2% of vote (9 percentage points ahead of Republican Bob Dole)	

Bush now had to contend with a Democrat-controlled Congress that was determined to resist much of his agenda and bring an end to the war in Iraq. The president was determined to continue with his policies, including the war in Iraq. On the day after the 2006 elections, Bush told reporters that "most Americans and leaders here in Washington from both political parties understand we cannot accept defeat"[62] in the war on terror. Responding to a reporter's question, he expanded on his resolution to continue the war in Iraq:

> [W]e will continue to adjust to achieve the objective. And I believe that's what the American people want…"Stay the course" means, let's get the job done, but it doesn't mean staying stuck on a strategy or tactics that may not be working…what's also important for the American people to understand is that if we were to leave before the job is done, the country becomes more at risk.[63]

Bush's resolve in the matter of the Iraq war and the larger war on terrorism combined with his overall style to invite conflict with Congress. Charles Jones characterized Bush's style as that of a "pure executive…believing that the president and Congress have distinctive functions."[64] This "pure executive" would focus on doing his job as he saw it, believing that the American public would ultimately understand what he was doing and why. As he told an interviewer after leaving office, what mattered to him was the perspective of history: "I hope I'm judged a success. But…I'm gonna be dead, Matt, when they finally figure it out. And I'm comfortable knowing that I gave it my all."[65]

Bargaining and Persuasion
The Democratic takeover of Congress had consequences for George Bush's ability to gain support on Capitol Hill. In the years when Republicans held majorities in Congress (the Senate had a one-vote Democratic majority in 2001 and 2002), Bush was successful in winning support for many of his legislative goals. He made compromises, such as winning support for tax cuts in 2001 by accepting them as temporary rather than permanent, but in his first six years in office he won support for important bills including the No Child Left Behind Act (2001), Medicare prescription drug coverage (2003), and the Military Commissions Act (2006). The

notable exception to this record of general success was Bush's inability to interest Congress or the public in his plan to overhaul Social Security, despite concerted administration efforts for several months in 2005.

As table 7 shows, congressional concurrence with Bush was strong in the first six years but fell sharply in the House and somewhat in the Senate following the 2006 midterm elections. The president achieved an average combined House and Senate concurrence rate of 80.9% during his first six years, but after the Democratic takeover of Congress, average combined concurrence fell almost by half (to 43.1%). House concurrence with Bush was only 15.4% in 2007, the lowest rate on record for any year in either chamber of Congress.

Table 7. Congressional Concurrence with the President, 2001–2008

Year	Total H&S Concurrence	House Concurrence	# of House Votes	Senate Concurrence	# of Senate Votes
2001	87.0	83.7	43	88.3	77
2002	88.0	82.5	40	91.4	58
2003	78.7	87.3	55	74.8	119
2004	72.6	70.6	34	74.0	50
2005	78.0	78.3	46	77.8	45
2006	80.9	85.0	40	78.6	70
Average	**80.9**	**81.2**		**80.9**	
Total			258		419
2007	38.3	15.4	117	66.0	97
2008	47.8	33.8	80	68.5	54
Average	**43.1**	**24.6**		**67.3**	
Total			197		151

Source. Compiled from data in *Vital Statistics on American Politics, 2009–2010* (p. 245) by Harold Stanley and Richard Niemi. Washington, DC: CQ Press, 2010.

Legislative Successes/Compromises/Concessions
George Bush's relations with the 110th Congress were marked more by conflict than by agreement. As table 7 highlights, Congress concurred

with the president much less often than it disagreed with him. As a result, other than continued funding for the wars in Iraq and Afghanistan, there was little in the way of legislative successes or compromises for most of this period. Indeed, various accounts of the 110th Congress identify few significant acts other than those related to the war on terror or to the federal government's response to the economic crisis that erupted in the fall of 2008. In 2007, Congress agreed to the Protect America Act, which removed the requirement for a warrant in cases when the government conducts surveillance of foreign intelligence targets, as part of its overall endorsement of antiterrorist measures in the wake of the 9/11 attacks. The following year it passed the Foreign Intelligence Surveillance Act Amendments of 2008, which further enhanced the government's power to conduct surveillance against terrorism suspects.

In October 2008, responding to the worldwide financial crisis, Congress and the president agreed on emergency legislation to create the $700 billion Troubled Asset Relief Program (TARP). The administration's handling of the crisis focused on having Treasury Secretary Henry Paulson (working closely with Ben Bernanke, chairman of the Board of Governors of the Federal Reserve System) take the lead in constructing a plan. That plan, which initially met sharp resistance from Congress, passed after intense negotiations between administration officials and congressional leaders, as well as a growing sense of urgency over the economic situation and a major presidential address to stress the need for swift legislative approval. In the end, the crisis atmosphere of the period as much as bargaining or Bush's going public led to agreement on the creation of TARP.[66]

Failed Attempts at Legislative Bargaining/Compromise

Bush was at odds with the 110th Congress more often than they found terms for agreement. In 2007, Congress made two attempts to pressure the president to commit to a timetable for withdrawal of U.S. troops from Iraq. The first was a resolution that set a nonbinding goal of redeploying all U.S. troops from Iraq by March 2008. This proposal died in the Senate after intense opposition from Republicans. In May, Congress passed a supplemental appropriations bill that contained a timetable for withdrawal, which Bush vetoed. Unable to overcome the president's opposition, legislators subsequently conceded on the timetable issue and passed a revised version of the bill, and Bush approved it.

Bush was also unable to win congressional approval for an immigration reform plan. Earlier in his presidency, different proposals had been passed by the House and Senate, but none was able to win support by both chambers. When the Democrats assumed the majority on Capitol Hill, some observers thought Bush would be able to work out a compromise with Congress.[67] But a bipartisan bill on the issue—the Comprehensive Immigration Reform Act—failed to overcome a filibuster in the Senate in June 2007. At this point Bush called on senators to give the bill a chance, and the measure was taken up for consideration later that month.[68] Despite his efforts, however, opposition to the bill's provision of a path to citizenship for immigrants already in the United States illegally led to its defeat.

Executive Actions

As a "pure executive," George Bush made extensive use of unilateral presidential powers, including the veto, executive orders, and signing statements. He employed the veto to block legislation he found objectionable, especially any measure he saw as interfering with his conduct of the war in Iraq or other policy goals. In October and December 2007, he vetoed attempts to extend the State Child Health Insurance Program (S-CHIP), asserting that the program encouraged dependency on the federal government. In January 2007, he issued Executive Order 13422, which tightened White House control over rulemaking by administrative agencies.[69] He also continued the use of signing statements as a device to affect the implementation of laws passed by Congress. Of the thirteen signing statements he issued in 2007–2008, seven were significant; most of these contained warnings that his administration would interpret provisions in bills "in a manner consistent with the constitutional authority of the President."[70]

Foreign Policy Initiatives and Actions

Despite the fact that the 2006 midterm elections were widely seen as a referendum on Bush and the Iraq war, the president was determined to see the war through to a successful conclusion. Shortly after the elections, Bush told the Iraq Study Group (ISG), a bipartisan commission of former senior government officials and political heavyweights, "The word that captures what we want to achieve is victory...We want an ally [Iraq] in the war on terror, a government that can govern, sustain and defend itself."[71] Consistent with his "pure executive" style of governing, he also told the ISG, "I am running this war."[72] As he maintained even after leaving office, his decisions would be judged by history. Between the 2006 midterms and the end of his presidency, he adhered to this unilateralist approach.

Bush launched the war in 2003 (helped by a blank-check authorization to use force to overthrow the regime of Saddam Hussein), and by 2006, many in Congress and the public feared it had become a "quagmire" on the order of the Vietnam War.[73] Frustrated with the situation, in March 2006 Congress created the ISG (with reluctant White House support), and the group conducted an intensive study of the war. By the end of the year, the situation in Iraq seemed bleak—sectarian violence was rampant and anarchy seemed imminent[74]—and pressure was mounting (from both inside and outside the administration) for a change in American policy.

Less than a week after the midterm elections, a formal administration review of the war was set into motion. As the *New York Times* later described the political situation of the time,

> The Republicans had taken a beating at the polls and the Iraq Study Group...was preparing to publish its recommendations—to step up efforts to train Iraqi troops and withdraw virtually all American combat brigades by spring 2008...A document prepared for the [administration's own] review stated: "Our center of gravity —public support—is in jeopardy because of doubts that our Iraq efforts are on a trajectory leading to success."[75]

When the ISG released its report in December 2006, Bush praised its work but made it clear that he would make his own decision regarding any change in the war.[76] The administration's own review continued into 2007, but the president had already made up his mind about the direction he would take.

That new direction was to order a "surge" of U.S. forces in Iraq. Bush had signaled his advisors that he wanted to pursue some kind of troop increase when the National Security Council met early in December, but he had not yet determined how big the surge should be.[77] Over the next few weeks, administration officials coalesced around the idea of a five-brigade surge (20,000 troops). Particularly influential in shaping the final decision was General David Patraeus, a top counterinsurgency expert in the military who was the leading candidate to take over command of U.S. forces in Iraq.

The idea of a surge did not attract universal support inside the administration, but resistance to it was overcome by the end of 2006. Some skeptics softened their reservations to go along with a policy that had clear presidential support. Others were removed from positions that made them obstacles to a surge: General George Casey, the American commander in Iraq, was named chief of staff of the army, and the U.S. ambassador to Iraq Zalmay Khalilzad was nominated to be ambassador to the United Nations. Both had opposed the surge; their replacements—especially General Patraeus as the commander in Iraq—supported it. The president approved the plan and announced it to the nation on January 10, 2007.[78]

There was considerable backlash against Bush's decision, but he did have support from key quarters. On one hand, many on Capitol Hill attacked the surge as the wrong course of action. The Democratic senator Barack Obama predicted that 20,000 additional troops would exacerbate sectarian violence in Iraq, and the Republican senator Chuck Hagel called the plan "the most dangerous foreign policy blunder in this country since Vietnam."[79] On the other hand, Bush had support or acquiescence from administration officials who had been skeptical of a surge (e.g., Secretary of State Condoleezza Rice), Senator John McCain (an influential voice on defense policy), and others. Bush could also claim that the ISG endorsed the idea. Although the commission's recommendations emphasized a reduction of forces in Iraq, its report had stated, "We could, however, support a short-term redeployment or surge of American combat forces to stabilize Baghdad."[80] Bush thus had sufficient political support to block attempts in Congress to interfere with the surge.

The surge and its aftermath took up most of 2007 and 2008. The additional brigades began deploying to Iraq early in 2007 and reached their peak that September. Noncombat violence in Iraq, especially the sectarian violence that had threatened anarchy, was reduced by 40% or more.[81] Over the next several months, American troop levels in Iraq declined, and the Pentagon declared the surge over in July 2008 (although the number of American soldiers still in Iraq was greater than it had been before the surge began).[82] In November 2008, the Bush administration concluded an agreement on a strategic framework for relations between the United States and Iraq, as well as a "status of forces" agreement that laid out plans for eventual reduction of American combat forces.

Many observers viewed the surge as producing ambiguous results (until 2009, when President Obama acknowledged that it had succeeded[83]), and by the end of Bush's presidency the public was divided on whether the surge had been effective. In general, the public had turned against the war. Nevertheless, Bush was able to conduct the war as he saw fit. Although he was pressured into a review of American strategy in 2006, he was able to develop and implement his own plan without effective resistance from inside his administration, from Congress, or from the public. He had told the members of the Iraq Study Group "I am running this war," and that is how he proceeded.

Organizational Changes
The unmandate of 2006 had organizational/personnel consequences for the Bush administration. Most immediate was the departure of Defense

Secretary Donald Rumsfeld. One day after the 2006 midterm elections, Bush announced Rumsfeld's resignation and the nomination of Robert Gates to succeed him. Rumsfeld had been an especially controversial figure in the administration, and if the elections were a referendum on the war, they also rendered a negative judgment on him. Indeed, some Republicans would have preferred that he had left sooner because it might have helped them in the midterm elections.[84] Gates, by contrast, was welcomed with bipartisan support (and remained in the post under President Obama).

One key consequence of Rumsfeld's departure was that it removed a major obstacle to the troop surge as the idea was debated inside the administration. Other obstacles, including General George Casey and Ambassador Zalmay Khalilzad, were removed by their placement in different jobs.

The other major organizational change that occurred as a consequence of the 2006 unmandate took place in the Department of Justice in August 2007. In December 2006, seven U.S. attorneys were dismissed by President Bush. A scandal erupted because of allegations that these officials had been fired to halt investigations into wrongdoing by Republican politicians or because they had not pursued investigations against Democrats. As the scandal grew hotter over the summer of 2007, many Democrats in Congress decried what they saw as the politicization of the Justice Department. Eventually, Attorney General Alberto Gonzales and eight other senior Justice Department officials resigned, helping to put aside the controversy, and the president appointed new leadership at the department.

Going Public

President Bush employed the strategy of going public on a limited basis. Beyond the conventional public addresses that presidents give (e.g., the State of the Union, a Farewell Address), he spoke to the nation to address the war and the financial crisis that erupted in the fall of 2008. Regarding the war, Bush's rhetoric continued to state the case for his decisions and emphasize that he prosecuted the war because of his responsibility for protecting the nation and its interests. In announcing the troop surge in January 2007, he declared, "Failure in Iraq would be a disaster for the United States...For the safety of our people, America must succeed in Iraq."[85] After vetoing a spending bill that contained a timetable for withdrawal from Iraq, he returned to this theme of responsibility, criticizing those who used the bill for political purposes. He told the nation, "I recognize that many Democrats saw this bill as an opportunity to make a political statement about their opposition to the war. They've sent their message. And now it is time to put politics behind us and support our troops with the funds they need."[86] Concerning the economic crisis of 2008, Bush repeated his responsibility theme: "With the situation becoming more precarious by the day, I faced a choice: to step in with dramatic government action or to stand back and allow the irresponsible actions of some to undermine the financial security of all."[87]

Overall, Bush used public politics to explain and defend his handling of the nation's business rather than to rally support for himself. His rhetoric tended to echo the "pure executive" approach—"*I* faced a choice..." (emphasis added)—that Jones identified as his characteristic style. His rhetoric seemed to flow from the idea that the public wanted reassurance that he was in charge instead of appealing for public support.

Epilogue
George Bush finished his second term as president with a public approval rating of 33% but certain that he had met his responsibility to protect the nation.[88] He left office awaiting the judgment of history on his war in Iraq. His response to political adversity is summarized in table 8.

Table 8a. Summarizing the President's Response to Adversity—Unmandate—George W. Bush 2007-2008

Type of response	*Summary data & significant examples*
1. Bargaining & persuasion	*House-Senate concurrence with president—average for 2007-2008:* 43.1% *Legislative successes/compromises/concessions:* • May 2007: Appropriations bill (revised after veto) • Aug 2007: Protect America Act (no warrant needed to monitor foreign intelligence targets) • Feb 2008: Economic Stimulus Act • July 2008: FISA Amendments of 2008 • Oct 2008: Emergency Economic Stabilization Act *Failed attempts at legislative bargaining/compromise:* • June 2007: Immigration reform • Nov 2007: Water resources (veto overridden) • May 2008: Farm bill (veto overridden) *Other:* Mar 2007: Vote against Iraq troop surge failed
2. Executive actions constitutional	*Vetoes:* 10 regular (60% sustained), 1 pocket • May 2007: Appropriations bill with timetable for Iraq withdrawal (sustained); Congress conceded • Oct & Dec 2007: twice vetoed extension of S-CHIP (child health insurance) program (sustained) *Pardons & clemency:* 84 *Proclamations:* 236 *Executive orders:* 62 • 13422—more pres control over agency rulemaking *Signing statements:* 13 (7 significant)—several warnings on keeping pres's "constitutional authority" *Claims of executive privilege:* at least 4 • Jun 2007: Aides not testify on firing of US attorneys • Jun 2008: EPA withheld documents from Cong • July 2008: Former aide not testify to House committee on firing of US attorneys • July 2008: Documents related to CIA employee Valerie Plame withheld from House comm
Outcome of case: Bush left office with approval rating of 33% (66% disapproval), but most of his foreign policy still intact	

Table 8b. Summarizing the President's Response to Adversity—Unmandate—
George W. Bush 2007–2008 (Cont.)

Type of response	*Summary data & significant examples*
other actions	Sept 2008: White House mtg on financial crisis Nov 2008: Convened special meeting of G20 nations to discuss international financial crisis
3. Foreign policy initiatives & actions	*National security directives:* 16 (plus 8 Homeland Security Directives) *Executive agreements:* number undetermined • Nov 2007: US-Iraq—long-term military relations *Significant treaties:* N/A *Uses of force:* Continuation of US military operations in Iraq, Afghanistan, Kosovo, and elsewhere • Jan 2007-July 2008: Troop surge in Iraq *Other:* Nov 2008: Strategic framework and "Status of Forces Agreement" between US & Iraq
4. Organizational changes	Nov 2006: Defense Sec Rumsfeld resigned one day after Democrats won congressional majorities Jan 2007: new US military & diplomatic leadership in Iraq Aug 2007: Atty Gen Gonzales & 8 top Justice Dept officials resigned over firing of US attorneys
5. Going public	*Major speeches:* 5 (2007-3; 2008-2) *News conferences:* 57 (2007-30; 2008-27) *Key events/activities:* • Jan 2007: State of the Union Address • Jan 2007: Iraq troop surge • May 2007: On veto of bill with timetable for Iraq withdrawal • Sept 2007: Progress & future of Iraq troop surge • Jan 2008: State of the Union Address • Sept 2008: Address to nation on the economy & the bailout of financial institutions • Jan 2009: Farewell Address to nation
6. Unconventional actions?	N/A
Outcome of case: Bush left office with approval rating of 33% (66% disapproval), but most of his foreign policy still intact	

Table 8c. Comparing the President's Response to Non-Adverse Circumstance—George W. Bush 2007–2008

Type of response	*Comparison to non-adverse circumstances* (2001-06)
1. Bargaining & persuasion	*House-Senate concurrence with president—average for 2001-2006:* 80.9% *Legislative successes/compromises/concessions:* • June 2001: tax cut • Oct 2001: USA PATRIOT Act • Jan 2002: No Child Left Behind Act • Oct 2002: Authorize force in Iraq • Nov 2002: Homeland Security Act • Nov 2003: Medicare drug coverage • May 2006: extended certain tax cuts • Oct 2006: Military Commissions Act *Failed attempts at legislative bargaining:* • 2005: No action on Bush plan for Soc Security *Other:* • 2005: Agreed to submit nuclear arms agreement as treaty (eventually negotiated & ratified as Treaty of Moscow)
2. Executive actions constitutional	*Vetoes—total:* 11 reg (64% sustained), 1 pocket • All but one of Bush's vetoes came in 2007-2008 *Pardons & clemency:* 200 total *Proclamations:* 940 total *Executive orders:* 291 • 13435—blocked most stem-cell research *Signing statements:* 162 (69 challenged part of a law) • Dec 2005: Detainee Treament Act— invoked authority to protect nation *Claims of executive privilege:* several • 2002: Withheld docs on VP's energy task force
other actions	2005: Pres disaster declarations to give federal aid to states affected by Hurricane Katrina
Outcome of case: Bush left office with approval rating of 33% (66% disapproval), but most of his foreign policy still intact	

Table 8d. Comparing the President's Response to Non-Adverse Circumstance—George W. Bush 2007–2008 (Cont.)

Type of response	Comparison to non-adverse circumstances (2001-06)
3. Foreign policy initiatives & actions	*National security directives:* 66 (plus 25 Homeland Security Directives) *Executive agreements—total:* undetermined *Significant treaties:* • 2002: Treaty of Moscow (on arms reduction) *Uses of force:* several, most involving war on terrorism or UN-sponsored operations • Oct 2001: Invasion of Afghanistan • Mar 2003: Invasion of Iraq *Other:* Ended US participation in several internatl agreements, including Kyoto (Mar 2001) & ABM Treaty (Dec 2001)
4. Organizational changes	Nov 2004: Cabinet shakeup after midterm elections Mar 2006: New chief of staff,more Cabinet changes
5. Going public	*Major speeches:* 36 (total)—yrs with most: 2001, 2003, 2005-7 in each *News conferences:* 209 (total) *Key events/activities:* • Sept 2001: On attacks of September 11, 2001 • Oct 2002: Iraq threat • Mar 2003: Beginning of invasion of Iraq • May 2003: "Mission accomplished" speech • 2005: Extensive campaign for Social Security reform, many pres appearances • Sept 2005: Rebuilding New Orleans after Hurricane Katrina • 2005-2008: Several speeches/appearances to defend Iraq war
6. Unconventional actions?	May 2003: Flew onto deck of *USS Abraham Lincoln* in Navy jet to announce end of major combat operations in Iraq
Outcome of case: Bush left office with approval rating of 33% (66% disapproval), but most of his foreign policy still intact	

OUTCOME AND ASSESSMENT

An unmandate is a blow to an incumbent president. In each of the cases examined previously, the chief executive suffered a political setback in midterm elections and, in three of the cases, faced a Congress determined to change the direction of national policy. Each of the presidents responded in a way intended to maintain his ability to govern despite his party's loss of a congressional majority.

Did the President's Actions Make Any Difference?

In two of these cases—Truman and Clinton—the president confronted the opposition Congress and in doing so revived his political fortunes. Truman vetoed legislation (sometimes unsuccessfully) and asserted a leadership role in foreign policy, but eventually he used a special session to challenge congressional Republicans to act on key issues. When they did not, he campaigned effectively and successfully against the "do nothing" 80th Congress. Clinton used the veto to stand his ground against the Republican juggernaut and in the process revived his fortunes and forged a base of public support that had eluded him earlier in his presidency. Eisenhower was able to maintain good relations with the Democratic Congress, which may have had the consequence of enhancing his preferred position as a president above party. George W. Bush fought a kind of rearguard action, determined to keep Congress from interfering with his conduct of the Iraq war.

Table 9 presents an assessment of how significant the various factors examined in these cases were to their outcomes. In each of the cases, factors other than bargaining and persuasion were important. Only in the Truman case were bargaining and persuasion highly significant (mostly in relation to the Truman Doctrine). In the other cases, the significance was mixed at best.

Table 9a. Assessing the President's Response to Adversity—Unmandates

President	Response types (and significance)
Truman, 1947-48 _Outcome:_ **Won 1948 election; Democrats reclaimed House & Senate**	1. **Bargaining & persuasion:** Truman won approval of key foreign-policy measures, but battled repeatedly with the "do-nothing 80th Congress" **(Significance: Mixed)** 2. **Executive actions:** Truman employed unilateral actions to oppose Congress and to make policy **(Significance: High)** 3. **Foreign policy initiatives & actions:** Truman drew on bipartisan support for his foreign policy in 1947-48, but his initiatives and actions made him a significant foreign policy leader **(Significance: High)** 4. **Organizational changes:** Changes from administration of FDR came slowly and incrementally **(Significance: Low)** 5. **Going public:** Truman Doctrine speech highly effective and 1948 campaign activities also successful **(Significance: High)** 6. **Unconventional actions:** Calling special session gave Truman ammunition to run against the "Do-Nothing 80th Congress" in successful 1948 campaign **(Significance: High)**
Eisenhower, 1955-56 _Outcome:_ **Reelected in 1956 by a landslide**	1. **Bargaining & persuasion:** Divided government resulted in limited legislative action—with exception of interstate highway bill— but Ike had bipartisan support for his foreign policy **(Significance: Mixed)** 2. **Executive actions:** Used veto, but also used signing statements to issue warnings to Congress; EO 10598 important to covert operations **(Significance: Low)** 3. **Foreign policy initiatives & actions:** Eisenhower had bipartisan support for his foreign policy, which continued containment of communist influence but was also marked by restraint **(Significance: High)** 4. **Organizational changes:** N/A **(Significance: N/A)** 5. **Going public:** Already popular & aided by strong economy and stable international scene, Eisenhower able to draw strong public support & campaign effectively to win reelection in landslide **(Significance: High)** 6. **Unconventional actions:** N/A **(Significance: N/A)**

Table 9b. Assessing the President's Response to Adversity—Unmandates

President	Response types (and significance)
Clinton, 1995-96 _Outcome_: **Reelected, 1996**	1. **Bargaining & persuasion:** Contentious relations with Congress led to government shutdown and little legislative success for Clinton **(Significance: Mixed)** 2. **Executive actions:** Veto was significant weapon; expansion of other executive actions, including signing statements, executive orders, etc. **(Significance: High)** 3. **Foreign policy initiatives & actions:** Aside from N. Korea, Clinton was able to conduct foreign policy and use force as he saw fit **(Significance: High)** 4. **Organizational changes:** Dick Morris became key strategist for "triangulation" that proved effective for Clinton's political recovery **(Significance: High)** 5. **Going public:** Use of "voice" and public appearances key to maintaining political presence and winning 1996 election **(Significance: High)** 6. **Unconventional actions:** Govt. shutdown was pivotal to Clinton's political turnaround **(Significance: High)**
Bush, 2007-2008 _Outcome_: **Finished term with 33% approval, but foreign policy largely intact**	1. **Bargaining & persuasion:** Contentious relations with Congress led to confrontation more than cooperation, but Congress supported war on terror **(Significance: Mixed)** 2. **Executive actions:** Veto key to holding off congressional attempts to alter war policy or pass bills Bush opposed **(Significance: High)** 3. **Foreign policy initiatives & actions:** Troop surge carried out despite opposition **(Significance: High)** 4. **Organizational changes:** Controversial figures removed to avoid conflict with Congress, but others reassigned to remove obstacles to troop surge **(Significance: Mixed)** 5. **Going public:** Bush used public politics mostly to explain his decisions; he did little to rally support for his policies and this may have contributed to his low approval ratings **(Significance: Mixed)** 6. **Unconventional actions:** N/A **(Significance: N/A)**

In all of these cases, unilateral executive powers and presidential control of foreign policy were significant. Some of these presidents—Truman and Clinton—also employed unconventional actions to help alter the political landscape, and three of the four used public politics (especially in the context of a reelection campaign). It is noteworthy that of the four presidents examined in this chapter, all three facing an upcoming election won. George W. Bush concentrated on managing the Iraq war and, late in 2008, in presiding over a response to the economic crisis managed mostly by his treasury secretary. He left office with much public disapproval but with the conviction that he would be vindicated in the long run.

How Did Adversity Limit What the President Could Do or Accomplish?

All of these presidents experienced a significant limitation of what they could accomplish in the matter of a domestic legislative program, but in foreign policy, each president retained a large degree of freedom. Of course, limited opportunities for persuasion in domestic affairs encouraged Clinton and Bush to use unilateral actions (signing statements, White House control over rulemaking, and other measures) to advance their domestic goals.

Did Adversity Open Opportunities in Any Way?

In the cases of Truman and Clinton, adversity spurred each to take a bold gamble to turn the tables on an unfriendly Congress. In both cases, an unconventional action by the president helped revive his fortunes. Clinton is the most clear-cut example because it was his willingness to shut down the government, combined with the larger strategy of "triangulation," that saved his presidency. Newt Gingrich and the Republicans were convinced they could "break" Clinton, and many political observers thought the president would give in under pressure (as he had done earlier in his political career). But Clinton's showdown with the Republican majority—an act of "command" that violated Neustadt's major lesson for presidents—demonstrated he was a force to be reckoned with. For the rest of his presidency, Clinton had bargaining leverage when negotiating with Congress over the budget.

What Powers Did the President Retain Despite Adversity, and How Did the President Exercise Them in a Relevant Way?

In each case, the president retained a variety of powers: powers over foreign policy and defense, unilateral executive powers, and the ability to go public. Each of these presidents was able to continue directing foreign policy in a significant way: the Truman Doctrine and the Marshall Plan were developed and enacted during the period of 1947–1948; Eisenhower dealt with the PRC's threat to Taiwan; Clinton was able to act in Bosnia and Herzegovina and oversee the Dayton Accords; and Bush was able to carry out a troop surge in Iraq and hold off attempts to impose even a symbolic timetable for withdrawing American troops.

The unmandate, which Jones identified as a decisive judgment by voters against an incumbent, is not a final judgment on a president. Even faced with a Congress controlled by the other party—and in the Truman, Clinton, and Bush cases, dominated by congressional majorities eager to put their stamp on policy—the chief executives in these examples demonstrated a variety of tools they could use to assert power. Perhaps the president's situation was best summarized by George W. Bush in a comment he made to Bob Woodward in answer to the question "Does the president ever have a last card?" (i.e., Can the president run out of options?). Bush replied, "No. There's always another card."[89]

ENDNOTES

1. Quoted in Charles Krauthammer, "But He Never Asked for a Mandate," *Washington Post*, January 11, 1988, A23.
2. C. O. Jones, *Presidency in a Separated System*, 196.
3. David McCullough, *Truman* (New York: Simon & Schuster, 1992), 490.
4. Ibid., 529.
5. House and Senate concurrence scores (discussed in other cases) are not available for years before 1953.
6. Joseph M. Jones, *The Fifteen Weeks* (New York: Viking, 1955), 89–99.
7. Harry Truman, "Special Message to the Congress on Greece and Turkey," March 12, 1947, accessed January 3, 2011, http://www.presidency.ucsb. edu/ws/index.php?pid = 12846&st = &st1 = .
8. Samuel Kernell, "The Truman Doctrine Speech: A Case Study of the Dynamics of Presidential Opinion Leadership," *Social Science History* 1 (Autumn 1976): 23.
9. Alonzo Hamby, *Man of the People: A Life of Harry S Truman* (New York: Oxford University Press, 1995), ch. 22.
10. McCullough, *Truman*, 551.
11. See ibid., 552–553.
12. Quoted in ibid., 552.
13. Quoted in ibid., 553.
14. Hamby, *Man of the People*, 435.
15. Harry S. Truman, "The President's News Conference," August 5, 1948, accessed January 3, 2011, http://www.presidency.ucsb.edu/ws/index.php? pid = 12973&st = &st1 = .
16. For more on Truman's use of national security directives and a text of NSC-4, see "National Security Council [NSC]: Truman Administration [1945-1953]". http://www.fas.org/irp/offdocs/nsc-hst/index.html (accessed January 3, 2011).
17. Dale Sorenson, "The Language of a Cold Warrior: A Content Analysis of Harry Truman's Public Statements," *Social Science History* 3 (Winter 1979): 172.
18. Hamby, *Man of the People*, 400.
19. McCullough, *Truman*, 569.
20. For a text of the address, see Harry S. Truman, "Address Before the National Association for the Advancement of Colored People," June

29, 1947, accessed January 3, 2011, http://www.presidency.ucsb.edu/ws/
index.php?pid = 12686&st = &st1 = . See also Monroe Billington, "Civil
Rights, President Truman, and the South," *Journal of Negro History* 58
(April 1973): 132.

21. Quoted in ibid., 132.
22. McCullough, *Truman*, 644.
23. Stephen Ambrose, *Eisenhower*, vol. 2, *The President* (New York: Simon
& Schuster, 1984), 220.
24. Ibid.
25. Ibid., 221.
26. Lyn Ragsdale, *Vital Statistics on the Presidency: Washington to Clinton*
(Washington, DC: CQ Press), 362.
27. For an excellent discussion of the matter, see Robert A. Divine, *Eisenhower and the Cold War* (New York: Oxford University Press, 1981), ch.
2.
28. See Ambrose, *Eisenhower*, 301.
29. Ibid., 252.
30. Dwight Eisenhower, "The President's News Conference," March 16,
1955, accessed January 7, 2011, http://www.presidency.ucsb.edu/ws/
index.php?pid = 10434&st = &st1 = .
31. Ambrose, *Eisenhower*, 266.
32. See Divine, *Eisenhower and the Cold War*, ch. 4.
33. Dwight Eisenhower, "Television Broadcast: 'The People Ask the President,'" October 12, 1956, accessed January 7, 2011, http://www.presi-
dency.ucsb.edu/ws/index.php?pid = 10640&st = &st1 = ; Dwight Eisenhower, "Radio and Television Broadcast: 'The Women Ask the President,'" October 24, 1956, accessed January 7, 2011, http://www.presi-
dency.ucsb.edu/ws/index.php?pid = 10669&st = &st1 = .
34. Data reported in Ragsdale, *Vital Statistics*, 194–195.
35. William C. Berman, *From the Center to the Edge: The Politics and Policies of the Clinton Presidency* (Lanham, MD: Rowman & Littlefield,
2001), 42.
36. Ibid.
37. See ibid., 47–50; Nigel Hamilton, *Bill Clinton: Mastering the Presidency* (New York: Public Affairs, 2007), especially ch. 44; David Gergen,
Eyewitness to Power (New York: Simon & Schuster, 2000), 314; Elizabeth Drew, *Showdown: The Struggle Between the Gingrich Congress and
the Clinton White House* (New York: Simon & Schuster, 1996), especially

ch. 4; and John F. Harris, *The Survivor: Bill Clinton in the White House* (New York: Random House, 2005), ch. 14.

38. Drew, *Showdown.*
39. Berman, 69.
40. Harris, *Survivor*, 169.
41. Berman, *From the Center*, 64–65.
42. Richard S. Conley, "President Clinton and the Republican Congress, 1995–2000:Vetoes, Veto Threats, and Legislative Strategy" (paper presented at the Annual Meeting of the American Political Science Association, San Francisco, CA, August 30–September 2, 2001), 16.
43. Ibid., 1.
44. A continuing resolution allows the government to continue to operate temporarily until a budget is approved or the resolution expires.
45. Leon Panetta, recounting a meeting with Newt Gingrich, as reported by Hedrick Smith for his public television series, "People and the Power Game," transcript, accessed February 22, 2011, http://hedricksmith.com/site_powergame/files/panetta.html.
46. Conley, "President Clinton," 24–25.
47. Quoted in Berman, *From the Center*, 55.
48. See "People and the Power Game."
49. http://www.gallup.com/poll/124922/Presidential-Approval-Center.aspx.
50. William J. Clinton, "Statement on Signing the Fisheries Act of 1995," November 3, 1995, accessed February 23, 2011, http://www.presidency.ucsb.edu/ws/index.php?pid = 50735&st = Fisheries+Act+of+1995&st1 = .
51. William J. Clinton, "Statement on Signing the Cuban Liberty and Democratic Solidarity [LUBERTAD] Act of 1996," March 12, 1996, accessed February 23, 2011, http://www.presidency.ucsb.edu/ws/index.php?pid = 52532&st = &st1 = .
52. Berman, *From the Center*, 57.
53. Ibid., 58–59.
54. See Hamilton, *Bill Clinton*, ch. 64.
55. Quoted in Richard Behar, "Rummy's North Korean Connection," *Fortune* [online], May 12, 2003, accessed February 23, 2011, http://money.cnn.com/magazines/fortune/fortune_archive/2003/05/12/342316/.
56. For a discussion of the incident and Elder's dismissal, see Hamilton, *Bill Clinton*, 385–387.

57. The story of the rise and fall of Dick Morris is told in several accounts of the Clinton presidency. See, for example, Hamilton, *Bill Clinton*, ch. 44 and 82.

58. Charles O. Jones, *Passages to the Presidency* (Washington, DC: Brookings, 1998), 193.

59. Ibid.

60. Gingrich quoted in Berman, *From the Center*, 59.

61. Gary C. Jacobson, "The War, the President, and the 2006 Midterm Congressional Elections" (paper presented at the Annual Meeting of the Midwest Political Science Association, Chicago, IL, April 12–15, 2007), 2.

62. George W. Bush, "The President's News Conference," November 8, 2006, accessed February 24, 2011, http://www.presidency.ucsb.edu/ws/index. php?pid = 24269&st = &st1 = .

63. Ibid.

64. Charles O. Jones, *The American Presidency: A Very Short Introduction* (New York: Oxford University Press, 2007), 114.

65. George W. Bush interview, "Decision Points," November 2010, accessed February 24, 2011, http://www.msnbc.msn.com/id/40076644/ns/politics-decision_points/.

66. http://afp.google.com/article/ALeqM5h40yrrEcqeJEeVRgcrDXB7 egDo2A. Accessed February 25, 2011.

67. See, for example, Robert McMahon, ed., "The 110th Congress and Immigration Reform," accessed February 25, 2011, http://www.cfr.org/population-and-demography/110th-congress-immigration-reform/p12628.

68. "US Senate to Reconsider Immigration Reform Next Week," *VOA News*, June 23, 2007, accessed February 25, 2011, http://www.voanews.com/english/news/a-13-2007-06-23-voa21-66560197.html.

69. Exec. Ord. 13422, January 18, 2007, accessed February 25, 2011, http://www.presidency.ucsb.edu/ws/index.php?pid = 24456.

70. George W. Bush, "Statement on Signing the National Defense Authorization Act for Fiscal Year 2008," January 28, 2008, accessed February 25, 2011, http://www.presidency.ucsb.edu/ws/index.php?pid = 76389.

71. Quoted in Bob Woodward, *The War Within: A Secret White House History, 2006–2008* (New York: Simon & Schuster, 2008), 210.

72. Quoted in ibid.

73. The term *quagmire* was used early on by critics of the war, but by late 2006 even sympathetic observers began to grudgingly conclude that the war seemed to be stalled. See Caitlin Johnson, "What Ben Stein Thinks Bush

Should Do," *CBS Sunday Morning*, October 29, 2006, accessed February 28, 2011, http://www.cbsnews.com/stories/2006/10/29/sunday/main2135 739.shtml.

74. *The Iraq Study Group Report*, December 6, 2006, accessed February 28, 2011, http://media.usip.org/reports/iraq_study_group_report.pdf.

75. Michael R. Gordon, "Troop 'Surge' Took Place Amid Doubt and Debate," *New York Times*, August 30, 2008, accessed February 28, 2011, http://www.nytimes.com/2008/08/31/washington/31military.html?_r = 1.

76. Woodward, *War Within*, 262–264.

77. Gordon, "Troop 'Surge' Took Place."

78. Woodward, *War Within*, 310–311; Gordon, "Troop 'Surge' Took Place."

79. Obama and Hagel quoted in Woodward, *War Within*, 316.

80. *Iraq Study Group Report*, 50.

81. "Pentagon: Violence Down in Iraq Since 'Surge,'" CNN, June 23, 2008, accessed February 28, 2011, http://www.cnn.com/2008/WORLD/meast/0 6/23/iraq.security/.

82. "Military Surge in Iraq Ends; 150,000 Troops Remain," *USA Today*, July 16, 2008, accessed February 28, 2011, http://www.usatoday.com/news/world/iraq/2008-07-16-iraq-surge_N.htm.

83. Walter Alarkon, "Patraeus Says Obama Told Him Iraq Surge Was a Success," *The Hill*, December 6, 2009, accessed February 28, 2011, http://thehill.com/homenews/administration/70787-petraeus-says-obama-told-him-iraq-surge-was-a-success.

84. Woodward, *War Within*, 206.

85. George W. Bush, "Address to the Nation on the War on Terror in Iraq," January 10, 2007, accessed March 1, 2011, http://www.presidency.ucsb.edu/ws/index.php?pid = 24432&st = &st1 = .

86. George W. Bush, "Remarks on Returning Without Approval to the House of Representatives the 'U.S. Troop Readiness, Veterans' Care, Katrina Recovery, and Iraq Accountability Appropriations Act, 2007,'" May 1, 2007, accessed March 1, 2011, http://www.presidency.ucsb.edu/ws/index.php?pid = 73974&st = &st1 = .

87. George W. Bush, "Address to the Nation on the National Economy," September 24, 2008, accessed March 1, 2011, http://www.presidency.ucsb.edu/ws/index.php?pid = 84355&st = &st1 = .

88. See George W. Bush, "Farewell Address to the Nation," January 15, 2009, accessed March 1, 2011, http://www.presidency.ucsb.edu/ws/index.php?pid = 85423&st = &st1 = . See also George Bush interview, November

2010, as well as other interviews and George W. Bush, *Decision Points* (New York: Crown, 2010).
89. Quoted in Woodward, *War Within*, 305.

CHAPTER 3

SCANDALS AND
PRESIDENTIAL POWER

Periods of scandal present presidents with unique challenges, especially in their relations with Congress and the public. As James Ceaser commented in reference to the Iran-Contra affair,

> What we know today as a presidential "affair" is a special case in the dialogue on the public Presidency. During an affair, the President is rhetorically disarmed and the initiative lies with his critics and with "objective" analysts. A presidential affair emerges from a blunder, impropriety, or illegality, plus a possible cover-up, which is charged to the President or to high administration officials and which puts the Presidency on the defensive in the eyes of the nation.[1]

Scandals weaken the chief executive and distract all actors in the political system.

This chapter examines three scandals in the post–World War II presidency: Richard Nixon and Watergate (1973–1974); Ronald Reagan and the Iran-Contra affair (November 1986–December 1987); and the Clinton-

Lewinsky scandal (January 1998–June 1999). Reflecting on them, David Abshire, special counselor to President Reagan during Iran-Contra, observed, "Each president and the country were profoundly injured. One resigned, one was tarnished, and a third was impeached and tried…There is no redeeming factor in these three episodes if future presidents do not learn from them."[2]

RICHARD NIXON AND WATERGATE

The scandal that led to the only presidential resignation in American history began on June 17, 1972, as five individuals were arrested for breaking and entering into the national headquarters of the Democratic Party in Washington, DC's Watergate office building.[3] There was immediate suspicion of White House involvement because one of the burglars was James McCord, Jr., security coordinator for the Nixon reelection committee.[4] Within three days, Democratic National Committee chairman Lawrence O'Brien filed a $1 million lawsuit against Nixon's reelection committee.[5] Although campaign manager John Mitchell denied any wrongdoing on behalf of Nixon and the president himself disavowed responsibility, Nixon did acknowledge on June 22 that he would no longer comment on the incident because of an ongoing investigation by both the Washington, DC, Police Department and the FBI.[6]

Despite allegations of wrongdoing, on November 7, 1972, Nixon won one of the biggest landslide elections in American history, winning 49 states and 520 electoral votes. The glow of his victory soon faded. In February 1973, the U.S. Senate formed a special Watergate committee in order to investigate the matter. Former White House counsel John Dean III disclosed to the Senate committee the intention of the White House to pay $1 million to seven Watergate defendants in exchange for secrecy regarding the matter. Additional witnesses pointed fingers directly at campaign manager Mitchell and the White House chief of staff H. R. Haldeman, whereas Nixon continued to claim innocence in the matter.[7]

As the investigation proceeded, a stunning revelation in mid-July 1973 refocused the attention on the president himself. Alexander Butterfield, a former White House aide, told the Senate Watergate Committee that Nixon had a tape-recording system in place within the White House in order to document all conversations with the president.[8] Over the next twelve months, the White House battled with Congress over whether tapes of these conversations should be handed over to the Senate committee. In the meantime, a grand jury investigating the Watergate break-in, and working alongside special Watergate prosecutor Archibald Cox, subpoenaed nine of the White House tapes. In response, Nixon invoked executive privilege and refused to comply with the subpoena. Cox responded by filing an action against the president in federal court, and both the U.S. District Court and the U.S. Court of Appeals sided with the special prosecutor. These courts determined that a federal district judge would first review the tapes to ensure that national security would not be compromised through the release of the tapes and would then turn the tapes over to the special prosecutor.[9]

Following the courts' rulings, Nixon's legal team attempted to strike a deal with Cox regarding the tapes. Upon Cox's refusal, Nixon ordered Attorney General Elliot Richardson to fire Cox. Both Richardson and Deputy Attorney General William Ruckelshaus refused to comply and resigned.[10] As a result, Nixon turned to Solicitor General Robert Bork to carry out the termination. These events, which occurred on Saturday, October 20, 1973, subsequently became known as the Saturday Night Massacre. In response to the Saturday Night Massacre, many in Congress began to consider the possibility of impeachment, and twenty-one separate presidential impeachment resolutions were submitted in the House on October 23.[11] Nixon eventually complied with the subpoena, but this did him little good, given that there was an eighteen-minute gap on one of the crucial tapes.

In February 1974, as the House Judiciary Committee began its impeachment investigation, Nixon once again found himself in a battle over additional tape recordings. The House itself voted 410–4 to grant the committee subpoena power as it investigated the president.[12] In July, the committee approved three articles of impeachment against Nixon, including charges of obstruction of justice, abuse of presidential powers, and contempt of Congress. In the meantime, the Supreme Court, which included four Nixon appointees, issued a unanimous decision ordering the president to turn over all of the tapes requested by the special prosecutor. Ultimately, these events led to President Nixon's nationally televised announcement on August 9 that he would resign.

Bargaining and Persuasion

During the Watergate investigation, Richard Nixon made efforts at bargaining and persuasion in a variety of ways, most notably in his effort to pass a series of economic reforms to combat the continued economic decline. He also attempted to control the direction of the Watergate investigation. The results of these efforts were mixed, given that the president achieved relatively high levels of success with regard to his legislative agenda but ultimately failed to control the congressional investigation that resulted in the end of his presidency.

Legislative Successes/Compromises/Concessions

Just as Congress began its investigation into Watergate, Nixon received the troubling news that inflation had increased from 3.4% late in 1972 to 9% in May 1973.[13] In response, on June 13, 1973, Nixon took to the airwaves and challenged Congress to provide him with increased authority to reduce tariffs and to initiate the construction of the Alaska pipeline.[14] Two weeks later, he further demanded that Congress establish a new cabinet department to handle energy and natural resource issues.[15] It seems likely that even if Nixon had never faced Watergate, many of his domestic initiatives would have been the same because he could not ignore the economic crisis.

Surprisingly, in spite of the immense obstacles faced by Nixon during 1973 and 1974, his success in Congress stayed above the 50% threshold. As illustrated in table 10, though his overall success rate in the two chambers dropped from 66.3% in 1972 to 50.6% in 1973, it increased once again to 59.6% in 1974. Furthermore, his success in the House actually increased nearly 20% between 1973 and 1974, and his success in the Senate remained stagnant beginning in 1972. More specifically, during 1973, President Nixon achieved victory with the passage of a bill approving the construction of a trans-Alaskan pipeline (part of Nixon's energy plan), a bill that authorized nearly $20 billion for mass transit (part of Nixon's economic plan); and though it did not make it through the Senate in time, the House approved a bill that significantly increased presidential authority to negotiate trade deals.[16] Although not as successful in 1974, Nixon achieved victory in a weapons procurement bill and two additional bills that replaced categorical grants with block grants in community development and education.[17]

Table 10. Congressional Concurrence with the President, 1969–1974

Year	Total H&S Concurrence	House Concurrence	# of House Votes	Senate Concurrence	# of Senate Votes
1969	74.8	72.3	47	76.4	72
1970	76.9	84.6	65	71.4	91
1971	74.8	82.5	57	69.5	82
1972	66.3	81.1	37	54.3	46
Average	**73.2**	**80.1**		**67.9**	
Total			206		291
1973	50.6	48.0	125	52.4	185
1974	59.6	67.9	53	54.2	83
Average	**55.1**	**58.0**		**53.3**	
Total			178		268

Source. Compiled from data in *Vital Statistics on the Presidency: Washington to Clinton* (p. 390) by Lyn Ragsdale. Washington, DC: CQ Press, 1998.

Failed Attempts at Legislative Bargaining/Compromise

Although these aggregate concurrence scores indicate that Nixon continued to exhibit bargaining influence within Congress, his weakened position contributed to the passage of two bills that had long-term implications for the operations of the presidency. First, Congress passed the War Powers Resolution of 1973, which mandated that presidents could send U.S. armed forces into combat only upon authorization from Congress or if the nation were under attack. In particular, the legislation required that a president notify Congress within forty-eight hours of sending troops into combat and prohibited the use of troops for more than sixty days if the president did not receive congressional authorization to continue beyond that deadline. Despite Nixon's veto on October 24, by November 7 both houses of Congress successfully overrode his veto. Second, Congress passed the Budget and Impoundment Control Act of 1974. This act accomplished several goals, including the establishment of the House and Senate Budget Committees, but it most pointedly prohibited the president from impounding funds appropriated by Congress. Through these bills, Congress sent a clear message that it intended to reclaim broader authority over both the sword and the purse.

Other Efforts at Bargaining and Negotiation

In May 1973, Nixon tried to forestall an aggressive investigation of Watergate by nominating Defense Secretary Elliot Richardson to be attorney general. He hoped that Richardson's ties to the Republican Eastern Establishment and good reputation on Capitol Hill would assuage Congress. At that time, he believed that he needed to do something to change the direction of events, which were unraveling his administration. His previous attorney general, Richard Kleindienst, had resigned under pressure at the end of April because he was closely associated with John Mitchell (Nixon's first attorney general, now discredited).[18] Two top White House aides, chief of staff H. R. Haldeman and domestic policy advisor John Ehrlichman, also resigned, and White House counsel John Dean was fired. Nixon's presidency seemed on the verge of collapse.

The Richardson appointment can be seen as Nixon's attempt to maximize personal power and conserve political capital for two reasons. First, Richardson brought with him personal integrity and ties to an important constituency; the Republican Eastern Establishment. He was respected on Capitol Hill and among the Washington press, and Nixon thought his appointment might shield the president from unwarranted criticisms. Second, Nixon hoped that the appointment of Richardson would undercut demands for an independent Watergate special prosecutor. In a nationally televised address announcing the appointment, Nixon declared that Richardson would have "absolute authority to make all decisions bearing upon the Watergate case and related matters."[19] Nixon feared that a special prosecutor would lead to "prosecutorial zeal [that] would assume a life of its own."[20] In short, he hoped to dampen the growing pressure for a full-blown investigation that could lead directly to the Oval Office.

Unfortunately for Nixon, the appointment backfired. As confirmation hearings began in the Senate, it became apparent that "the Senate would hold his nomination hostage until an independent Watergate Special Prosecutor was appointed."[21] As Nixon put it, Richardson chose to "yield to the pressure" and eventually appointed Harvard professor and long-time Kennedy ally Archibald Cox to this extraordinary role. Nixon further explained, "Richardson then compounded the mistake by approving a charter for the Special Prosecution Force that, instead of limiting its responsibility to the area of Watergate, gave it virtual *carte blanche* to investigate the executive branch."[22]

Thus, the appointment of Richardson as attorney general was a case of extreme bargaining failure for President Nixon. Richardson did not shield the president in any way. His appointment not only failed to prevent the creation of a special prosecutor, but it led to the appointment of a combative prosecutor. Eventually the conflict between Nixon and Cox would result in the Saturday Night Massacre, leaving both Richardson and Cox jobless. Despite Nixon's hope that the appointment of Richardson could help salvage his presidency, it produced an even greater threat to his hold on the office.

Executive Actions

Although President Nixon preserved a relatively good success rate in Congress throughout 1973 and 1974, he also relied heavily on unilateral powers during his last nineteen months in office. First, Nixon carried out an effective veto strategy. In fact, Nixon's second-term veto strategy proved more successful than his first-term one. Nixon vetoed eleven bills during the 91st Congress (1969–1970), with a success rate of 62.5%; twenty bills during the 92nd Congress (1971–1972), with a success rate of 66.7%; and twelve bills during the 93rd Congress (1973–1974), with a success rate of 83.3%. And although one of his defeats during the 93rd Congress included the War Powers Resolution, his ability to sustain ten out of twelve vetoes during this period of adversity is quite amazing.

In addition, Nixon employed unilateral executive actions to combat the growing economic problems referenced earlier. For instance, on July 1, Nixon announced that the White House, through the Cost of Living Council, had begun investigating the 3,100 largest American corporations to determine "any whose price increases since January cannot be justified by cost increases." Moreover, he explained his decision to create a new White House energy office. Additionally, in an effort to decrease agricultural prices, he announced his decision to free forty million acres for planting and to control exports on certain agricultural products.[23]

Finally, though he ultimately failed, during the Watergate investigation President Nixon tried to invoke executive privilege on three different occasions. When Special Prosecutor Cox subpoenaed nine tape recordings from the White House, the president refused to comply with the order.[24] He took the same position when the Senate Select Committee sought the same tapes as Cox, and again when Cox's predecessor Leon Jaworski subpoenaed sixty-four additional tapes during jury trial proceedings.[25] Many scholars argue that Nixon's noncooperation and extreme secrecy cost him his presidency. In fact, this appears to be Nixon's biggest mistake in regard to how he responded to the situation. For instance, a recent CQ Press documentary history publication contended, "If Nixon had come forward with the facts during the early stages of the scandal, he might have saved his presidency. It was the continuing cover-up that dragged him down, not the earlier break-in. But Nixon tended toward secrecy."[26]

Foreign Policy Initiatives and Actions

Throughout the Watergate scandal, Nixon continued to pursue a successful foreign policy. During this nineteen-month period, Nixon carried out an extensive bombing of Cambodia (ignoring congressional opposition), oversaw the complete withdrawal of American forces from Vietnam, carried out a weeklong airlift of supplies to Israel, convinced Arab oil ministers to lift the oil embargo, and completed two trips to the Middle East and the Soviet Union. Thus, despite his problems on the domestic front, President Nixon's endeavors in foreign policy never waned.

It was also during this period that Nixon maintained his commitment to continue his pursuit of détente with the Soviet Union. On April 10, 1973, the president sent Congress what he termed the Trade Reform Act of 1973, which included a provision that would extend most-favored-nation status to the Soviet Union (this measure passed the House but did not make it to the Senate for a vote prior to the 1973 recess).[27] Two months later, in mid-June, Nixon hosted Brezhnev for several days at Camp David, the White House, and Nixon's California home. By the end of the meetings, not only did the two leaders sign the Prevention of Nuclear War (PNW) treaty, but they agreed on a wide range of issues, including transportation, agriculture, commercial aviation, use of atomic energy, and trade.[28] In addition, Nixon successfully persuaded Brezhnev to concur to establish a "permanent agreement" regarding strategic offensive limitations by late 1974.[29]

Almost immediately after his meetings with Brezhnev, Nixon asserted himself further in the foreign policy realm as he vetoed Congress's attempt to cut off funding for military actions in Cambodia. Although a majority of the House (241 members) voted to override the president's veto, this was thirty-five votes short of the two-thirds required, and thus Nixon proved victorious.[30] Although funding would ultimately be cut off on August 15, 1973, it did not occur until "the U.S. Air Force dropped more than 240,000 tons of bombs on Cambodia, which was 50 percent more than the total conventional explosives dropped on Japan in World War II."[31]

Later that year, Nixon successfully used his commander in chief powers to respond to the attacks on Israel by Syria and Egypt, as American planes flew 550 missions between October 13 and October 20.[32] The importance of Nixon's bold action cannot be underestimated. Indeed, Stephen Ambrose noted,

> Had Nixon not acted so decisively who can say what would have happened? The Arabs probably would have recovered at least some of the territory they had lost in 1967. They might even have destroyed Israel. But whatever the might-have beens, there is no doubt that Nixon played a central role in courageous action.[33]

The following week, Nixon vetoed the controversial War Powers Act, declaring the act "both unconstitutional and dangerous" because it would "seriously undermine the Nation's ability to act decisively and convincingly in times of international crisis."[34] Ultimately, Nixon lost this battle, because both the House and Senate overrode his veto, but he set the foundation for future presidents to virtually ignore Congress's attempted power grab.

Overall, the Nixon administration's efforts in foreign policy during the first year of the Watergate scandal were quite successful. In fact, they were so successful that Kissinger received the Nobel Peace Prize in 1973. Kissinger himself acknowledged that the prize came as a result of policies, oftentimes unpopular, initiated by his boss in the Oval Office.[35]

The foreign policy success of the Nixon administration continued throughout 1974. Although extreme tension remained between the United States and the Arab world as a result of the American support for Israel in

October 1973, in the first week of March 1974, the United States reestablished diplomatic relations with Egypt, and on March 18, Kissinger was able to convince the Arab oil ministers to unconditionally lift the oil embargo.

Consequently, although Nixon's presidency will always be remembered for the Watergate scandal, one cannot take away from his extraordinary advances in the foreign policy realm throughout the scandal. Nixon remained active in diplomatic efforts with the Soviet Union, defied Congress with his continued aerial assault in Cambodia, helped establish peace in the Middle East, and pressured an end to the oil embargo. With such success in foreign policy, perhaps it should not be a surprise that the public, in late June 1974, gave President Nixon a 54% job approval rating for his handling of foreign affairs, all the while only giving him an overall job approval rating of 26%.[36]

Organizational Changes
With the scandal focused directly on those closest to the president, organizational changes were bound to occur within the Nixon White House. The biggest shake-up occurred on April 30, 1973, as Nixon announced the firing of White House counsel John Dean, along with the resignations H. R. Haldeman (Nixon's chief of staff), John Ehrlichman (the assistant to the president for domestic affairs), and Richard Kleindienst (attorney general). Nixon immediately asked Secretary of Defense Elliot Richardson to transfer to the Department of Justice to fill Kleindienst's role. In the weeks that followed the announcement, Nixon further reorganized his administration as he moved James Schlesinger from CIA director to defense secretary and filled Schlesinger's position with William Colby, Schlesinger's deputy at the CIA. In addition, he appointed Clarence Kelley, the chief of the Kansas City Police Department, to direct the FBI; Mel Laird and Bryce Harlow became counselors to the president; John Connally joined the staff as an unpaid advisor; and Fred Buzhardt (a general counsel in the Defense Department) was added to Nixon's White House legal team.[37]

Perhaps the most important organizational change occurred in October 1973. On October 10, Vice President Spiro Agnew resigned because of criminal charges brought against him stemming from when he was the governor of Maryland. Two days later, in accordance with the Twenty-fifth Amendment, President Nixon nominated Representative Gerald Ford to fill Agnew's post. Ford was confirmed on December 6, 1973.

Going Public

Nixon attempted to use a "going public" strategy that he hoped would result in Americans effectively lobbying Congress to get behind the president's economic agenda and ultimately force Congress to drop the Watergate investigation. For instance, on March 29, 1973, as he announced the complete withdrawal of American troops from Vietnam, he turned to the domestic front and urged the public to rally behind his economic program by demanding that their members of Congress get on board with the president.[38] Eventually President Nixon expanded his attacks against the "do nothing Congress" to several other areas as well. At a press conference on September 5, 1973, Nixon scolded Congress for not dealing with inflation, national defense, the growing energy crisis, education, building better communities, and the need for new housing.[39] In November, Nixon used two televised speeches that further challenged Congress to take effective action with regard to the looming energy crisis. The president proposed increased coal initiatives, fewer commercial flights, a national speed limit of 50 miles per hour, an Alaskan pipeline, more nuclear power plants, and relaxed environmental regulations.[40]

In addition, the president sought to use other publicity events to garner popular support from the public. For example, on May 24, 1973, President Nixon held an unprecedented event at the White House, where he, along with Sammy Davis, Jr., Bob Hope, and John Wayne, hosted 1,300 guests comprising former POWs and their families.[41] Later, in November 1973, he also took to the road and made campaign-style appearances in Macon,

Georgia, and Memphis, Tennessee. Similarly, in March 1974, Nixon once again held campaign-style events in Nashville, Chicago, and Houston.[42]

Finally, Nixon used the "going public" strategy to deny wrongdoing in Watergate. Perhaps the best example of this came on April 29, 1974, when Nixon sat at his desk in the Oval Office and addressed the country as he was about to hand over 1,200 pages of transcripts of 46 taped conversations to the House Judiciary Committee. President Nixon confidently told the American people that when he handed these materials over to Congress, this action "will at last, once and for all, show that what I knew and what I did with regard to the Watergate break-in and cover-up were just as I have described them to you from the very beginning."[43]

Unconventional Actions

The Watergate scandal brought two of the most historic unconventional actions by a president. The first came in October 1973, in what became known as the Saturday Night Massacre. As previously indicated, when two federal courts sided with special prosecutor Archibald Cox regarding subpoenaed White House tape recordings, the White House sought to strike a deal with Cox concerning the tapes. When Cox refused, the president demanded that Attorney General Richardson fire Cox. Ambrose explained, "[F]iring Cox...would free him [Nixon] from further subpoenas for Watergaterelated tapes. He could expect to continue to defy the Ervin Committee and the Watergate grand jury successfully, on the basis of separation of powers, confidentiality, and executive privilege. If he got rid of Cox, the prosecution of Watergate crimes would be done by the Justice Department."[44] However, both Richardson and Deputy Attorney General William Ruckelshaus refused to comply, leading to the resignations of both Richardson and Ruckelshaus.[45] Nixon ultimately turned to Solicitor General Robert Bork to carry out the termination.

The second unconventional action came when Nixon chose to resign rather than face impeachment in the House and a trial in the Senate.

Unlike Andrew Johnson before him and Bill Clinton after him, President Nixon willingly relinquished power instead of allowing the constitutional process to take its course.

Epilogue

Of all the modern cases of presidential adversity, given that the Watergate scandal ended with the resignation of President Nixon, this case had the most detrimental impact on the presidency. Not only did the scandal limit what the president could accomplish, it ultimately led to the president voluntarily handing over the reins of the office to the vice president. The president's actions had further damaging effects on the Republican Party, because the 1974 midterm elections resulted in the Republican Party losing forty-eight seats in the House of Representatives and four seats in the Senate, giving the Democrats a 291–144 advantage in the House and a veto-proof 61–38 advantage in the Senate (one Independent also caucused with the Democrats).

RONALD REAGAN AND IRAN-CONTRA

In the fall of 1986, as Ronald Reagan neared completion of his sixth year in office, his presidency seemed as strong as ever. On October 22, Reagan signed into law the Tax Reform Act of 1986, which "reduced the brackets to three, cut the maximum rate for individuals from 50 percent to 28, nearly doubled the personal exemption, and destroyed thousands of shelters."[46] Given the pending midterm elections during a second-term presidency, such passage, as one historian noted, "shocked conventional wisdom."[47] His public approval ratings that year were impressive: they peaked at 68% and averaged 64% for the year, which made Reagan "the most popular sixth-year president since the advent of polling."[48]

Table 11a. Summarizing the President's Response to Adversity—Scandal—
Nixon 1973–1974

Type of response	*Summary data & significant examples*
1. Bargaining & persuasion	*House & Senate concurrence with president— average for 1973-1974*: 55.1% *Legislative successes/compromises/concessions:* • Sept 1973: Highway/Transit Bill (success) • Nov 1973: Alaska Pipeline (success) • Aug 1974: Weapons procurement (success) *Failed attempts at legislative bargaining/compromise:* • Nov 1973: War Powers Act (veto override) • Sept 1973: min wage raise (veto sustained) • July 1974: Budget Reform Act (opposed) *Other:* Elliot Richardson apptd as Atty General
2. Executive actions constitutional	*Vetoes:* 12 regular (83.3% sustained), 0 pocket • July 1973: Attempt to cut $ for Cambodia • Oct 1973: War Powers Act (overridden) *Pardons & clemency:* 401 (389 pardons, 12 commutations) *Proclamations:* 6 *Executive orders:* 104 *Signing Statements:* 39 *Claims of executive privilege:* • July 1973: Refused to comply with Senate & spec prosecutor subpoenas on testimony, pres documents, tapes • Oct 1973: Refused more tapes sought by prosecutor Jaworski & Senate comm
other actions	N/A
3. Foreign policy initiatives & actions	*National security directives:* 64 *Executive agreements:* 319 *Significant treaties:* • June 1973: Prevent of Nuclear War Treaty
Outcome of case: Nixon resigned, Democrats won landslide congressional election in 1974	

Table 11b. Summarizing the President's Response to Adversity—Scandal—Nixon 1973–1974 (Cont.)

Type of response	Summary data & significant examples
Foreign policy initiatives & actions *continued*	*Uses of force:* Continuation of Vietnam War *Other:* • Jan 1973: Paris Peace Accords • June 1973: Summit with Brezhnev in US • Oct 1973: Airlift of supplies to Israel • Mar 1974: Re-estd relations with Egypt Mar 1974: OPEC convinced to lift embargo
4. Organizational changes	Apr 1973: Haldeman & Ehrlichman resign May 1973: New directors at CIA and FBI; new Def Sec; new legal team within White House Oct 1973: "Saturday Night Massacre": Atty Gen & Deputy AG resign; prosecutor Cox fired Dec. 1973: Ford confirmed as Vice President Dec. 1973: Wm Saxbe confirmed as Atty General
5. Going public	*Major speeches:* 13 (1973-9; 1974-4) *News conferences:* 9 (1973-7; 1974-2) *Key events/activities:* Mar 1973: Withdrawal of troops from Vietnam; Called for support of economic policy June 1973: Phase IV of economic recovery plan Sept 1973: Used press confer to attack Congress Nov 1973: 2 TV addresses on energy Nov 1973: Campaign-style events in GA & TN Dec 1973: Televised broadcast regarding energy Mar 1974: Campaign-style events in Nashville, Chicago, and Houston Mar 1974: Released docs & tapes; denied crime in Watergate Aug 1974: Nixon resigns
6. Unconventional actions?	• Oct. 1973: Saturday Night Massacre • Aug. 1974: Nixon resigns
*Outcome of case: **Nixon resigned, Democrats won landslide congressional election in 1974***	

Table 11c. Comparing the President's Response to Non-Adverse Circumstances—Nixon 1973–1974

Type of response	Comparison to non-adverse circumstances (1969-70)
other actions	• 1969: FBI wiretaps to track leaks • 1970: Estd EPA and NOAA
3. Foreign policy initiatives & actions	*National security directives:* 96 *Executive agreements:* 341 *Significant treaties:* • Oct 1969: Nuclear Non-Prolif Treaty *Uses of force:* • Continuation of Vietnam War • Mar 1969: Secret Cambodia bombing • Apr 1970: Invasion of Cambodia *Other:* • Feb 1970: Nixon Doctrine
4. Organizational changes	June 1970: Replaced HEW Secy R Finch with Elliot Richardson July 1970: Moved George Shultz (Labor Secy) to OMB Dir; James Hodgson as Labor Secy
5. Going public	*Major speeches:* 11 (1969-5; 1970-6) *News conferences:* 14 (1969-8; 1970-6) *Key events/activities:* May 1969: Addressed nation about Vietnam War Aug 1969: Announced domestic initiatives Nov 1969: "Silent Majority" Speech Dec 1969: Troop reductions in Vietnam Apr 1970: More troop reductions in Vietnam Apr 1970: Addressed Cambodia invasion July 1970: Plan to establish EPA and NOAA Oct. 1970: Speech called for Indochina cease-fire and widened peace talks
6. Unconventional actions?	N/A
Outcome of case: Nixon resigned, Democrats won landslide congressional election in 1974	

Table 11d. Comparing the President's Response to Non-Adverse Circumstances—Nixon 1973–1974 (Cont.)

Type of response	Comparison to non-adverse circumstances (1969-70)
other actions	• 1969: FBI wiretaps to track leaks • 1970: Estd EPA and NOAA
3. Foreign policy initiatives & actions	*National security directives:* 96 *Executive agreements:* 341 *Significant treaties:* • Oct 1969: Nuclear Non-Prolif Treaty *Uses of force:* • Continuation of Vietnam War • Mar 1969: Secret Cambodia bombing • Apr 1970: Invasion of Cambodia *Other:* • Feb 1970: Nixon Doctrine
4. Organizational changes	June 1970: Replaced HEW Secy R Finch with Elliot Richardson July 1970: Moved George Shultz (Labor Secy) to OMB Dir; James Hodgson as Labor Secy
5. Going public	*Major speeches:* 11 (1969-5; 1970-6) *News conferences:* 14 (1969-8; 1970-6) *Key events/activities:* May 1969: Addressed nation about Vietnam War Aug 1969: Announced domestic initiatives Nov 1969: "Silent Majority" Speech Dec 1969: Troop reductions in Vietnam Apr 1970: More troop reductions in Vietnam Apr 1970: Addressed Cambodia invasion July 1970: Plan to establish EPA and NOAA Oct. 1970: Speech called for Indochina cease-fire and widened peace talks
6. Unconventional actions?	N/A
Outcome of case: Nixon resigned, Democrats won landslide congressional election in 1974	

Unfortunately for Reagan, this beneficent situation soon changed. In fact, as early as November 29, 1986, John Felton of *Congressional Quarterly* wrote,

> Ronald Reagan is heading into the final to two years of his Presidency with his credibility damaged, the competency of his administration questioned and investigations under way into the conduct of his foreign policy...Reagan's ability to govern has been severely damaged.[49]

Indeed, November brought a series of reverses that threatened not only Reagan's influence, but even his hold on the Oval Office. First, the congressional midterm elections brought an end to the Republican majority in the Senate. In the coming Congress, Democrats would dominate Republicans in the Senate by a 55–45 margin. A few days later, rumors surfaced in the media that members of the administration, and possibly the president himself, had sanctioned covert weapons deliveries to Iran. Moreover, the story suggested that such shipments were made in exchange for the release of American hostages in Lebanon, held by the Iranian-supported militant group Hezbollah.

The story emerged a few weeks prior to the November elections when a CIA-leased supply plane was shot down in Nicaragua. Upon capture, the pilot, former marine Eugene Hasenfus, told his captors that his mission was a CIA-led effort, a charge that brought an immediate rejection by the White House.[50] The story regained life when, on November 3, *Al-Shiraa*, a magazine published in Beirut, included a story that described a secret meeting that had occurred between former national security advisor Robert McFarlane and senior Iranian officials in September 1986 (although the meeting actually took place in May 1986).[51] Although the account was not entirely accurate, Theodore Draper explained that the story "succeeded in making known that there had been a secret deal between the United States and Iran by which the United States had provided weapons to Iran in exchange for an Iranian promise to stop supporting 'liberation movements in the world.'"[52] One day later, the

Iranian Majlis Speaker, Hashemi Rafsanjani, spoke publicly and corroborated *Al-Shiraa*'s story.[53]

In his analysis of the Iran-Contra affair, the historian Michael Flamm described why the events posed such a threat to the Reagan presidency. Flamm explained that the allegations meant the Reagan administration had (1) violated the 1984 Boland Amendment, "which banned aid or assistance to the Contras"; (2) violated a U.S. law prohibiting deals with terrorists; and (3) violated a U.S. arms embargo against Iran.[54] These storylines provided the media with numerous narratives. According to Peter Wallison, President Reagan's White House counsel throughout the Iran-Contra affair, between early November 1986 and the end of January 1987, the *Washington Post* ran 555 stories regarding the scandal, which only barely out-covered the 509 stories printed by the *New York Times* during the same timeframe.[55]

As the media pressured the White House for details, Congress recognized the necessity to investigate the matter. Although the president announced on November 25 that an independent commission would be established to investigate wrongdoing by administration officials, incoming leaders in the House and Senate both announced their intentions to create investigatory panels within Congress.

By December 1986, as Reagan entered his seventh year in office, his once-intimidating job approval ratings had plummeted: the Gallup organization reported a drop of sixteen points, from 67 to 46%.[56] Even worse, a December 2 *New York Times*/CBS poll placed his approval at 36%.[57] These declining numbers no doubt reflected what a December 1986 *Newsweek* poll found: 90% of Americans did not believe Reagan had been truthful about his knowledge of the scandalous events.[58] Republican congressman Newt Gingrich lamented, "He will never again be the Reagan that he was before he blew it. He is not going to regain our trust and our faith so easily."[59]

Bargaining and Persuasion

During this period, Reagan not only amassed significant legislative losses in Congress, but he also lost a Supreme Court nomination battle and could not prevent a full-scale congressional investigation of his administration, even though he initiated an independent commission to investigate the matter. Reagan attempted to maintain persuasive influence over Congress as he announced an "Up from Dependency" welfare proposal, an initiative to promote American competitiveness, a White House Conference on a Drug Free America, and an Economic Bill of Rights for Americans, but these proved to be largely symbolic gestures. In fact, unlike the other cases in this analysis, there are no notable legislative successes, concessions, or compromises during the Iran-Contra scandal. Simply put, his persuasive abilities in Congress during this period of his presidency should be deemed a failure.

Failed Attempts at Legislative Bargaining/Compromise

As illustrated in table 12, throughout 1987 Reagan achieved an abysmal 43.5% congressional concurrence rate, earning him "the lowest success rate since CQ began its voting studies in 1953 and the first time a president lost more votes than he won."[60] Even worse, when *Congressional Quarterly* examined "key votes" for 1987, they found that of the twenty-nine key votes, Reagan took a position on sixteen and only won two. This was a stark contrast from his 65% success rate on key votes in 1986.[61] Furthermore, *Congressional Quarterly* reported, "The House and Senate flouted Reagan's will by approving trade bills he considered protectionist and arms control amendments that brazenly contradicted his policies" and "drove Reagan to sign a bill he believed unconstitutional" (an independent counsel statute).[62]

Table 12. Congressional Concurrence with the President, 1985–1988

Year	Total H&S Concurrence	House Concurrence	# of House Votes	Senate Concurrence	# of Senate Votes
1985	59.9	45.0	80	71.6	102
1986	56.5	33.3	90	80.7	83
Average	**58.2**	**39.2**		**76.2**	
Total			170		185
1987	43.5	33.3	99	56.4	78
1988	47.4	32.7	104	64.8	88
Average	**45.5**	**33.0**		**60.6**	
Total			203		166

Source. Compiled from data in *Vital Statistics on the Presidency: Washington to Clinton* (p.391) by Lyn Ragsdale. Washington, DC: CQ Press, 1998.

Interestingly, Reagan's awful 33.3% success rate in the House in 1987 was the same score he received throughout 1986 when his popularity was at a high, and it stayed roughly the same throughout 1988, after Reagan regained his popularity. However, his success scores in the Senate appear to be significantly related to the adverse circumstances he faced. Not only did his success rate drop from 80.7% to 56.4%, but on the fourteen "key votes" before the Senate in 1987, Reagan took a position on eight and lost all but one.[63] Certainly, some of this decline in support can be attributed to the Democratic takeover of the Senate in the 1986 midterm elections, but his support among Republican senators decreased dramatically during the Iran-Contra scandal. In fact, Reagan lost a majority of Republican senators in sixteen of the thirty-four votes he lost in the Senate in 1987.[64] His loss of influence among Republican senators was highlighted on October 23, 1987, when the Senate rejected the president's Supreme Court nominee Robert Bork by a vote of forty-two in favor and fifty-eight against, which included six Republican votes in the "nay" column.

Other Efforts at Bargaining and Negotiation

Besides his failed efforts to maintain his legislative leadership in Congress, Reagan took at least two significant actions that can be deemed relevant to Neustadt's notion of enhancing personal power through persuasion and bargaining: he established the President's Special Review Board (later dubbed "the Tower Commission" by reporters), and he initiated an independent counsel to investigate whether members of his administration had broken any laws. In fact, these were two of the first actions taken by the president in response to the adverse circumstances he faced, given that he announced the establishment of the board on November 25, 1986, and the plans for an independent counsel investigation on December 2.[65] On November 26, President Reagan announced that the board would comprise three well-respected individuals: former senator John Tower, who had served as the chairman of the Senate Armed Services Committee; former national security advisor Brent Scowcroft; and former senator Edmund Muskie, who had also served briefly as President Carter's secretary of state.[66] Weeks later, on December 19, a panel of judges chose Lawrence E. Walsh, a former district court judge, diplomat, and deputy attorney general, to serve as the independent counsel.[67]

The initial goal of this two-pronged investigation was avoiding congressional investigation. Based on this standard, Reagan's efforts failed, because both the House and Senate announced on December 4 their plans to appoint select committees to investigate the matter.[68] Still, for at least two reasons, Reagan's strategy should not be deemed a complete failure. First, the president did preempt Congress, given that he established his own inquiry prior to congressional action. In doing so, Reagan effectively delineated his scandal from Watergate and seemed to publicly display his desire to determine whether or not unlawful acts had occurred. Second, White House counsel Wallison described that beyond avoiding a congressional investigation, the administration recognized the necessity of the Tower Commission because if the White House "did not have this investigation, the only story ever told about the Iran-Contra matter would be the account provided by the Democratically-controlled Congress and in the press through leaks from the Hill."[69]

Executive Actions

With his persuasive influence significantly diminished, Reagan initially attempted to carry out an effective veto strategy but learned very early on that his clout in Congress was quite low. During the thirteen-month period between November 1986 and December 1987, President Reagan vetoed eight bills, but four of these vetoes came prior to the Iran-Contra story breaking. Thus, only four vetoes during the scandal are left: a pocket veto of a NASA Authorization bill on November 14, 1986; a veto of the Water Quality Act on January 30, 1987; a veto of the Surface Transportation and Uniform Relocation Assistance Act (STURAA) on March 27, 1987; and a veto of the Fairness in Broadcasting Act on June 19, 1987.[70] Despite the president's best efforts, Congress overcame the president's veto in all but the broadcasting bill.

Congress defeated the first veto, of the NASA Authorization bill, approximately one year after Reagan refused to sign the bill. It passed an almost identical piece of legislation, which the president signed on October 30, 1987.[71] More significant battles came with the Water Quality Act of 1987 and the STURAA. The veto of the Water Quality Act was easily overturned because it contained the sorts of pet constituency projects that usually win support in Congress.[72] Reagan's other major veto, of the STURAA, was almost sustained, but in a complex series of parliamentary moves the veto was narrowly overridden. Although Reagan went to the Capitol and told Republican senators (thirteen of whom voted to override) "I beg you for your vote," he was unable to win the support he needed.[73] This episode illustrates the political damage caused by the Iran-Contra affair: most analysts interpret his failure as a consequence of losing political capital because of the scandal.[74]

However, in his analysis, Charles Jones viewed this as an important facet of Reagan's strategy for responding to the crisis. Jones argued,

"Although he lost both battles [the water-pollution-control bill and the highway bill], the President established his own combative posture in the face of the Iran-*contra* distraction. This aggressiveness probably benefited him later in the year when the impact of the hearings had abated."[75] Even at the time, Senator George Mitchell, a Democrat, remarked in the aftermath of the successful veto-override of the highway bill, "I don't think it's a total loss for the President. This was an opportunity for the President to demonstrate aggressive, personal involvement in government."[76]

Given the limited success of his veto strategy, it is not surprising that Reagan decided to rely heavily on additional unilateral executive powers. Most notably, the administration proceeded to use signing statements to circumvent Congress and shape policy. For example, in the August 22, 1987, signing statement that Reagan issued to accompany the Federal Triangle Development Act, the president directed all federal agencies to ignore one provision of the act that established a congressional review mechanism (i.e., a legislative veto) and decreed that the mayor of the District of Columbia could not vote on any binding decisions of the International Cultural and Trade Commission created by the law.[77] The following month, in the signing statement on the Federal Debt Limit and Deficit Reduction Bill, Reagan identified four provisions that he thought "require[d] technical comment as a matter of legislative history."[78] He made it clear that he would treat four problematic provisions as strictly "precatory."

Still, Reagan did not use his executive authority flippantly. Most importantly, Reagan made the decision not to invoke executive privilege. This decision, which stood in sharp contrast to Richard Nixon's attempt to use executive privilege to shield tapes of Oval Office conversations from the Watergate special prosecutor (and Bill Clinton's later attempt to protect himself from an investigation of his affair with Monica Lewinsky), helped the president to shake off much of the taint of scandal.

Foreign Policy Initiatives and Actions

Even though the scandal that shook the foundations of the Reagan presidency came via the foreign policy realm, throughout these "tough times" several substantial foreign policy developments occurred. The major international theme of Reagan's presidency was to confront the Soviet Union, and in 1987 this policy took two tracks. On one hand, he held to his policy of making the Cold War too expensive for Moscow, by keeping up defense spending, proceeding with the Strategic Defense Initiative, maintaining pressure on the pro-Moscow Sandinista government of Nicaragua, and even putting rhetorical pressure on the Soviet leadership. Most famously, on June 12, 1987, Reagan spoke before the Brandenburg Gate in Berlin (which marked the line between the Communist and non-Communist sectors of the divided city) and admonished the Soviet president, "General Secretary Gorbachev, if you seek peace, if you seek prosperity for the Soviet Union and Eastern Europe, if you seek liberalization: Come here to this gate! Mr. Gorbachev, open this gate! Mr. Gorbachev, tear down this wall."[79]

On the other hand, the Reagan administration entered negotiations on an Intermediate Nuclear Forces (INF) treaty with the Soviet Union, hoping to control or reduce nuclear arms. The agreement was signed by Reagan and Gorbachev on December 8, 1987. As the historian William Pemberton explained, this treaty, "in line with Reagan's zero-zero proposal of 1981, required the Soviets to abandon many of the objections to it that they had raised in the past."[80] Furthermore, "[t]he INF Treaty was the first time in history that nations had agreed to destroy nuclear weapons rather than just slow down the arms race."[81]

Reagan took other actions to show that he was still in charge of foreign policy. In December 1986, he issued Proclamation 5595, which imposed a surcharge on imports of certain types of softwood lumber from Canada (as part of a long-running dispute between the two neighbors over this commodity).[82] In February 1987, he lifted economic sanctions that had been imposed against Poland for repression of pro-democracy activities. He also sent Congress notice that he was continuing declarations of national emergencies regarding Iran and Nicaragua, thus retaining power over trade with those nations. Finally, in October 1987, the Reagan administration engaged in a brief military encounter with Iran: in reprisal for the Iranian military firing a SILKWORM missile against a U.S.-flagged merchant ship, Reagan ordered an attack on an armed Iranian oil platform in the Persian Gulf. He informed Congress of his foreign policy activities but did not ask for permission to act.

Organizational Changes

Given that Reagan maintained that the Iran-Contra scandal emerged largely as the result of administration officials acting improperly and taking actions that had not been approved by the president, it is no surprise that organizational changes took place almost immediately. Perhaps much of Reagan's response came from lessons learned from Watergate. As Charles Jones explained, "No doubt having the Watergate debacle in mind, the President acted quickly to manage the Iran-*contra* affair. National Security Council personnel were fired, an independent counsel was requested, an investigating commission appointed, and a Department of Justice probe was launched."[83]

On November 25, 1986, National Security Advisor John Poindexter resigned, and Oliver North was removed from his post on the National Security Council. A few days later, on December 2, Reagan chose former deputy defense secretary Frank Carlucci to fill the national security advisor position.[84] The appointment of Carlucci was an important step because Carlucci was well respected in Washington, DC. Days after his appointment, one reporter described that Carlucci "will bring some important qualities that his predecessor, Adm. John Poindexter, lacked: a wide experience in government, a vision of the broad objectives of U.S. foreign policy, a preference for teamwork and planning over adventurism and cloak-and-dagger operations."[85]

President Reagan's next substantial organizational move came as the scandal continued to grow and it was clear that his presidency could be in jeopardy. Late in December 1986, Reagan appointed Ambassador David Abshire as a special counselor to the president, with a seat in the cabinet, to serve as Reagan's liaison and assistant in all matters related to the affair.[86]

Additional organizational adjustments came two months later. On February 27, 1987, one day after the Tower Commission released its findings, chief of staff Donald Regan was forced to resign. In fact, when the president addressed the nation on March 4 to give his response to the Tower Commission's report, he also utilized the event to begin a new chapter in his administration. Beyond endorsing the commission's findings, he announced that a "new team" would take over in his White House. Most importantly, former senator Howard Baker became his chief of staff. With Baker at the helm, additional personnel changes soon followed. In particular, Baker sought to establish a new relationship with the press. In order to accomplish this task, Baker replaced press secretary Larry Speakes with Marlin Fitzwater and director of communications Patrick Buchanan with Baker's close aide Thomas Griscom.[87]

Going Public
President Reagan immediately recognized the need to speak to the American people. In his diary, on November 12, 1986, Reagan wrote, "This whole irresponsible press bilge about hostages and Iran has gotten totally out of hand. The media looks like it's trying to create another Watergate…I want to go public personally and tell the people the truth."[88] The following day, in a national address, the president admitted that he had "authorized the transfer of small amounts of defensive weapons and spare parts for defensive systems in Iran."[89] However, he further explained, "The United States has not made concessions to those who hold our people captive in Lebanon. And we will not. The United States has not swapped boatloads or planeloads of American weapons for the return of American hostages. And we will not."[90] In this address, Reagan acknowledged that he was responsible for the actions taken by his administration but claimed that he

was not privy to the details of what had occurred. He also declared that he would not invoke executive privilege to shield himself or his administration from scrutiny and would cooperate with investigations into the scandal. This initial address failed to convince the American people that the president was being completely forthright. In fact, a *Los Angeles Times* poll indicated that only 14% of Americans "believe[d] the president's statement that he had not been trading arms for hostages."[91]

As a result of his failed efforts, the president held a press conference six days later. Once again, the "Great Communicator" failed to communicate effectively. In his seminal text regarding the Iran-Contra affair, Theodore Draper described, "The press conference of November 19 was the most disastrous in President Reagan's presidency."[92] Although Reagan told reporters that he personally had ordered "no further sales of any kind to be sent to Iran," he damaged his image by giving contradictory answers to seemingly similar questions.[93]

In spite of Reagan's attempts to quell the emergence of a major scandal, developments continued to worsen. On November 24, chief of staff Donald Regan confided in White House counsel Peter Wallison that "a situation is developing now that looks like Watergate."[94] The next day, Reagan read a four-paragraph statement to the press in which he acknowledged "seriously flawed" policy but maintained he had not been "fully informed" of the actions carried out.[95] Draper wrote, "President Reagan's worst enemy in this crisis was himself, because his evident lack of mastery of the facts deprived him of the public's willingness to take his word on trust and give him credit for knowing what he was doing or what was done in his name."[96]

As such, his initial attempts at forthrightness appeared to worsen the situation. The *New York Times* raised a question no doubt on the minds of many observers: "It's hard to know which would be more alarming, Presidential ignorance or arrogance."[97] By the end of November, a *New York Times*/CBS News poll reported that nearly three-fifths of the American public believed the looming crisis was "at least as serious as Watergate."[98]

Unconventional Actions

President Reagan attempted at least two unconventional strategies in an effort to overcome his adverse circumstances. First, unlike many presidents (including Nixon and Clinton) who try to prevent or stall investigations against the chief executive, in Reagan's case, within weeks of the scandal breaking he announced his own intention to inquire into the matter. As previously indicated, President Reagan announced on November 25, 1986, his plan to form an independent commission that would investigate wrongdoing by administration officials. Though this did not prevent Congress from establishing its own investigations, the president preempted Congress and effectively differentiated his scandal from Watergate.

His second unconventional strategy was to reverse course. When his initial attempts at "going public" failed, "the Great Communicator" essentially stopped communicating. In 1986 Reagan had made forty-eight political appearances, and in 1988 he would make forty-nine. In 1987, however, he made only nine such appearances and hosted only three press conferences.[99] Instead, Busby explained, "It was principally left to Vice President Bush to speak for the upper echelons of the administration."[100]

In essence, this shift was a response to the charge by Reagan's critics that he was too aloof and not active enough in everyday policy; his approach, some believed, may have led to the Iran-Contra affair. Likewise, the Tower Commission determined that the Iran-Contra affair "had arisen as a result of the president's disengaged style of management which made it possible for policy-making and implementation to be hijacked by amateurs and adventurers."[101] Reagan thus worked to bolster his image as an active president involved in everyday tasks of government. He would return to a more public and rhetorical style of governing in 1988, but for a time Reagan became too busy to travel and to speak much.

Epilogue

Although the independent counsel's investigation of the Iran-Contra affair continued for several years, the congressional investigators issued their final report in November 1987, and by year's end Ronald Reagan had largely put the scandal behind him. By January 1988, in spite of the stock market collapse of October 19, 1987, the *Los Angeles Times* reported that his public approval ratings were back up to 67%.[102] In fact, by the time he left office in January 1989, he had the highest presidential job approval ratings since Franklin Roosevelt: 63% according to the Gallup organization and 68% according to the *New York Times*.[103] The scandal remained a black mark on his presidency, but Reagan's reputation would not be permanently damaged by it. Even Richard Neustadt, a noted critic of Reagan's leadership style, acknowledged that Reagan's "presidency restored the public image of the office to a fair (if perhaps rickety) approximation of its Roosevelt mold: a place of popularity, influence, and initiative…like or hate his politics—a presence many of us loved to see as Chief of State."[104]

BILL CLINTON AND THE MONICA LEWINSKY SCANDAL

Prior to the eruption of the Monica Lewinsky scandal, Bill Clinton's political future seemed bright. As the journalist Marvin Kalb described the situation,

> At the start of 1998, the Clinton presidency seemed to be at the peak of its power and influence. The budget was being balanced. Unemployment was low. While problems persisted in parts of the world, the Cold War was history, American troops were not dying on distant battlefields, and nuclear war was widely regarded as inconceivable.[105]

His job approval rating held at 59% in early January 1998 and had not dipped below 54% throughout all of 1997.[106] This situation changed, however, when the Monica Lewinsky scandal took center stage.

Table 13a. Summarizing the President's Response to Adversity—Scandal—Reagan Nov 1986–Dec 1987

Type of response	Summary data & significant examples
1. Bargaining & persuasion	House & Senate concurrence with president —1987: 43.5% Legislative successes/compromises/concessions: • 1987: Independ Counsel Act (concession) Failed attempts at legislative bargaining/compromise: • 1987: Water Quality Act • 1987: Surface Transportation Act • 1987: Bork Supreme Court nomination Other: Tower Commission & indep counsel failed to stop congressional investigation
2. Executive actions constitutional	Vetoes: 3 regular (33% sustained), 1 pocket • Jan 1987: Water Quality Act (overridden) • Mar1987: Surfc Transport Act (overridden) Pardons & clemency: 78 (all pardons) Proclamations: 193 Executive orders: 50 • 12575 – Special Revw Bd (Tower Commn) Signing Statements: 36 Claims of executive privilege: None
other actions	April 1987: Privatization of CONRAIL
3. Foreign policy initiatives & actions	National security directives: 42 • NSDD 261 – Restructuring of SDI program • NSDD 266 – Implement Tower Commn International agreements: 94 Significant treaties: • Sept.1987: Nucl Risk Reduction Ctrs Treaty • Dec. 1987: Intermed Nuclear Forces Treaty Uses of force: • Oct. 1987: Attacked Iranian oil platform in response to Iran missile at US merchant ship
Outcome of case: Reagan left office with approval ratings over 60% and his Vice President won the 1988 election	

Table 13b. Summarizing the President's Response to Adversity—Scandal—
Reagan Nov 1986–Dec 1987

Type of response	Summary data & significant examples
Foreign policy initiatives & actions *continued*	*Other:* • Pressure on Sandinista govt-Nicaragua • Feb 1987: End sanctions against Poland • Jun 1987: "tear down this wall" speech • Jun 1987: Tariffs on Japan lifted
4. Organizational changes	Nov 1986: Fired Oliver North from NSC staff; Security Advisor Poindexter resigns Dec 1986: Carlucci as Natil Security Advisor Dec 1986: Amb Abshire apptd as Specl Counselor Feb 1987: Fired Don Regan as chief of staff Mar 1987: New chief of staff & new CIA Director Mar. 1987: New press secy; new commun director
5. Going public	*Major speeches:* 8 (1986-2, 1987-6) *News conferences:* 3 (only includes 1987) *Key Events:* • Nov 1986: Iran-contra • Nov 1986: Press conference on Iran-contra • Nov 1986: Acknowledged "flawed policy" • Nov 1986: Announcing Tower Commission • Dec 1986: Iran-contra • Jan 1987: State of the Union • Mar 1987: Endorsed Tower Comm report, announced "new team" • Aug 1987: Iran-contra affair • Oct 1987: Bork Supreme Court nomination • Dec 1987: On summit with Gorbachev
6. Unconventional actions?	• Creation of Tower Commission • Withdrew from the public in order to prove he was "active" in governing; 1987: only 9 political appearances (1986: 48, 1988: 49)
Outcome of case: Reagan left office with approval ratings over 60% and his Vice President won the 1988 election	

Table 13c. Comparing the President's Response to Non-Adverse Circumstances—Reagan Nov 1986–Dec 1987

Type of response	Comparison to non-adverse circumstances (1981)
1. Bargaining & persuasion	*House & Senate concurrence with president* – *1981: 82.4%* *Legislative successes/compromises* • Aug: tax cut (Success) • Sept: O'Connor confirmed (Success) • Oct: Saudi arms deal (Success) • Nov: MX Missile program • Dec: Restore funding for B-1 bomber program (success) *Failed attempts at legislative bargaining:* • None significant
2. Executive actions constitutional	*Vetoes:* 1 regular (100% sustained), 1 pocket • Nov: Continuing Appropriations Bill *Pardons & clemency:* 2 (both pardons) *Proclamations:* 71 *Executive orders:* 76 • 12296 – Econ Advisory Policy Board • 12301 –Grace Commn estd to review fed programs *Signing statements:* 19 *Claims of executive privilege:* • Interior Secy kept from answering cong probe of Canadian oil leases
other actions	Aug.: Fired over 11,000 air traffic controllers
3. Foreign policy initiatives & actions	*National security directives:* 14 • NSDD 12- Strategic Forces Modernization *International agreements:* 249 (194 Executive Agreements, 55 Treaties) *Significant treaties:* N/A *Uses of force:* • Aug: US planes down Libyan jets
*Outcome of case: **Reagan left office with approval ratings over 60% and his Vice President won the 1988 election***	

Table 13d. Comparing the President's Response to Non-Adverse Circumstances—Reagan Nov 1986–Dec 1987 (Cont.)

Type of response	Comparison to non-adverse circumstances (1981)
Foreign policy initiatives & actions *continued*	*Other:* • Sent military advisors to El Salvador • Japan limited car exports to avoid quotas • Jul: G-7 Summit • Sept: Addressed IMF & World Bank • Dec: Speaks against martial law in Poland
4. Organizational changes	N/A
5. Going public	*Major speeches:* 6 *News conferences:* 6 *Key Events:* • Jan: Inaugural Address • Jan: Ceremony for released Iran hostages • Feb: Econ recovery program speech to Cong • Apr: First public appearance after being shot; spoke to joint session of Congress • Jul: Address on Tax Reduction • Sept: National address on economic recovery
6. Unconventional actions?	N/A
*Outcome of case: **Reagan left office with approval ratings over 60% and his Vice President won the 1988 election***	

Though the Lewinsky scandal did not truly emerge until January 1998,
a key event that precipitated it occurred on May 27, 1997, when the
Supreme Court unanimously rejected the president's claim of immunity
from a civil lawsuit in the case of *Clinton v. Jones*. The sexual harassment
suit filed against Clinton by former Arkansas state employee Paula Jones
proceeded, serving as an embarrassment for the president.[107] Matters
grew worse in August 1997 when *Newsweek* reported on allegations that
Clinton had made inappropriate advances toward Kathleen Willey and
that he may have had an additional relationship with a White House

intern.[108] The following week, the Clinton legal team attempted to end the harassment case, offering Paula Jones a $700,000 settlement, which she refused. Upon her refusal, Jones's lawyers withdrew from the case and she obtained representation from a team of politically motivated lawyers supported in part by a conservative advocacy group.[109]

Jones's new legal team found that Clinton had been involved in a relationship with a White House intern named Monica Lewinsky. In December 1997, the Jones attorneys subpoenaed Lewinsky, and she was scheduled to appear for a deposition. On January 7, 1998, however, Lewinsky signed an affidavit stating that she had "never had a sexual relationship with the President."[110] Ten days later, Clinton gave his own deposition. One day after Clinton's deposition, the *Drudge Report* broke the story of a 23-year-old former White House intern who had been in a sexual affair with the president.[111]

On January 20, news broke that independent counsel Kenneth Starr, who had originally been appointed to investigate other matters, intended to pursue obstruction-of-justice charges against the president because of his apparent attempt to influence Lewinsky's testimony in the Jones case. The next day, the *Washington Post* included the headline, "Clinton Accused of Urging Aide to Lie; Starr Probes Whether President Told Woman to Deny Alleged Affair to Jones's Lawyers."[112] On January 22, that paper acknowledged the possibility of impeachment.[113] Some of Clinton's closest aides thought that he might resign as a result of this emerging scandal.[114] In a short time, a consensus quickly developed among Washington pundits that, if Clinton were found to be lying about his relationship with Lewinsky, this would create "a crisis that could sink his presidency."[115]

Throughout 1998, the scandal worsened for the president. In July, Lewinsky and Starr finalized an agreement whereby she would provide a detailed account of her relationship with the president, and in return Starr would provide Lewinsky with immunity from possible perjury charges.[116] By August, a number of leading Democrats, including Senators Joe Lieberman, Bob Kerrey, and Daniel Patrick Moynihan, publicly expressed their concern with the president's lack of candor regarding the scandal and his overall poor judgment. As he recounted the situation, Lanny Davis, part of Clinton's legal defense team, commented, "I'm pretty convinced that Clinton was within inches of losing the presidency then."[117] In September, following the release of Starr's report on the Clinton-Lewinsky matter, Democratic senator Kent Conrad told Clinton's special counsel Greg Craig, "You are about three days from having the senior Democrats come down and ask for the president's resignation."[118]

On December 19, 1998, the House of Representatives formally impeached President Clinton, charging him with perjury before a federal grand jury and obstruction of justice. The Senate impeachment trial began on January 7, 1999. Nearly five weeks later, on February 12, the Senate rejected both charges. The obstruction of justice charge resulted in a tie vote, whereas the perjury charge was rejected by a 45–55 vote, meaning that neither vote came close to the two-thirds necessary for removal.[119]

Interestingly, rather than finding a president crippled by scandal, we find a president who was quite successful. As Peri Arnold suggested, "One would expect these events to have greatly burdened Clinton's ability to lead; remarkably, however, he was able to overshadow those proceedings with his own presidential activity."[120]

Bargaining and Persuasion
Clinton wanted to pursue an ambitious legislative agenda in 1998, including Social Security reform, campaign finance reform, and a patients' "bill of rights." Instead, he had to settle for victories on minor issues. He also attempted to use bargaining and persuasion to control both his testimony in the Lewinsky matter and the impeachment trial in Congress.

Legislative Successes/Compromises/Concessions

Although Clinton was a lame-duck president who faced a Republican Congress seeking to remove him from office, he won key victories on individual votes throughout 1998 and, to some extent, in 1999. *Congressional Quarterly* reported that the Republican emphasis on impeachment throughout 1998 "created a political vacuum that allowed the president and a few congressional lone wolves...to step in and win passage of legislation that would have likely met with defeat in the earlier, headier days of the Republican revolution."[121] Clinton attained victory with the expansion of NATO's borders, a massive transportation bill, the approval for his initiative to hire 100,000 new teachers, the expansion of Head Start, and the investment of the budget surplus in Social Security, rather than a new tax cut advocated by the Republican Congress.[122] Such success led Barbara Sinclair to conclude, "Given the constraints of that political environment—conservative Republican majorities in both chambers of Congress, news media more interested in scandals than in policy choices —Clinton did about as well as was possible."[123] Most importantly, President Clinton remained in office because the Senate rejected both charges brought against him by the House impeachment managers.

Failed Attempts at Legislative Bargaining/Compromise

In spite of these victories, it was during the 1998 session that Clinton lost on what he considered the most important issues on the agenda, given that he failed to achieve victory on tobacco legislation, campaign finance reform, "fast track" trade authority, and a patients' "bill of rights."[124] More importantly, he could not overcome the House leadership's decision to proceed with impeachment and eventually lost votes on two of the articles of impeachment. The losses continued to mount during the 1999 session, but the overall scorecard of the Republicans did not fare much better, because the two houses of Congress often could not agree upon legislation. As a result, *Congressional Quarterly* found that "Clinton did manage to win a few big votes, although victories in one chamber were often undone in the other."[125] Such disparities were found on bills pertaining to HMO protections, campaign finance reform, and gun control.

Overall, statistical evidence (see table 14) suggests that Clinton's legislative success in Congress declined throughout the scandal. Although his vote concurrence in Congress had declined from 86% in 1993 and 1994 to a record-low 36.2% in 1995, Clinton learned to bargain with his Republican counterparts in Congress, and his success increased to 55.1% in 1996 and 53.6% in 1997. During the Lewinsky scandal, however, his success again declined. By 1999, his overall vote concurrence plummeted to 37.8%, which included a precipitous drop in the Senate from 66.7% in 1998 to 42.2% in 1999. Even worse, *Congressional Quarterly* reported that when they excluded Senate votes regarding nominations, his overall success in the Senate declined to a mere 28.6% in 1999 (as compared to 57.1% in 1998).[126] Much of this decline appears scandal-driven, given that his success once again increased in 2000.

Table 14. Congressional Concurrence with the President, 1997–2000

Year	Total H&S Concurrence	House Concurrence	# of House Votes	Senate Concurrence	# of Senate Votes
1997	53.6	38.7	75	71.4	63
1998	50.6	36.6	82	66.7	72
1999	37.8	35.4	82	42.2	45
2000	55.0	49.3	69	65.0	40
Average	49.3	40.0		61.3	
Total			308		220

Source. Compiled from data in *Vital Statistics on American Politics, 2007–2008* (p. 265) by Harold Stanley and Richard Niemi. Washington, DC: CQ Press, 2008.

Other Efforts at Bargaining and Negotiation

One of the more unique developments during the Lewinsky scandal illustrated a rather successful example of presidential bargaining. In July 1998, the Office of Independent Counsel subpoenaed the president for grand jury

testimony. Some believed that because this was a completely "unprecedented act...the White House might have been able to challenge it in
court."[127] Clinton and his legal team decided not to challenge the subpoena
but instead chose to negotiate an agreement whereby the president would
provide testimony under guidelines satisfactory to the president, which led
to the withdrawal of the subpoena. Instead of Clinton appearing before the
grand jury in person, he would appear via closed-circuit television broad-
casted from the White House. Daniel Cohen explained that because of
these negotiations, "President Clinton had some advantages that an ordinary grand-jury witness does not have. His lawyer would be in the room
with him, not on camera, but in easy consultation range."[128]

Another attempt at bargaining, though unsuccessful, came in early
October 1998, when the president engaged in conversations with Democratic senators Bob Torricelli and John Breaux. Clinton sought their assistance on a plan to get at least thirty-four senators to sign a letter explaining
their position against removing the president from office, which in effect
would undermine the House impeachment proceedings. According to
Peter Baker of the *Washington Post*, the arrangement failed when "Tom
Daschle stepped in and put a halt to the plan, telling Clinton it would be
improper and imprudent."[129]

Executive Actions

During the scandal, President Clinton effectively wielded his veto power.
He used the veto ten times throughout 1998 and 1999, all of which
were sustained. It should be noted, however, that the five vetoes of 1999
occurred during the "post-scandal" period. Nevertheless, Clinton had a
great deal of success using this tool, given that lawmakers did not even
attempt to override any of his vetoes during 1998. The five vetoes covered
a wide range of issues, including school vouchers, sanctions against Iran,
agriculture appropriations, education savings accounts, and foreign affairs
reform. Furthermore, *Congressional Quarterly* explained that the president not only achieved success through the use of vetoes, but he maintained influence in Congress merely by threatening vetoes. In particular,

he threatened "vetoes on a battery of issues from tax cuts to restrictions on overseas family planning funds" and, as a result, "stymied congressional conservatives just when it seemed that they should be piling up political points."[130]

In addition to his veto strategy, Clinton relied heavily on executive orders and signing statements. During this eighteen-month period, Clinton issued fifty-six executive orders on a plethora of topics, including the expansion of Equal Employment Opportunity Commission protections to incorporate discrimination based on sexual orientation (E.O. 13087), the prohibition of transactions with Osama bin Laden and other terrorists (E.O. 13099), the implementation of human rights treaties (E.O. 13107), the expansion of federal programs for Asian Americans (E.O. 13125), and the implementation of the Chemical Weapons Convention (E.O. 13125). In addition, he issued a series of orders dealing with U.S. policy toward the former Yugoslavia as he declared the region a combat zone (E.O. 13119), activated members of the Selective Reserve to fight in the region (E.O. 13120), and prohibited trade with Serbia and Montenegro (E.O. 13121). He further utilized his unilateral executive powers to limit congressional authority pertaining to combat in the former Yugoslavia; on October 17, 1998, the president attached a signing statement to the Department of Defense Appropriations Act, whereby Clinton determined that Congress's restrictions on additional deployment of troops for combat in the former Yugoslavia only pertained to ground forces and thus was not an across-the-board restriction on the deployment of troops.

Finally, like Nixon, Clinton invoked executive privilege as he attempted to shield himself and some of his closest allies from further investigations. According to Morton Rosenberg of the Congressional Research Service, Clinton claimed executive privilege on five different occasions throughout 1998.[131] The claims pertained to his dealings with Nancy Hernreich, director of Oval Office operations; Sidney Blumenthal, senior advisor to the president; Cheryl Mills, deputy White House counsel; Lanny Breuer, a special White House counsel for the impeachment trial; and Bruce

Lindsey, senior advisor to the president. Overall these claims had mixed results: Clinton's legal team withdrew their claim regarding Hernreich prior to the hearing, lost on their claims pertaining to Blumenthal and Breuer, and succeeded in their claims concerning Mills and Lindsey.[132]

Foreign Policy Initiatives and Actions

John Harris described that throughout 1998 and 1999, "[f]oreign policy, in particular, rolled on, seemingly unshaken by the potholes of scandal."[133] Besides the aforementioned executive orders and signing statements, diplomacy remained high atop the president's agenda. In late January 1998, just as the scandal broke, Clinton continued his personal efforts to broker peace between Israel and the Palestinians.[134] Then, in March, Clinton took a much-anticipated trip to Africa. Harris explained, "Clinton was now taking the longest trip of his presidency—six nations in eleven days—on an itinerary designed to highlight progress and potential in a continent that tended to make news in America only for its horrors."[135] It was during this trip that the president, as he visited Uganda, famously apologized for America's involvement in the slave trade.[136] One day later, as he visited Rwanda, Clinton further apologized for American policy during the Rwandan genocide of 1994 as he confessed, "[A]ll over the world there were people like me sitting in offices, day after day, who did not fully appreciate the depth and speed with which you were being engulfed in this unimaginable terror."[137]

Diplomatic efforts continued throughout the summer of 1998. In June, Clinton visited China. Up until that point in his presidency, critics claimed that Clinton had "fumbled" U.S. policy toward China, but remarkably, Clinton used this visit to achieve what the foreign policy analyst William Hyland called "probably the high point of his policy."[138] After all, Clinton not only used the trip for diplomatic reasons, but he openly spoke out against China's human rights record and reasserted America's policy regarding Taiwan.[139] Then, in September, just weeks after Russia's financial markets crumbled, the president traveled to Moscow, where he not only met with President Yeltsin to discuss Russia's economic woes but also signed an agreement concerning strategies to prevent nuclear acci-dents.[140] Following his summit with Yeltsin, Clinton then spoke before the UN General Assembly on September 21.[141]

Besides his continued diplomatic efforts throughout his scandal, Clinton also used his war powers on three different occasions. Days after the Lewinsky story broke, the White House leaked information about a possible plan for "a four-day, around-the-clock bombing campaign" in Iraq because of fear that Saddam Hussein was once again stockpiling chemical and biological weapons.[142] Clinton spoke at the Pentagon to explain why action against Iraq was necessary, whereas Secretary of State Madeleine Albright, Secretary of Defense William Cohen, and National Security Advisor Sandy Berger took part in a televised town-hall meeting at the Ohio State University outlining the proposed actions.[143] Although the UN secretary-general Kofi Annan effectively postponed U.S. air strikes, Hussein's continued noncompliance led to Clinton ordering a four-day assault in December 1998. In fact, the House of Representatives delayed its impeachment vote one day in order to allow the president to carry out his military actions.[144]

In addition to the continued tension in Iraq, Clinton responded to the Serbian army's wholesale assault on Albanians living in Kosovo. Although Clinton's initial policy proved inconsistent, he eventually concluded that the Serb forces must completely withdraw from Kosovo; otherwise NATO would take action.[145] Tensions subsided in late 1998, but on January 15, 1999, Serbian forces broke the ceasefire and killed fifty civilians.[146] The president recognized the necessity of intensifying pres-sure on Milosevic and thus negotiated with members of NATO to develop a unified response.[147] On February 13, 1999, one day after the Senate voted against removal, Clinton announced the necessity of taking action against Milosevic and the Serbs as he argued that continued violence could cause a regional crisis and that ethnic conflicts often cause the loss of millions of people.[148] Just over six weeks later, Clinton achieved his desired "consensus" among NATO members, and NATO bombing operations commenced on March 24.[149] Ultimately, throughout the ongoing Lewinsky scandal, President Clinton provided international leadership that led to a June 9, 1999, agreement whereby the Serbs withdrew from Kosovo. According to one account, this marked "the first successful intervention to forestall ethnic mass slaughter in Europe in a century."[150]

The third arena in which President Clinton used military force during the Lewinsky scandal came in response to the terrorist strikes against two U.S. embassies in Kenya and Tanzania on August 7, 1998, leaving at least 220 dead and more than 4,000 wounded.[151] On August 20, President Clinton announced Operation Infinite Reach, whereby he ordered cruise missile strikes on terrorist camps in Afghanistan and a pharmaceutical factory in the Sudan.

Organizational Changes
President Clinton's scandal can be differentiated from those of the Nixon and Reagan administrations because the Lewinsky situation dealt exclusively with wrongdoing of the president, whereas the Nixon and Reagan scandals included several administration officials. Consequently, Clinton did not have to restructure his administration in the same way witnessed under Nixon and Reagan. Still, crucial changes did take place. First, in September 1998, just as Starr had concluded his report and sent it to the House, President Clinton asked attorney Greg Craig to leave his position in the State Department, where he was a senior advisor to Secretary of State Madeleine Albright and director of policy planning, to serve as assistant to the president and special White House counsel. The White House viewed Craig as "the 'quarterback' of the defense team, a description that was later written into the announcement of his appointment."[152] Additional changes came during the first week of October 1998, as press secretary Mike McCurry, senior advisor Rahm Emanuel, and Chief of Staff Erskine Bowles all resigned. Although it did not appear that Emanuel's resignation had any connection with the scandal, evidence suggests that McCurry and Bowles grew increasingly embittered with the president. As the *Washington Post* suggested, "Whatever their motivations, the depar-

tures of McCurry, Bowles, and Emanuel stripped the president of some of the strongest assets at a critical juncture."[153]

Going Public

Like Reagan, Clinton's immediate reaction to the scandal was to utilize the strategy of "going public." One scholar commented, "Clinton's public response to the impeachment drama was to conduct a presidency of high visibility and grand gestures."[154] However, unlike Reagan, who immediately took responsibility for his administration's actions and sought an investigation, Clinton vehemently denied any wrongdoing. Miroff described how this initial strategy included a four-pronged response: (1) denial of a sexual relationship, (2) a shift from character issues to substantive issues, (3) a refusal to answer questions regarding the matter, and (4) the utilization of his closest political allies to attack "the motives and methods" of independent counsel Kenneth Starr.[155] Apparently this initial strategy succeeded, because Clinton's pubic approval actually grew stronger during the first weeks following the story breaking.[156]

The first direct response from the president came on January 21, 1998, in a series of interviews that had already been scheduled as part of the White House strategy to gear up for the upcoming State of the Union address on January 27. President Clinton made himself available for three interviews: one on *The NewsHour with Jim Lehrer*, one with Mara Liasson of National Public Radio, and one with the Capitol Hill newspaper *Roll Call*. In all three interviews Clinton reiterated that no improper sexual relationship occurred between him and Lewinsky, his cooperation with the investigation, and the need to "get back to the work of the country."[157]

Clinton did not feel that these refutations were enough, leading to his famous January 26 public denial of the affair. The denial came at an event announcing the expansion of after-school programs, which had originally been scheduled to be hosted by the First Lady and the vice president. At the last minute, the president decided that he would join them. White House speechwriter Michael Waldman explained, "It was unstated, but obvious, that the purpose was to give him a chance to say something about the Lewinsky affair."[158] Following the remarks about the new funding initiatives, Clinton looked directly into the cameras and boldly stated, "I want to make one thing clear to the American people...I did not have sexual relations with that woman, Miss Lewinsky. I never told anybody to lie, not a single time—never. These allegations are false. And I need to get back to work for the American people."[159] Miroff said that this denial was quite important for the president, because "it bought him time by allowing the public to get used to the idea that a president might be a reprobate in his private behavior yet talented and effective in his public performance."[160]

These series of denials set the stage for his State of the Union address, in which he made no mention of the pending scandal but instead proposed an ambitious agenda. Most importantly, Clinton called on Congress to "Save Social Security first," prior to the Republican's proposed tax cut. Caught off-guard, Gingrich and the Republicans applauded the president's rhetoric. As one of Clinton's speechwriters recollected, "In that instant, a trillion dollars silently shifted on the budget ledger from the column marked 'tax cut' to the column marked 'Social Security.'"[161] Miroff noted that Clinton utilized his 1998 State of the Union address to propose "a long string of popular, poll-tested proposals," which led to a surge in the polls (over 70% according to some polling agencies).[162] The *Washington Post* reported that following the State of the Union address, President Clinton held a 52–35% advantage over the Republican Congress when people were asked whom they trusted more in dealing with the country's problems.[163] The day after his 1998 State of the Union address, Clinton, along with Vice President Gore, took to the road in an effort to get the public behind his policy initiatives.[164]

Throughout the scandal, Clinton utilized his "going public" strategy to try to illustrate to the American public that there were larger issues facing the country than his personal sins. He continued to emphasize his need to "get back to work" for the American people.[165] The speechwriter Waldman recounted, "Clinton's determination to keep doing the public job of his presidency entailed, above all else, public appearances, a relentless reliance on the bully pulpit."[166] As one scholar described, "Clinton turned the struggle into a question of whether a president who was performing well should be removed for actions unconnected to his official duties."[167]

As the scandal wore on, Clinton increased his number of public appearances.[168] Even on August 17, 1998, when the president gave his grand jury testimony, admitting that he had lied about the affair, Clinton sought the public's assistance to focus the country's attention on more important matters. In this national address, the president took "complete responsibility for all [his] actions, both public and private," and admitted misleading the American people. Clinton concluded his remarks by urging the public that it was time to move on. In particular, he stated, "This has gone on too long, cost too much, and hurt too many innocent people. It is time to stop the pursuit of personal destruction and the prying into private lives, and get on with our national life. Our country has been distracted by this matter for too long."[169]

Weeks later, when the House decided to release the Starr Report to the public, the White House immediately responded, condemning the independent prosecutor for drafting a report that focused on private sexual matters rather than constitutional offenses sufficient for removing a president from office.[170] Once again, we find evidence of an effective "going public" strategy by Clinton and his aides, given that the president's approval ratings actually increased throughout September 1998, whereas support for impeachment declined.[171]

Even after the Democratic success in the November 1998 midterm elections, the White House recognized the need to maintain public support and thus strategized ways to strengthen Clinton's relationship with the American people. In fact, on the very day he lost the impeachment vote in the House, Harris reported that the White House offered "an unusual response. Clinton would greet the news not with remorse but with exuberant defiance."[172] This included a "pep rally"–style event with House Democrats on the South Lawn of the White House. Harris noted, "The world would see Clinton not as a solitary and embattled figure like Richard Nixon walking the beach in his wingtips at San Clemente, but surrounded by friends."[173] Two days later, on December 20, 1998, the *New York Times* ran an article entitled, "Impeachment: Beyond the Vote: President Maps Out a Strategy for Governing While on Trial," which explained how Clinton had already planned "a blaze of campaign-style events" in early 1999.[174]

Weeks later, as critics called on the president to forgo his 1999 State of the Union address because of the pending Senate trial, Clinton not only refused but used the speech to illustrate his political strength. Just as he had done the previous year when he caught the Republicans off-guard concerning using the surplus to "save" Social Security, in 1999 he inserted a paragraph not released to the Republicans prior to the speech, with which he announced "that the Justice Department is preparing a litigation plan to take the tobacco companies to court—and with the funds we recover, to strengthen Medicare."[175] Waldman explained, "It was a powerful moment —a reminder, in terms as stark as the Constitution allowed, that *he* was still President, that *he* didn't need Congress for everything, that he wasn't pulling back from anything."[176]

Finally, on February 12, 1999, hours after the Senate voted against removing Clinton from office, the president addressed the American people and sought to put the scandal behind him. Clinton remarked, "Now that the Senate has fulfilled its constitutional responsibility, bringing the process to a conclusion, I want to say again to the American people how profoundly sorry I am for what I said and did to trigger these events and the great burden they have imposed on the Congress and on the American people."[177]

Epilogue

The scandal during the Clinton presidency is a stellar illustration of how presidents not only cope with tough times but in many ways can overcome extreme adversity. In fact, according to one study, prior to the scandal, Clinton's approval ratings only topped 60% seven times in the Gallup polls, but after the scandal broke, Clinton received 60% or higher in thirty-one consecutive polls. Thus, the study found, "Clinton was more popular in crisis than most presidents have ever been."[178] This high popularity helped lead to the unexpected Democratic success during the midterm congressional elections of 1998, just two months after House Speaker Newt Gingrich predicted a net gain of thirty seats for Republicans and Robert Novak boasted of the potential for a sixty-seat, filibuster-proof Senate for the Republicans.[179] Instead, Democrats gained five seats in the House and broke even in the Senate, which marked "the first time that an incumbent president's party had gained seats in the midterm election of a second term since 1822" and "only the second time in the twentieth century that an incumbent president's party had gained seats at all in a midterm election."[180] With this disaster at the polls, Speaker Gingrich not only gave up his position as Speaker but resigned his congressional seat. Two years later, just weeks before Clinton left office, his approval rating topped 70% for the first time in his presidency.[181] Though his final Gallup job approval rating dipped down to 66% on the week he left office, this was the highest job approval rating ever calculated by Gallup for a president leaving office.

OUTCOME AND ASSESSMENT

Periods of scandal are increasingly problematic for presidents; not only do they lead to a further divide between the president and Congress, but they also present the possibility that the incumbent will be removed from power. Furthermore, scandal-plagued administrations face growing mistrust among the American people, an additional impediment for successfully overcoming adversity.

Table 15a. Summarizing the President's Response to Adversity—Scandal—
Bill Clinton, Jan 1998–June 1999

Type of response	Summary data & significant examples
1. Bargaining & persuasion	*House & Senate concurrence with president— average for 1998-1999:* 44.2 % *Legislative successes/compromises/concessions:* • Mar 1998: No new tax cuts (success) • Jun 1998: Transportation Bill (success) • Oct 1998: Expansion of Head Start (success) • Feb 1999: Senate acquits president (success) • Mar 1999: Hire 100,000 new teachers (success) *Failed attempts at legislative bargaining/compromise:* • Feb 1998: Campaign finance reform • Jun 1998: Tobacco legislation • Dec 1998: House impeaches Clinton • Feb 1999: Comprehensive Nuc Test Ban Treaty
2. Executive actions constitutional	*Vetoes:* 5 regular (100% sustained) *Pardons & clemency:* 34 pardons *Proclamations:* 144 *Executive orders*: 56 • 13087 – Expanded EEOC protections to gays • 13120 –Reserves sent to fmr Yugoslavia • 13121 – No trade with Serbia & Montenegro *Signing Statements:* 59 *Claims of executive privilege:* 5 • Feb 1998 – Aide not testify (rejected by court) • Mar 1998 – Aide not testify (withdrawn) • Aug 1998 – Aides not testify (1 claim denied)
other actions	N/A
3. Foreign policy initiatives & actions	*Presidential Decision Directives:* 8 *Executive agreements:* 458 *Significant treaties:* • Apr 1998: Expansion of NATO borders
Outcome of case: Clinton more popular than any outgoing president, but character issues limited his role in 2000 election	

Table 15b. Summarizing the President's Response to Adversity—Scandal—
Bill Clinton, Jan 1998–June 1999

Type of response	*Summary data & significant examples*
Foreign policy initiatives & actions *continued*	*Uses of force:* • Aug 1998: Missile strikes: Afghanistan/Sudan • Dec 1998: Four-day air assault against Iraq • Mar –Jun 1999: NATO ops against Serbia *Other:* • Jan 1998: Sought Israel/Palestine peace deal • Mar 1998: Apologies for US role in slave trade and delayed response to Rwanda • Jun 1998: Criticized China human rights violations while in China • Sep 1998: Agreement w/Russia on preventing nuclear accidents
4. Organizational changes	Sept. 1998: Greg Craig from State Depart to White House to be Special Counselor for Lewinsky scandal. Oct. 1998: Resignations of press secy McCurry, senior advisor R Emanuel, and Chief of Staff Bowles
5. Going public	*Major speeches:* 7 (1998-5; Jan-Jun 1999-2) *News conferences:* 17 (1998-9; Jan-Jun 1999-8) *Key Events:* • Jan 1998: 3 interviews about Lewinsky affair • Jan 1998: "I did not have sexual relations with that woman, Miss Lewinsky." • Aug 1998: Admitted to lying about Lewinsky • Dec 1998: White House event to show defiance (following impeachment) • Feb 1999: Time to move on from scandal
6. Unconventional actions?	N/A
Outcome of case: Clinton more popular than any outgoing president, but character issues limited his role in 2000 election	

Table 15c. Comparing the President's Response to Non-Adverse Circumstances—Bill Clinton, Jan 1998–June 1999

Type of response	Comparison to non-adverse circumstances (Jan 1993-June 1994)
1. Bargaining & persuasion	*House & Senate concurrence with pres—average for 1993-1994:* 86.4% *Legislative successes/compromises/concessions:* • Feb 1993: Family/Medical Leave Act • May 1993: Motor Voter • Aug 1993: budget • Nov 1993: Brady handgun law • Nov 1993: Don't Ask, Don't Tell (concession) *Failed attempts at legislative bargaining/compromise:* • 1993-1994: Health care reform • Apr 1993: Economic stimulus • Jun 1993: Freedom of Choice Act
2. Executive actions constitutional	*Vetoes:* None *Pardons & clemency:* 0 *Proclamations:* 180 • 6641 – Implementation of NAFTA *Executive orders:* 88 • 12839 – Fed workforce reduction • 12846 – More restrictions dealing w/Yugoslavia • 12853 – Forbid transactions with Haiti • 12889 – Implement NAFTA • 12918 – Restrict transactions with Rwanda *Signing statements:* 40 *Claims of executive privilege:* None
other actions	Apr 1993: Clinton authorizes assault on Branch Davidian sect, Waco, TX
3. Foreign policy initiatives & actions	*Presidential Decision Directives:* 25 *Executive agreements—total:* 2048 • 1994: Agreed Framework to halt N. Korean nuclear weapons program
Outcome of case: ***Clinton more popular than any outgoing president, but character issues limited his role in 2000 election***	

Did the President's Actions Make Any Difference?
Presidential actions certainly make a difference during periods of scandal. First, the way a president responds to the scandal significantly influences the overall outcome of the case. Reagan chose a strategy of not only cooperating with the investigation but initiating his own. This stands in sharp contrast to Nixon and Clinton, who both became increasingly defiant, eventually leading to a resignation and an impeachment.

Table 15d. Comparing the President's Response to Non-Adverse Circumstances—Bill Clinton, Jan 1998–June 1999 (Cont.)

Type of response	Comparison to non-adverse circumstances (Jan 1993-June 1994)
Foreign policy initiatives & actions *continued*	*Significant treaties:* • Dec 1993: NAFTA *Uses of force:* • Jun 1993: Missile attack on Iraq to retaliate for attempt to kill GHW Bush • Oct 1993: Somali militia kill US troops ("Blackhawk Down" incident) *Other:* • Sept 1993: US helps to broker Oslo Accords (Israel & PLO), signed at White House • Feb. 1994: End embargo on Vietnam
4. Organizational changes	Dec 1993: Les Aspin out as Secy of Def; likely due to Somalia & battles with OMB over budget
5. Going public	*Major speeches:* 10 (1993-5; 1994-5) *News conferences:* 72 (1993-28; 1994-44) *Key Events:* • Jan. 1993: Inaugural address • Feb 1993: Response to WTC attacks • Feb 1993: Economic program. • Apr 1993: Branch Davidian incident • Jan 1994: State of the Union
6. Unconventional actions?	N/A
Outcome of case: *Clinton more popular than any outgoing president, but character issues limited his role in 2000 election*	

Second, the contrasting "going public" strategies of the three presidents seem to indicate presidential actions make a difference during periods of scandal. In Nixon's case, his seclusion and lack of forthrightness led to increased suspicions and helped cause the Republican collapse in the 1974 midterm elections. In Reagan's case, his initial attempts at utilizing his communication skills failed, leading him also to follow a strategy of seclusion, but the White House effectively communicated this strategy to the public as President Reagan's intent to "do the work of the American people." Finally, in Clinton's case, we find a chief executive who lied about his conduct but in doing so "bought time," which allowed him to rebuild his public image and ultimately resulted in the American people getting upset at the continued investigations. This helped lead to the surprising gains for Democrats in Congress during the 1998 midterm congressional elections.

Table 16 further illustrates that in all of these cases, unilateral executive powers and presidential control of foreign policy were more significant than bargaining and persuasion. Nixon and Clinton utilized the veto power effectively, and all three men displayed the importance of either executive orders or signing statements. Furthermore, all three presidents analyzed here illustrated extraordinary leadership in the foreign policy realm: Nixon led a weeklong airlift in Israel, Reagan signed the INF treaty, and Clinton directed NATO into combat against Serbia. In addition, organizational changes were of particular importance to Nixon and Reagan, given the severity of the allegations against members of both administrations.

How Did Adversity Limit What the President Could Do or Accomplish?

Table 16 highlights how scandals hindered each president's ability to implement successful bargaining and persuasion tactics. Nixon failed to prevent Congress from reasserting its authority with regard to the budget and war powers, Reagan had virtually no significant policy measures pass and lost a Supreme Court nomination, and Clinton failed in his attempts to get his major agenda items through. Still, Nixon and Clinton achieved levels of success in Congress that would undoubtedly surprise many observers.

Table 16a. Assessing the President's Response to Adversity—Scandals

President	Response types (and significance)
Nixon, 1973-74 *Outcome:* **Resigned; Democrats won landslide congressional elections in 1974**	1. **Bargaining & persuasion:** Maintained relatively high level of success in Congress, including passage of significant legislation & ability to carry out effective veto strategy. Failed to prevent assertion of congressional authority regarding war powers & budget process; appointment of Elliot Richardson to Attorney General failed to shield president—ultimately led to the "Saturday Night Massacre." **(Significance: Mixed)** 2. **Executive actions:** Very successful in ability to overcome Congress through veto strategy, but failed in his claims of executive privilege. **Significance: High)** 3. **Foreign policy initiatives & actions:** Showed international leadership on several fronts and received high levels of public approval for such actions. **(Significance: High)** 4. **Organizational changes:** Several changes in personnel in April/May 1973, but did not deflect criticism from the president. Appointed Ford Vice Pres upon resignation of Agnew. **(Significance: High)** 5. **Going public:** Repeatedly tried to get public to support his economic & energy initiatives & thus draw attention away from the Watergate, but never received the support he hoped for. **(Significance: High)** 6. **Unconventional actions:** Saturday Night Massacre helped lead to twenty-one articles of impeachment filed against Nixon; only president to resign. **(Significance: High)**

Table 16b. Assessing the President's Response to Adversity—Scandals (Cont.)

President	Response types (and significance)
Reagan, Nov 1986-Dec 1987 _Outcome_: **Left office with high approval & his VP succeeded in 1988 election**	1. **Bargaining & persuasion:** The combination of a new Congress dominated by Democrats and the withdrawal of Reagan from the public significantly limited his persuasive abilities. **(Significance: Low)** 2. **Executive actions:** Reagan utilized unilateral executive powers in a number of areas, but most notably in the creation of the Tower Commission. **(Significance: High)** 3. **Foreign policy initiatives & actions:** Remained the most important area for Reagan during the scandal, as he achieved success in a number of ways. **(Significance: High)** 4. **Organizational changes:** During two separate phases Reagan turned to a well-respected Washington insider to help reestablish confidence in his administration. **(Significance: High)** 5. **Going public:** The combination of withdrawal and acceptance of responsibility led to a restoration of confidence in Reagan during his final year in office. **(Significance: High)** 6. **Unconventional actions:** Creation of Tower Commission indicated willingness to investigate wrongdoing by administration officials. Withdrawal from public displayed Reagan's active role in governing. **(Significance: High)**

Table 16c. Assessing the President's Response to Adversity—Scandals (Cont.)

President	Response types (and significance)
Clinton, Jan. 1998-July 1999 **_Outcome_: Left office as the most popular outgoing president since polling began, but character issues limited his ability to help Gore in 2000 election.**	1. **Bargaining & persuasion:** Failed on biggest legislative objectives, but remained quite successful on minor issues. Succeeded in grand jury testimony negotiation, but failed in attempt to undermine House Impeachment with letter from Senate. **(Significance: Mixed)** 2. **Executive actions:** Vetoes, veto threats, executive orders, and signing statements all proved pivotal for Clinton during the scandal. **(Significance: High)** 3. **Foreign policy initiatives & actions:** Very active in diplomacy and used unilateral executive powers to pursue objectives. **(Significance: High)** 4. **Organizational changes:** Limited; the scandal was about his own personal mistakes, rather than mistakes made by administration officials. **(Significance: Low)** 5. **Going public:** Used three-phase approach (deny, "move on," and apology). Though he eventually admitted that he lied to the American people, his public image never suffered due to the scandal. **(Significance: High)** 6. **Unconventional actions:** N/A **(Significance: Low)**

Did Adversity Open Opportunities in Any Way?

Given the domestic obstacles that scandals inherently bring to presidents, it should come as no surprise that in many ways periods of scandals may open up more opportunities for presidents to exhibit international leadership. Nixon led a weeklong airlift in Israel, Reagan maintained his pressure on the Soviet Union, and Clinton directed NATO into combat against

Serbia. Moreover, each president made important strides in their diplomatic endeavors, including Nixon's continued pursuit of détente, Reagan's signing of the INF treaty, and Clinton's historic trip to Africa.

What Powers Did the President Retain Despite Adversity, and How Did the President Exercise Them in a Relevant Way?

Undoubtedly, one of the most glaring findings is the continued importance of unilateral executive actions during such periods. First and foremost, Nixon and Clinton exhibit the continued value of veto powers, even when faced with divided government. And though Reagan failed to implement an effective veto strategy like Nixon and Clinton, all three men displayed the utter significance of unilateral executive authority, through the use of executive orders and signing statements. Nixon, four days before he resigned, used an executive order to limit spending on what he deemed wasteful military spending; Reagan used an executive order to form the Tower Commission, which ultimately helped him effectively respond to the scandal itself; and Clinton used several executive orders to implement progressive social policies not supported by Congress and to carry out military operations in the former Yugoslavia.

Within a twenty-five-year period, American politics witnessed three presidents plagued by scandals and cover-ups of actions taken by the respective presidents and/or their subordinates. In each case, we find that the periods of scandal presented the particular president with unique challenges in his interaction with other governmental officials, the media, and the American people. Again, as Ceaser so aptly suggested, scandals place "the Presidency on the defensive in the eyes of the nation"[182] and thus significantly weaken the president. In spite of this weakened position, the cases of Richard Nixon, Ronald Reagan, and Bill Clinton demonstrate that presidents do not become politically paralyzed by such circumstances. In particular, each case illustrates the extremely important role of unilateral actions, both domestically and internationally.

ENDNOTES

1. James W. Ceaser, "The Reagan Presidency and American Public Opinion," in *The Reagan Presidency: Promise and Performance*, ed. Charles O. Jones (Chatham, NJ: Chatham House, 1988), 202.
2. David M. Abshire, *Saving the Reagan Presidency* (College Station: Texas A&M Press, 2005), 187.
3. Alfred E. Lewis, "5 Held in Plot to Bug Democrats' Office Here," *Washington Post*, June 18, 1972, accessed March 1, 2011, http://www.washingtonpost.com/wp-srv/national/longterm/watergate/articles/061872-1.htm.
4. Bob Woodward and Carl Bernstein, "GOP Security Aide Among Five Arrested in Bugging Affair," *Washington Post*, June 19, 1972, accessed June 23, 2012, http://www.washingtonpost.com/wp-dyn/content/article/2002/05/31/AR2005111001228.html.
5. David Hosansky, ed., *Eyewitnesses to Watergate: A Documentary History for Students* (Washington, DC: CQ Press, 2007), 2.
6. Richard Nixon, "The President's News Conference," June 22, 1972, accessed December 5, 2009, http://www.presidency.ucsb.edu/ws/index.php?pid = 3472&st = &st1.
7. This paragraph is drawn mostly from Hosansky, *Eyewitnesses to Watergate*, 2–3.
8. Elizabeth Drew, *Richard M. Nixon*, large print ed. (Detroit: Thomson Gale, 2007), 211.
9. This paragraph is drawn mostly from Hosansky, *Eyewitnesses to Watergate*, 3.
10. Carroll Kilpatrick, "Nixon Forces Firing of Cox; Richardson, Ruckelshaus Quit President Abolishes Prosecutor's Office; FBI Seals Records," *Washington Post*, http://www.washingtonpost.com/wp-srv/national/longterm/watergate/articles/102173-2.htm.
11. Stephen E. Ambrose, *Nixon*, vol. 3, *Ruin and Recovery 1973–1990* (New York: Simon & Schuster, 1991), 252.
12. Ibid., 300.
13. Ibid., 155.
14. Richard Nixon, "Address to the Nation Announcing Price Control Measures," June 13, 1973, accessed December 5, 2009, http://www.presidency.ucsb.edu/ws/index.php?pid = 3868&st = &st1.

15. Richard Nixon, "Radio Address About the Nation's Economy," July 1, 1973, accessed December 5, 2009, http://www.presidency.ucsb.edu/ws/index.php?pid = 3890&st = &st1.
16. Congressional Quarterly, *CQ Almanac: 93rd Congress 1st Session, 1973* (Washington, DC: CQ Press, 1974), 2.
17. Congressional Quarterly, *CQ Almanac: 93rd Congress 2nd Session, 1974* (Washington, DC: CQ Press, 1975), 2. It should be noted that both the community development bill and the education bill were signed by President Ford but had passed both houses of Congress prior to President Nixon resigning the presidency.
18. Richard Nixon, *RN: The Memoirs of Richard Nixon* (New York: Gosset & Dunlap, 1978), 848.
19. Richard Nixon, "Address to the Nation About the Watergate Investigation," April 30, 1973, accessed December 5, 2009, http://www.presidency.ucsb.edu/ws/index.php?pid = 3824&st = &st1.
20. Nixon, *RN*, 909.
21. Ibid.
22. Ibid., 910.
23. Nixon, "Radio Address About the Nation's Economy."
24. Hosansky, *Eyewitnesses to Watergate*, 3.
25. Morton Rosenberg, "Presidential Claims of Executive Privilege: History, Law, Practice, and Recent Developments," in *CRS Report for Congress* (Washington, DC: Congressional Research Service, 1998), CRS-37.
26. Hosansky, *Eyewitnesses to Watergate*, 5.
27. Henry Kissinger, *Years of Upheaval* (Boston: Little & Brown, 1982), 253, 291.
28. Ambrose, *Nixon*, 174, 177.
29. Raymond L. Garthoff, *Détente and Confrontation: American-Soviet Relations from Nixon to Reagan* (Washington, DC: The Brookings Institution, 1994), 329.
30. Ambrose, *Nixon*, 178.
31. Ibid., 204.
32. Kissinger, *Years of Upheaval*, 537.
33. Ambrose, *Nixon*, 240.
34. Richard Nixon, "Veto of the War Powers Resolution," October 24, 1973, accessed December 7, 2009, http://www.presidency.ucsb.edu/ws/index.php?pid = 4021&st = &st1.
35. Kissinger, *Years of Upheaval*, 371.
36. Ambrose, *Nixon*, 365.

37. Nixon, *RN*, 857.
38. Richard Nixon, "Address to the Nation About Vietnam and Domestic Problems," March 29, 1973, accessed December 7, 2009, http://www. presidency.ucsb.edu/ws/index.php?pid = 4161&st = &st1.
39. Richard Nixon, "The President's News Conference," September 5, 1973, accessed December 7, 2009, http://www.presidency.ucsb.edu/ws/index. php?pid = 3948&st = &st1.
40. Richard Nixon, "Address to the Nation About Policies to Deal with the Energy Shortages," November 5, 1973, accessed December 7, 2009, http://www.presidency.ucsb.edu/ws/index.php?pid = 4034&st = &st1; and Richard Nixon, "Address to the Nation About National Energy Policy," November 25, 1973, accessed December 7, 2009, http://www. presidency.ucsb.edu/ws/index.php?pid = 4051&st = &st1.
41. Richard Nixon, "Remarks at a Reception for Returned Prisoners of War," May 24, 1973, accessed December 7, 2009, http://www.presidency.ucsb. edu/ws/index.php?pid = 3856&st = &st1.
42. Ambrose, *Nixon*, 276, 313.
43. Richard Nixon, "Address to the Nation Announcing Answer to the House Judiciary Committee Subpoena for Additional Presidential Tape Recordings," April 29, 1974, accessed December 7, 2009, http://www.presidency.ucsb.edu/ws/index.php?pid = 4189&st = &st1.
44. Ambrose, *Nixon*, 233.
45. Kilpatrick, "Nixon Forces Firing of Cox."
46. William E. Pemberton, *Exit with Honor: The Life and Presidency of Ronald Reagan* (Armonk, NY: M. E. Sharpe, 1998), 146.
47. Ibid.
48. David Mervin, *Ronald Reagan and the American Presidency* (New York: Longman, 1990), 151.
49. John Felton, "Iran Arms and 'Contras': A Reagan Bombshell," *Congressional Quarterly Weekly Report*, November 29, 1986, p. 2971.
50. John Ehrman and Michael W. Flamm, *Debating the Reagan Presidency* (Lanham, MD: Rowman and Littlefield, 2009), 149.
51. Theodore Draper, *A Very Thin Line: The Iran-Contra Affairs* (New York: Hill and Wang, 1991), 457; Abshire, *Saving the Reagan Presidency*, 67.
52. Draper, *Very Thin Line*, 457.
53. Abshire, *Saving the Reagan Presidency*, 67.
54. Ehrman and Flamm, *Debating the Reagan Presidency*, 143–144.
55. Peter J. Wallison, *Ronald Reagan: The Power of Conviction and the Success of His Presidency* (Boulder, CO: Westview, 2003), 168.

56. Ibid., 210.
57. Pemberton, *Exit with Honor*, 188.
58. Jane Mayer and Donald McManus, *Landslide: The Unmaking of the President, 1984–1988* (Boston: Houghton Mifflin, 1988), 358.
59. Ehrman and Flamm, *Debating the Reagan Presidency*, 157.
60. Congressional Quarterly, *CQ Almanac: 100th Congress 1st Session, 1987* (Washington, DC: CQ Press 1988, 21-C.
61. Ibid., 3-C.
62. Ibid.
63. Congressional Quarterly, *CQ Almanac: 100th Congress, 1st Session, 1987.* Washington, DC: CQ Press, 1988.
64. Ibid., 21-C.
65. Ronald Reagan, "Remarks Announcing the Review of the National Security Council's Role in the Iran Arms and Contra Aid Controversy," November 25, 1986, accessed January 5, 2010, http://www.presidency.ucsb.edu/ws/index.php?pid = 36761&st = &st1; and Pemberton, *Exit with Honor*, 188.
66. Ronald Reagan, "Appointment of Three Members of the Special Review Board for the National Security Council," November 26, 1986, accessed January 5, 2010, http://www.presidency.ucsb.edu/ws/index.php?pid = 36 763&st = &st1.
67. Pemberton, *Exit with Honor*, 188; Draper, *Very Thin Line*, 552.
68. Pemberton, *Exit with Honor*, 188.
69. Wallison, *Ronald Reagan*, 205.
70. Congressional Quarterly, *CQ Almanac: 99th Congress 2nd Session, 1986* (Washington, DC: CQ Press, 1987), 24; Ronald Reagan Presidential Library, "Chronology of Ronald Reagan's Presidency, 1981–89," accessed March 1, 2012, http://www.reagan.utexas.edu/archives/reference/preschrono.html
71. Congressional Quarterly, *CQ Almanac: 99th Congress 2nd Session*, 24.
72. Richard S. Conley and Annie Krepel, "Presidential Influence: The Success of Vetoes and Veto Overrides" (paper presented at the Annual Meeting of the American Political Science Association, Atlanta, GA, August 1999), accessed March 1, 2011, http://web.clas.ufl.edu/users/kreppel/types.PDF, 20.
73. Federal Highway Administration, "President Ronald Reagan and the Surface Transportation and Uniform Relocation Assistance Act of 1987," accessed March 1, 2011, http://www.fhwa.dot.gov/infrastructure/rw01e.htm.

74. Ibid.; Conley and Krepel, "Presidential Influence," 20.

75. C. Jones, *The Presidency in a Separated System*, 49.

76. Quoted in ibid., 49.

77. Ronald Reagan, "Statement on Signing the Federal Triangle Development Act," August 22, 1987, accessed January 5, 2010, http://www.presidency. ucsb.edu/ws/index.php?pid = 34731&st = &st1.

78. Ronald Reagan, "Statement on Signing the Bill to Increase the Federal Debt Ceiling," September 29, 1987, accessed January 5, 2010, http:// www.presidency.ucsb.edu/ws/index.php?pid = 33467&st = &st1.

79. Ronald Reagan, *An American Life* (New York: Simon & Schuster, 1990), 663.

80. Pemberton, *Exit with Honor*, 195.

81. Ibid., 196.

82. Ronald Reagan, "Proclamation 5595—Imposition of Temporary Surcharge on Imports of Certain Softwood Lumber Products from Canada," December 30, 1986, accessed January 5, 2010, http://www.presidency.ucsb.edu/ws/index.php?pid = 36843&st = &st1.

83. C. Jones, *The Presidency in a Separated System*, 48.

84. Ronald Reagan, "Appointment of Frank C. Carlucci as Assistant to the President for National Security Affairs," December 2, 1986, accessed January 5, 2010, http://www.presidency.ucsb.edu/ws/index.php?pid = 36 773&st = &st1.

85. Oliver Trager, ed., *The Iran-Contra Arms Scandal: Foreign Policy Disaster* (New York: Facts on File, 1988), 50.

86. Abshire, *Saving the Reagan Presidency*, 71.

87. Pemberton, *Exit with Honor*, 189.

88. Reagan, *American Life*, 528.

89. Ronald Reagan, "Address to the Nation on the Iran Arms and Contra Aid Controversy," November 13, 1986, accessed January 5, 2010, http://www. presidency.ucsb.edu/ws/index.php?pid = 36728&st = &st1.

90. Ibid.

91. Draper, *Very Thin Line*, 474.

92. Ibid., 482.

93. Ehrman and Flamm, *Debating the Reagan Presidency*, 150; Draper, *Very Thin Line*, 482–484.

94. Wallison, *Ronald Reagan*, 196.

95. Ehrman and Flamm, *Debating the Reagan Presidency*, 150.

96. Draper, *Very Thin Line*, 483–484.

97. Ehrman and Flamm, *Debating the Reagan Presidency*, 150.

98. David E. Kyvig, *Reagan and the World* (New York: Praeger, 1990), 247.

99. Robert Busby, Ronald Reagan and the Iran-Contra Affair: The Politics of Presidential Recovery (New York: Macmillan, 1999).

100. Ibid., 99–100.

101. Mervin, *Ronald Reagan and the American Presidency*, 151.

102. Pemberton, *Exit with Honor*, 196.

103. Abshire, *Saving the Reagan Presidency*, 197.

104. Richard Neustadt, *Presidential Power and the Modern Presidents* (New York: Free Press, 1991), 269.

105. Marvin Kalb, *One Scandalous Story: Clinton, Lewinsky, and Thirteen Days that Tarnished American Journalism* (New York: The Free Press, 2001), 13.

106. "Presidential Job Approval: William J. Clinton," accessed January 22, 2010, http://www.presidency.ucsb.edu/data/popularity.php?pres = 42& sort = time&direct = DESC&Submit = DISPLAY

107. Kalb, *One Scandalous Story*, 28.

108. Ibid., 36.

109. Harris, *Survivor*, 293; Rich Lowry, *Legacy: Paying the Price for the Clinton Years* (Washington, DC: Regnery, 2003), 158.

110. Harris, *Survivor*, 301.

111. Kalb, *One Scandalous Story*, 81–94.

112. Michael Waldman, *POTUS Speaks: Finding the Words that Defined the Clinton Presidency* (New York: Simon & Schuster, 2000), 200.

113. Ibid., 204.

114. Ibid., 211.

115. Diane Hollern Harvey, "The Public's View of Clinton," in *The Postmodern Presidency: Bill Clinton's Legacy in U.S. Politics*, ed. Steven E. Schier (Pittsburgh: University of Pittsburgh Press, 2000), 130.

116. Harris, *Survivor*, 335.

117. Lowry, *Legacy*, 176.

118. Harris, *Survivor*, 347.

119. Ibid., 361.

120. Peri E. Arnold, "Clinton and the Institutionalized Presidency," in *The Post Modern Presidency: Bill Clinton's Legacy in U.S. Politics*, edited by Steven E. Schier, pp. 19-40 (Pittsburgh: University of Pittsburgh Press, 2000), 31.

121. Congressional Quarterly, *CQ Almanac: 105th Congress 2nd Session, 1998* (Washington, DC: CQ Press, 1999), 1–3.

122. Ibid., 1–5.

123. Barbara Sinclair, "The President as Legislative Leader," in *The Clinton Legacy*, ed. Colin Campbell and Bert A. Rockman (New York: Chatham House, 2000), 94.

124. Congressional Quarterly, *CQ Almanac: 106th Congress 1st Session, 1999* (Washington, DC: CQ Press, 2000), B-3.

125. Ibid., B-5.

126. Ibid., B-3.

127. Daniel Cohen, *The Impeachment of William Jefferson Clinton* (Brookfield, CT: Twenty-first Century Books), 66.

128. Ibid., 67.

129. Peter Baker, *The Breach: Inside the Impeachment and Trial of William Jefferson Clinton* (New York: Berkley Books, 2001), 117.

130. CQ Alamanac, 105th Congress, 2nd Session, 1998.

131. Rosenberg, "Presidential Claims of Executive Privilege," CRS-39.

132. Ibid.

133. Harris, *Survivor*, 325.

134. William G. Hyland, *Clinton's World: Remaking American Foreign Policy* (Westport, CT: Praeger, 1999), 164–166.

135. Harris, *Survivor*, 317.

136. William J. Clinton, "Remarks at the Kisowera School in Mukono, Uganda," March 24, 1998, accessed January 20, 2010, http://www.presidency.ucsb.edu/ws/index.php?pid = 55672&st = &st1.

137. William J. Clinton, "Remarks to Genocide Survivors in Kigali, Rwanda," March 25, 1998, accessed January 20, 2010, http://www.presidency.ucsb.edu/ws/index.php?pid = 55677&st = &st1.

138. Hyland, *Clinton's World*, 121, 123.

139. Ibid., 123.

140. Shirley Anne Warshaw, *Presidential Profiles: The Clinton Years* (New York: Facts on File, 2004), xvi.

141. Hyland, *Clinton's World*, 203.

142. Ibid., 181.

143. Ibid.

144. Harris, *Survivor*, 359.

145. Hyland, *Clinton's World*, 45–46.

146. Harris, *Survivor*, 366.

147. Peri E. Arnold, "Clinton and the Institutionalized Presidency," in *The Post Modern Presidency: Bill Clinton's Legacy in U.S. Politics*, edited by Steven E. Schier, pp. 19-40 (Pittsburgh: University of Pittsburgh Press, 2000), 31.

TO

148. William J. Clinton, "The President's Radio Address," February 13, 1999, accessed January 28, 2010, http://www.presidency.ucsb.edu/ws/index. php?pid = 56982.

149. Harris, *Survivor*, 367.

150. Waldman, *POTUS Speaks*, 263.

151. U.S. Department of State, "Report of the Accountability Review Boards: Bombings of the US Embassies in Nairobi, Kenya and Dar es Salaam, Tanzania on August 7, 1998," accessed January 23, 2010, http://www. state.gov/www/regions/africa/board_overview.html.

152. Baker, *Breach*, 95.

153. Ibid., 119.

154. Peri E. Arnold, "Clinton and the Institutionalized Presidency," in *The Post Modern Presidency: Bill Clinton's Legacy in U.S. Politics*, edited by Steven E. Schier, pp. 19-40 (Pittsburgh: University of Pittsburgh Press, 2000), 31.

155. Bruce Miroff, "Moral Character in the White House: From Republican to Democratic," *Presidential Studies Quarterly* 29 (September 1999): 708-712.

156. Harvey, "Public's View of Clinton," 130.

157. Haynes Johnson, *The Best of Times: America in the Clinton Years* (New York: Harcourt 2001, 230–231.

158. Waldman, *POTUS Speaks*, 210.

159. William J. Clinton, "Remarks on the After-School Child Care Initiative," January 26, 1998, accessed January 23, 2010, http://www.presidency. ucsb.edu/ws/index.php?pid = 56257&st = &st1.

160. Miroff, "Moral Character in the White House," 119.

161. Waldman, *POTUS Speaks*, 216.

162. Miroff, "Moral Character in the White House," 118.

163. Craig Allen Smith, "Bill Clinton in Rhetorical Crisis: The Six Stages of Scandal and Impeachment," in *Images, Scandal, and Communication Strategies of the Clinton Presidency*, ed. Robert E. Denton, Jr. and Rachel L. Holloway (Westport, CT: Praeger, 2003), 175.

164. Harris, *Survivor*, 313.

165. H. Johnson, *Best of Times*, 227, 230–231.

166. Waldman, *POTUS Speaks*, 219.

167. Peri E. Arnold, "Clinton and the Institutionalized Presidency," in *The Post Modern Presidency: Bill Clinton's Legacy in U.S. Politics*, edited by Steven E. Schier, pp. 19-40 (Pittsburgh: University of Pittsburgh Press, 2000), 31.

168. Waldman, *POTUS Speaks*, 219.
169. William J. Clinton, "Address to the Nation on Testimony Before the Independent Counsel's Grand Jury," August 17, 1998, accessed January 24, 2010, http://www.presidency.ucsb.edu/ws/index.php?pid = 54794& st = &st1.
170. Miroff, "Moral Character in the White House,"119.
171. Harvey, "Public's View of Clinton," 130.
172. Harris, *Survivor*, 360.
173. Ibid.
174. James Bennett, "Impeachment: Beyond the Vote President Maps Out a Strategy for Governing While on Trial," *New York Times*, December 20, 1998, A31.
175. William J. Clinton, "Address Before a Joint Session of Congress on the State of the Union," January 19, 1999, accessed January 28, 2010, http://www.presidency.ucsb.edu/ws/index.php?pid = 57577&st = &st1.
176. Waldman, *POTUS Speaks*, 260.
177. William J. Clinton, "Remarks on the Conclusion of the Senate Impeachment Trial and an Exchange with Reporters," February 12, 1999, accessed February 9, 2010, http://www.presidency.ucsb.edu/ws/index.php?pid = 56912&st = &st1.
178. C. A. Smith, "Bill Clinton in Rhetorical Crisis," 177.
179. Waldman, *POTUS Speaks*, 240, 241.
180. Ibid., 241.
181. American Presidency Project, "Presidential Job Approval."
182. Ceaser, "Reagan Presidency," 202.

CHAPTER 4

GOVERNING IN TIMES OF NATIONAL DIVISION

Though not as easily defined as cases of unmandates or scandals, periods of national division pose particular difficulties for chief executives. In such cases, presidents face not only divisions within the electorate at large but divisions within their own party, as the nation remains divided over the proper policies to combat instability within the political system. During such periods, political and economic factors combine to place pressure on the president that hinders his ability to lead effectively. Examples include the obstacles Lyndon Johnson faced throughout 1967 and 1968 as the country sought direction regarding the Vietnam War; the extreme difficulties Jimmy Carter encountered throughout 1979 and 1980, resulting from the weakened economy and the Iranian hostage crisis; and the impediments George H. W. Bush met in 1992 as the country faced a looming recession.

Although the particular crisis (or crises) that each president faced differed, these three cases have several definable characteristics that place them in their own category of "presidential adversity." Common factors include: (1) division within the president's own party, which led to a major challenge for renomination; (2) a loss in confidence among the American electorate regarding both political parties, which led to a significant third party or Independent challenger in the general election; (3) job approval ratings consistently below 40%; and (4) evidence that the American electorate's ideology moved toward the opposition party's stances on crucial issues, which ultimately led to the opposition party's victory in the subsequent election.

LYNDON JOHNSON, 1967–1968

Troubles began for Lyndon Johnson in the 1966 midterm elections as Republicans received a net gain of 47 seats in the House and 3 in the Senate, not to mention 8 governors and 677 state legislators.[1] Not only did the elections illustrate division across the country and a backlash against Johnson, but the results also led to significant divisions within the Democratic Party. George Reedy, who served as Johnson's first press secretary and special consultant to the president during his final year in office, argued that Johnson first lost support within the Democratic Party because of his failures in the 1966 election, not because of the Vietnam War.[2] Within weeks, Democratic governors held a national meeting, at which they openly questioned Johnson's effectiveness as both national and party leader.[3]

As a result, as Johnson entered 1967, he encountered a political climate significantly different from the time when he first took the oath of office following President Kennedy's death and from the time when he won the landslide election of 1964. The political scientist Irving Bernstein claimed, "Not since the 1850s had a chief executive confronted domestic turmoil on this scale."[4] Racial tensions alone resulted in 24 riots within 23 cities in 1967, including a riot in Newark that led to 26 dead, 1,500 wounded, and over 1,000 arrested and a riot in Detroit that led to 40 dead and 5,000 arrested.[5] At the same time, the president faced what Thomas Langston termed "a middle-class backlash...against the Great Society."[6]

In his memoirs, the president recognized this growing sentiment as he wrote, "The blue collar worker felt that the Democratic party had traded his welfare for the welfare of the black man. The middle class suburbanite felt that we were gouging him in order to pay for the antipoverty programs."[7]

In the meantime, as one Johnson biographer wrote, "Vietnam came to dominate the Johnson presidency. It could not be escaped, for it impinged on the economy, on appropriations for the Great Society, and on the gamut of desired legislation."[8] By March 1967, troop deployments in Vietnam reached over 670,000.[9] Interestingly, Johnson's policies continued to garner significant support, for in March 1967, a full 63% of Americans opposed the idea of stopping the bombing, and by early 1968, some 49% supported invading North Vietnam (only 29% opposed) and 47% supported invading the demilitarized zone (only 21% opposed).[10] Thus, while protests filled the evening news, throughout 1967, polling data indicated that more Americans actually supported escalation, not retreat.

Nevertheless, opposition to the war weakened Johnson during his final two years in office. In fact, 116 anti-Vietnam protests occurred outside the White House in 1967 alone.[11] February 25, 1967, proved pivotal, as Martin Luther King, Jr. attended his first antiwar protest accompanied by four Democratic senators, including Eugene McCarthy and George McGovern.[12] Months later, on September 26, Republican senator Clifford Case "surprised his colleagues and the President by going to the Senate floor to assail what he termed LBJ's irresponsible 'misuse' and 'perversion' of the Tonkin Gulf Resolution to deepen American involvement in Vietnam."[13] Perhaps even more troublesome for the administration, several former military leaders, including General David M. Shoup, Lieutenant General James Gavin, and General Matthew Ridgway, openly criticized Johnson's strategies.[14] By the end of 1967, Americans faced the startling statistics of 16,000 dead and 100,000 wounded. In response to the growing sentiment against the war, especially among Democrats, Senator

Eugene McCarthy announced his candidacy for the Democratic nomination for president in November 1967.[15]

Circumstances worsened throughout 1968. Joseph Califano, Johnson's top assistant for domestic affairs, termed 1968 the "Nightmare Year."[16] Similarly, the political scientist Irving Bernstein recalled, "This was one of the most dreadful periods any American President ever faced."[17] As the tumultuous year began, administration officials grappled over the legislative agenda for the upcoming year. Secretary of the Treasury Henry Fowler urged cuts in the Great Society, whereas others, led by Califano, sought increased domestic initiatives.[18] Division within the administration culminated with the resignation of HEW (Health, Education, and Welfare) secretary John Gardner in late January, when he told the president, "[A]t this point in time, I don't believe you can lead the country. I believe you can no longer pull the country together."[19]

Meanwhile, on January 23, 1968, North Korean forces attacked and captured the USS *Pueblo*, a U.S. Navy Communications vessel (not returned until December 1968). One week later, the North Vietnamese launched the Tet Offensive, which included an attack on five out of the six largest cities in South Vietnam, thirty-six out of the forty-four provincial capitals, and approximately sixty district capitals.[20] Although the North Vietnamese failed in achieving their ultimate goal of victory, Califano explained, "Victory or not, the sheer ability of the North Vietnamese and Vietcong to mount such a large-scale offensive had shattered the American people's confidence in the President's word. For the first time, large numbers of Americans thought their country might lose the war."[21] Johnson noted this very point in his memoirs, as he indicated that in their attempt to "erode the resolve of the American people," the North Vietnamese got "exactly the reaction they sought."[22]

During the Tet Offensive, Langston described, the nightly news "left Americans little doubt that they were involved in a bigger war than their president's optimistic rhetoric had prepared them to accept."[23] Most troublesome for the administration was Walter Cronkite's comment on

February 27, when he lamented, "It is increasingly clear to this reporter that the only rational way out…will be to negotiate, not as victors, but as honorable people who lived up to their pledge to defend democracy, and did the best they could."[24] Johnson privately commented, "If I've lost Cronkite, I've lost middle America."[25] The president's approval dropped from 48% to 36% in six weeks.[26]

The results of the New Hampshire presidential primary on March 12 provided further evidence of Johnson's eroding support, given that the incumbent barely defeated Senator McCarthy by a 49–42% margin.[27] Four days later, Senator Robert Kennedy entered the race, declaring, "[I]t is now unmistakably clear that we can change [the country's] disastrous divisive policies [in Vietnam and at home] only by changing the men who are now making them."[28] Two weeks later, on March 31, 1968, President Johnson finished a national speech regarding the Vietnam War and surprised onlookers as he explained that he would not run for reelection.[29]

President Johnson received great praise for his announcement, because politicians, pundits, and citizens admired his decision to put the country above his own career.[30] However, on April 3, an assassin's bullet took Martin Luther King, Jr.'s life. Johnson instantly realized, "Everything we've gained in the last few days we're going to lose tonight."[31] Violence erupted in 130 cities across the United States. Over 2,600 fires burned and 46 people died, which led to the deployment of 75,000 National Guardsmen.[32] Two months later, the country received further stunning news that an assassin had killed Robert Kennedy.

Consequently, as President Johnson and the Democratic Party prepared for their 1968 national convention, they had to deal with the assassinations of two iconic figures, a growing problem of urban violence, and a party and country divided over both the Vietnam War and the future of Johnson's Great Society. Democrats split into various camps, including pro-war liberals, antiwar liberals, and the traditionally conservative Southern Democrats.[33] Then, on August 10, just prior to the convention, Senator George McGovern announced his candidacy, hoping to win support as the peace candidate.[34] In response, President Johnson, who previously tried to steer clear of the partisan divisions, formally endorsed Vice President Humphrey on August 19 in an effort to promote party unity.[35]

The situation only grew worse as delegates arrived in Chicago. Califano described, "The 1968 Democratic National Convention was Lyndon Johnson's political crown of thorns. The convention had been set for the week of LBJ's sixtieth birthday, August 27, which was the day before the planned selection of the presidential candidate."[36] Instead, mass protests outside of the convention prevented the president from even attending. Over a four-day period, protesters damaged 81 vehicles and injured 192 law enforcement officials, leading to 668 arrests.[37] The country appeared more divided than any period since the Civil War.

Bargaining and Persuasion
Lyndon Johnson will forever be remembered for his extraordinary bargaining abilities, both as Senate majority leader and as president. Langston noted, "Lyndon Johnson was a master at handling Congress," given that he "would bargain, cajole, and if need be cry, plead, and threaten to get the votes he needed."[38] Johnson himself once stated, "There is only one way for a president to deal with Congress, and that is continuously, incessantly, and without interruption...He's got to know them even better than they know themselves."[39] Consequently, even throughout this period of extreme adversity, Johnson remained focused on an ambitious legislative agenda.

Legislative Successes/Compromises/Concessions
Table 17 demonstrates that although 1967 proved to be a difficult year for Johnson, he maintained a 78.8% concurrence rate, a rate not matched by another president until Ronald Reagan in 1981. Johnson signed into law the Public Broadcasting Act, creating the Corporation for Public Broadcasting and National Public Radio; an act establishing the National

Product Safety Commission; the Air Quality Act; and the Age Discrimination in Employment Act.[40] In addition, his nomination of Thurgood Marshall to the Supreme Court received Senate approval on June 13.[41]

Table 17. Congressional Concurrence with the President, 1964–1968

Year	Total H&S Concurrence	House Concurrence	# of House Votes	Senate Concurrence	# of Senate Votes
1964	87.9	88.5	52	87.6	97
1965	93.1	93.8	112	82.6	162
1966	78.9	91.3	103	68.8	125
Average	86.6	91.2		79.7	
Total			267		384
1967	78.8	75.6	127	81.2	165
1968	74.5	83.5	103	68.9	164
Average	76.7	79.6		75.1	
Total			230		329

Source. Compiled from data in *Vital Statistics on American Politics, 2007–2008* (p. 264) by Harold Stanley and Richard Niemi. Washington, DC: CQ Press, 2008.

The following year, Johnson continued to have high levels of success, with a concurrence rate of 74.5%. His most notable victory came on April 11, when he signed the Civil Rights Act of 1968, which prohibited discrimination in the sale and rental of housing—a measure rejected by the House the previous two years.[42] However, Johnson's other major legislative victories throughout 1968 included significant compromises. For instance, on January 2, Johnson signed into law a 13% increase in Social Security payments (Johnson proposed 15%), but a series of amendments included a freeze on Aid to Families with Dependent Children (AFDC) funds and a requirement that mothers on welfare register for jobs; the president opposed both provisions.[43] Similarly, when the president signed his proposed Crime Control and Safe Streets Act into law on June 19, he almost vetoed the bill because it included an amendment that expanded wiretapping capabilities for local, state, and federal offi-cials.[44] The pattern held true with the signing of Johnson's controversial tax hike in an effort to limit the budget deficit, first proposed in early 1967. Congress demanded that the tax increase be tied to cuts in existing federal programs. Johnson initially balked at this requirement, then offered only a $4 billion budget cut, and finally conceded a $6 billion cut, along with a federal reduction in employment.[45] Ironically, members of Congress could not agree to the budget cuts they demanded, so an initial compromise on Johnson's part became a victory for the president.[46] Finally, Johnson convinced Congress to pass the Gun Control Act of 1968, only to have Congress gut the strongest provisions concerning gun registration and owner licensing.[47]

Failed Attempts at Legislative Bargaining/Compromise

President Johnson largely avoided major legislative failures in 1967 and 1968. The first significant loss occurred on June 7, 1967, when the House voted down Johnson's initiative to increase the debt limit. Several liberal Democrats voted against the bill as a protest vote against the excessive spending on the Vietnam War, which they perceived resulted in less money for domestic programs.[48] His other major disappointments came in the Senate: the institution did not approve his proposal to promote Abe Fortas from associate justice to chief justice on the Supreme Court or the Nuclear Non-Proliferation Treaty he signed with the Soviet Union.[49]

Other Efforts at Bargaining and Negotiation

Johnson recognized the extreme political divisions that he faced during his final two years in office and thus limited his attempts to enhance personal power beyond the walls of the Capitol. Nevertheless, the pres-ident attempted to wield his influence during the 1968 presidential elec-tion. Upon announcing the decision that he would not seek reelection, he tried to convince Nelson Rockefeller to run, even though Rockefeller was a Republican. Johnson's lack of confidence in both Hubert Humphrey and Bobby Kennedy caused the president to spend six weeks (including a private dinner at the White House) trying to convince Rockefeller to enter the race. Ultimately, Johnson's efforts failed.[50] When Rockefeller declined, Johnson continued his attempt to influence the Democratic Party's contest by preventing all high-ranking administration officials from endorsing or participating in the nomination battle. Though Secretary of Agriculture Orville Freeman defied Johnson's order and endorsed Humphrey, the president got his way, with only one resignation, Postmaster General Larry O'Brien, who left the administration to work for the Kennedy campaign.[51]

Executive Actions

Johnson's success with legislative bargaining did not prevent him from recognizing the importance of unilateral executive actions. In his final two years in office, Johnson successfully vetoed 8 bills, entered into 385 executive agreements, signed 121 executive orders, issued 13 National Security Action memorandums, and penned 72 signing statements.

Urban unrest became the most important area in which Johnson used his unilateral powers during this period. In July 1967, he issued Executive Order 11364, which led to 4,700 federal troops being sent to Detroit in the wake of race riots. Four days later, the president issued Executive Order 11365, which established the National Advisory Commission on Civil Disorders (later dubbed the Kerner Commission) to investigate race riots across the country. The following year, in the aftermath of Dr. King's death, Johnson issued three more orders authorizing the use of federal troops to stem the spread of violence.

Executive orders also proved vital in Johnson's oversight of the economy, especially in dealing with labor disputes. The most notable example came on January 28, 1967, when President Johnson issued Executive Order 11324, which not only created an emergency board to oversee the dispute but prevented the union from striking for sixty days. Additionally, the president issued Executive Order 11375 on October 13, 1967, which expanded previous federally mandated affirmative action programs to women.

Foreign Policy Initiatives and Actions

Langston wrote, "The war in Vietnam continues to cast a large shadow over the accomplishments of the Johnson presidency."[52] This is especially true in the foreign policy realm. The two most important foreign policy actions in regard to the Vietnam War during Johnson's final two years in office included the commencement of the Paris Peace Talks in May 1968 and Johnson's announced bombing halt in North Vietnam on October 31, 1968.[53] However, a more detailed examination of the president's record finds that even during the turbulent years of 1967 and 1968, the beleaguered president remained quite active in foreign policy endeavors beyond the Vietnam War. In particular, these two years highlight Johnson's desire for diplomacy, given that he attended three historic summits, signed three historic treaties, and successfully managed the Six-Day War in the Middle East.

Diplomacy abounded throughout 1967 and 1968. On January 27, 1967, the president signed the Treaty on Principles Governing the Activities of States in the Exploration and Use of Outer Space with the Soviet Union and fifty-eight other countries. Most importantly, the treaty barred nuclear weapons in outer space.[54] Then, in April 1967, the president attended a three-day summit in Uruguay with fellow members of the Organization of American States. Two months later, he hosted Soviet premier Alexsei Kosygin in Glassboro, New Jersey. To finish the year, on December 19, he embarked on the "Round the World" trip as he visited leaders in Australia, Pakistan, South Vietnam, Thailand, and Italy, among others. Finally, on July 1, 1968, Johnson successfully completed the Nuclear Non-Proliferation Treaty with fifty-eight countries and established an agreement with the Soviet Union regarding missiles.[55] However, Soviet troops invaded Czechoslovakia and thus, according to Johnson, "slammed the door on the missile talks we had painstakingly worked out and planned to announce."[56]

Still, for two reasons, the president's handling of the Six-Day War was arguably the most remarkable non-Vietnam-related foreign policy action during his final two years in office. First, President Johnson and Premier Kosygin utilized the Hotline (a direct line of communication between the White House and the Kremlin; it was established after the 1962 Cuban Missile Crisis) several times throughout the crisis, the first time this tool was used. Second, when Israeli planes attacked the USS *Liberty*, a navy communications vessel, leaving thirty-four Americans dead, the president ignored initial advice to "handle" the situation "as if the Arabs or Russians had done it." Instead, Califano explained, "Johnson handled...the crisis coolly."[57]

Organizational Changes

Organizational changes did not prove too significant during Johnson's final two years in office. Minor personnel changes occurred when Ramsey Clark became attorney general in February 1967, after serving in an interim role since October 1966; Cyrus Smith replaced Alexander Trowbridge as secretary of commerce in March 1968 because of Trowbridge's declining health; Marvin Watson replaced Lawrence O'Brien as postmaster general in April 1968; and Joseph Barr succeeded Henry Fowler as secretary of treasury when Fowler chose to take a position at Goldman Sachs, literally weeks before Johnson left office.

Disagreements over the administration's policies in Vietnam led to the two most important organizational changes, Clark Clifford taking over the reins of the Defense Department from Robert McNamara and Wilbur Cohen replacing John Gardner as secretary of HEW. McNamara resigned in late November 1967 (though his resignation did not take effect until March 1, 1968) after the president rejected his recommendations for a scaled-down U.S. presence in Vietnam, which included a freeze on troop levels, a bombing halt, and a transition in the ground war to South Vietnamese troops.[58] Gardner resigned when he personally communicated to the president his dissention with the war and his belief that Johnson no longer could provide the leadership necessary for the country as a whole.[59]

Going Public

Divisions within the American public exacerbated the adversity Johnson faced in 1967 and 1968. Quite simply, whatever public proclamations the president made, he was sure to alienate large sectors of society. For example, Califano recalled that during the 1967 State of the Union address, "Remarkably, some of his strongest applause came when he expressed his intention to stand firm in Vietnam."[60] However, such rhetoric proved troublesome for the growing antiwar movement. Likewise, as Johnson received praise for his rhetorical campaign against the growing urban violence, critics claimed that increased law enforcement was not the answer; instead, they believed Johnson should pursue further actions to promote equal opportunities for minorities. As a result, to his detriment, Johnson selectively chose his appearances. Langston explained, "Johnson's difficulty with the public was intensified by his continued silence. In a time of war, Americans expect the president to lead the nation by providing information and inspiration."[61] In fact, his March 31, 1968, speech was only the second national speech he gave concerning the war. The limited appearances also displayed Johnson's increasing insecurities regarding public appearances. Johnson perceived that his style when speaking "before large audiences, and especially on television...appeared either wooden or so folksy as to lack credibility."[62]

However, Johnson's communication difficulties went beyond his silence on crucial issues. In fact, his greatest obstacle may have been an ever-growing "credibility gap." As the administration prepared for the 1967 State of the Union address, chief speechwriter Harry McPherson reported, "The President is simply not believed."[63] Langston added, "If the president had spoken with greater creditability about the war, he may have earned greater public backing, even sufficient to withstand Tet."[64] Similarly, Doris Kearns noted, "By 1968...[t]he issue was not simply Johnson's loss of popularity; it was his loss of credibility. A majority of people believed he regularly lied to them."[65] The historian Bruce Schulman added, "The credibility gap exploded into an uncrossable chasm during the Tet offensive."[66]

Lastly, extraordinary circumstances beyond the president's control diminished his ability to utilize public appearances successfully. The most striking example of this occurred following Johnson's announcement that he would not seek another term. Polls indicated he went from a 57% *disapproval* rating to a 57% *approval* rating.[67] However, as previously indicated, the public's mood quickly shifted with the assassination of Dr. King.

Unconventional Actions

Although he faced a splintering Democratic Party and a country shifting toward conservatism, President Johnson's decision not to seek reelection in 1968 seemingly qualifies as an "unconventional action." Johnson was a man known for his political muscle while serving as Senate majority leader, who successfully pushed through comprehensive civil rights reforms following the assassination of President Kennedy and who significantly expanded the role of the federal government in numerous areas with the implementation of the Great Society. In addition, Johnson became known for his personal ambition, yet he ultimately chose to relinquish willingly his grasp on power. As Randall Woods noted (ironically in his biography of Johnson, titled *LBJ: Architect of American Ambition*), when Johnson decided not to seek the presidency, his "overriding objective was to keep himself and the presidency above politics so that he could preserve as much of the Great Society as possible and secure what he believed would be an honorable peace in Vietnam, two goals, he believed, that were inextricably intertwined."[68]

Epilogue

Johnson's continued successes in both domestic and foreign policy were not enough to save his presidency. Instead, his inability to effectively communicate to the American people dealt a fatal blow to his leadership as he faced a credibility gap that he could not overcome. Ultimately, these factors, and more, led to Johnson's decision not to seek a second full term in office, the splintering of the Democratic Party into several factions,

Democratic losses in both the House and the Senate (though they kept solid majorities), and the election of Richard Nixon to the presidency.

Table 18a. Summarizing the President's Response to Adversity—National Division—Johnson 1967–1968

Type of response	Summary data & significant examples
1. Bargaining & persuasion	*House & Senate concurrence with president— average for 1967-1968:* 76.7% *Legislative successes/compromises/concessions:* • Jun 1967: Thurgood Marshall Sup Court nomination • Nov 1967: Public Broadcasting Act • Nov 1967: Natl Product Safety Commission • Nov 1967: Air Quality Act • Dec 1967: employment age discrimination • Jun 1968: Soc Sec Amdmnts (compromise) • Apr 1968: Civil Rights Act- Fair Housing • Jun 1968: Safe Streets Act (compromise) • Jun 1968: Income tax surcharge (compromise) • Sept 1968: Gun Control Act (compromise) *Failed attempts at legislative bargaining/compromise:* • Jun 1967: Raising debt limit • Oct 1968: Fortas nomin to Chief Justice • July – Dec 1968: Nuclear Non-Prolif Treaty
2. Executive actions constitutional	*Vetoes:* 2 regular (100% sustained), 6 pocket *Pardons & clemency:* 261 (235 pardons, 26 commutations) *Proclamations:* 9 *Executive orders:* 122 • 11364 – Ordered 4700 troops to Detroit riots • 11375 – No gender discrim in fed jobs • 11403 – 11405 – Troops to DC, Ill, & Md in aftermath of King assassination *Signing Statements:* 72 *Claims of executive privilege:* None
other actions	Jun 1968: Secret Service protect all pres candidates
Outcome of case: LBJ chose not to seek reelection, Nixon elected president	

Table 18b. Summarizing the President's Response to Adversity—National Division—Johnson 1967–1968

Type of response	Summary data & significant examples
3. Foreign policy initiatives & actions	*National security action memorandum:* 13 *Executive agreements:* 385 *Significant treaties:* (3 total) *Uses of force:* • 1967-68: Continuation of Vietnam War *Other:* • Jun 1967: Six Day War crisis • Jun1967: Hosted Soviet Premier in NJ • Dec 1967: Worldwide diplomacy tour • Jan 1968: USS *Pueblo* seized by N Korea • May 1968: Paris Peace talks • Aug 1968: Missile agreement w/Soviets, but voided after Soviet actions in Czech • Oct 1968: Bombing halt in North Vietnam • Dec 1968: Crew of USS *Pueblo* released
4. Organizational changes	1967-68: Several Cabinet changes, but only McNamara leaving seen as significant Mar 1968: Clark Clifford as new Secy of Defense
5. Going public	*Major speeches:* 9 (1967-3; 1968-6) *News conferences:* 41 (1967-22; 1968-19) *Key Events* Jan. 1967: State of the Union Jul 1967: Fed troops to Detroit for riot control Jul 1967: Civil disorder Jan 1968: State of the Union Jan 1968: USS *Pueblo* incident Mar 1968: Not seek another term Apr 1968: Mourning for Martin Luther King,Jr Jul 1968: Robert Kennedy assassination Oct 1968: Bombing halt of North Vietnam
6. Unconventional actions?	Mar 1968: Decision not to seek reelection
Outcome of case: LBJ chose not to seek reelection, Nixon elected president	

Table 18c. Comparing the President's Response to Non-Adverse Circumstances—Johnson 1967–1968

Type of response	Comparison to non-adverse circumstances (1964-65)
1. Bargaining & persuasion	*House & Senate concurrence with president— average for 1964-1965: 90.5%* *Legislative successes/compromises/concessions:* • Jul 1964: Civil Rights Act • Aug 1964: Gulf of Tonkin Resolution • Aug 1964: Economic Opportunity Act • Aug 1964: Food Stamp Act • Sept 1964: Wilderness Act • Apr 1965: Elem & Secondary Ed Act • Jul 1965: Medicare & Medicaid • Aug 1965: Voting Rights Act • Sept 1965: HUD Act • Oct 1965: Immigration Act • Oct 1965: Water Quality Act • Oct 1965: Highway Beautification Act • Nov 1965: Higher Education Act *Failed attempts at legislative bargaining:* • Sept. 1965: Home Rule bill for DC • Oct 1965: Senate not repeal "right-to-work"
2. Executive actions constitutional	*Vetoes:* 11 regular (100% sustained), 2 pocket *Pardons & clemency:* 481 (361 pardons, 120 commutations) *Proclamations:* 118 *Executive orders:* 130 • 11141 – Age discrimination policy • 11246 – Estd aff action in fed contracting *Signing statements:* 45 *Claims of executive privilege:* None
other actions	Aug. 1965: Postponed steel industry shutdown
3. Foreign policy initiatives & actions	*National security action memorandum:* 62 *Executive agreements:* 407
Outcome of case: LBJ chose not to seek reelection, Nixon elected president	

Table 18d. Comparing the President's Response to Non-Adverse Circumstances—Johnson 1967–1968 (Cont.)

Type of response	Comparison to non-adverse circumstances (1964-65)
Foreign policy initiatives & actions *continued*	*Treaties:* (3 total) *Uses of force:* • Aug 1964: Gulf of Tonkin incident • Apr 1965: Dominican Republic *Other:* • Feb 1964: Guantanamo Water Crisis • Apr 1964: Diplomatic relations with Panama restored after Jan incident when students raised U.S. flag in canal zone • Jul 1965: Halted aid to India & Pakistan without presidential approval Jul 1965: Increased troop levels in Vietnam from 75,000 to 125,000
4. Organizational changes	1965: Gradual replacement of most of JFK Cabinet Sept 1965: Robert Weaver as 1st HUD Secy & 1st African American in Cabinet
5. Going public	*Major speeches:* 11 (1964-5; 1965-6) *News conferences:* 47 (1964-30; 1965-17) *Key Events* Jan 1964: State of the Union May 1964: "Great Society" speech Jul 1964: Signing of Civil Rights Act Aug 1964: Acceptance of Dem Party nomination Jan 1965: Inaugural Address Mar 1965: Voting Rights message to Congress Apr 1965: "Peace Without Conquest" speech May 1965: Situation in Dominican Republic
6. Unconventional actions?	Oct 1964: Mrs. Johnson completes 1,682 mile "Whistle Stop" campaign
Outcome of case: LBJ chose not to seek reelection, Nixon elected president	

JIMMY CARTER, 1979–1980

The 1978 congressional elections illustrated the national political division President Carter faced during the final two years of his presidency. The political scientist Andrew Busch explained that although the Republicans only gained three seats in the Senate and fifteen seats in the House, the election resulted in the defeat of "five prominent liberal Democrats" in the Senate, "ten new senators deemed more conservative than their predecessors," and a House of Representatives in which "nearly all of the 77 freshmen across party lines were committed to tax and spending cuts."[69] Another commentator noted that Republicans successfully elected "thirty-six new breed Republican freshmen, the vanguard of a New Right swing toward Reagan conservativism."[70] The results signaled a shift to the right among American voters.

In response, Carter determined that decreased spending and fiscal responsibility would dominate his agenda. The historian Burton Kaufman noted that administration officials "maintained that budget austerity was not only good economics but also good politics."[71] Many within Carter's own party vehemently disagreed. In December 1978, Democrats held a "mini-convention" in Memphis. As a backlash against Carter's proposed cuts in spending for education, housing, jobs, and aid to cities, Senator Edward Kennedy received a rousing ovation from the 2,500 delegates after he claimed such budget cuts "would divide the party as badly as the Vietnam War."[72] Similarly, during a meeting with 100 African American delegates, Representative John Conyers predicted Carter's defeat in 1980 because of the president's focus on anti-inflation measures, rather than full employment and national health insurance.[73]

December 1978 also witnessed the crumbling of the progress made at the Camp David accords because the deadline to complete a peace agreement passed. Peter Bourne, who served as a special assistant to President Carter, recalled, "By the new year, the specter of Carter's greatest triumph turning to ashes was casting a long shadow over the White House."[74]

But the disturbing results of the 1978 congressional elections, infighting within the Democratic Party, and the breakdown of peace negotiations between Israel and Egypt only begin to tell the story of the extremely difficult circumstances President Carter faced as he entered 1979. Inflation increased from 10.8% in 1978 to 13.3% in 1979; "wholesale prices increased at an annual rate of 14.1 percent during the first three months of 1979"; and in spite of Carter's continued warning against overdependence on foreign oil, by 1979, the United States imported more oil than when Carter took office.[75]

Throughout 1979, Carter's fortunes only grew worse. On March 28, a major accident occurred at a nuclear power plant on Three Mile Island near Harrisburg, Pennsylvania. Kaufman noted, "For six days, Americans contemplated in horror the possibility of a nuclear meltdown or an explosion that would send lethal radioactive gases into the atmosphere."[76] Five weeks later, 65,000 protestors marched in Washington, urging Carter to close all of America's nuclear power plants.[77] Weeks later, OPEC announced "its fourth and largest price surge in five months."[78]

By mid-September, polls indicated that 70% of Americans did not believe Carter could be reelected.[79] Among Democrats, the president trailed Senator Kennedy in national polls by an astounding margin, 62–24%.[80] Carter made a personal appeal to Kennedy but could not garner his support. On November 6, Kennedy formally announced his candidacy.[81] A day later, California governor Jerry Brown also entered the race.[82] Two days prior to Kennedy's announcement, 3,000 Iranian students stormed the American embassy in Tehran and took sixty-six Americans hostage.[83] Not surprisingly, the hostage crisis and the upcoming presidential election dominated the headlines throughout 1980.

Bargaining and Persuasion
Throughout 1979 and 1980, as Jimmy Carter faced an electorate increasingly hostile to government spending, a growing insurgency within the Democratic Party, and a pending international crisis, the president made

efforts at bargaining and persuasion in a variety of ways. Most notably, Carter attempted to use bargaining efforts to combat the worsening economic situation and to prevent a formidable challenge for the Democratic nomination.

Legislative Successes/Compromises/Concessions

When Carter entered 1979, his legislative leadership appeared to be significantly diminished, yet (as indicated in table 19) he still received a 71.7% concurrence rate in the House and an 81.4% rate in the Senate. He achieved victories with the passage of a $5.7 billion welfare reform bill, a $3.7 billion aid package for the Chrysler Corporation, and despite months of opposition in Congress, a bill to implement gasoline rationing.[84] His biggest success in 1979 came on September 27, when Congress approved the creation of the Department of Education, despite an opposition force composed of the American Federation of Teachers and a group called the Committee Against a Separate Department of Education, which included presidents from over fifty leading universities across the country. This win proved crucial for the president because it occurred just as Senator Kennedy was about to launch his presidential campaign. The following day, the board of directors of the National Education Association announced their endorsement of Carter's reelection.[85]

Carter's overall success with Congress remained high the following year, as his concurrence rate in the House increased to 76.9%, whereas his Senate rate dropped to 73.3%. In 1980, Congress finally passed a windfall profits tax bill that Carter had pushed for since 1977, and Congress granted Carter's request for the creation of a new program that disbursed "loans, loan guarantees, price supports, and purchase agreements" to synthetic fuel companies.[86] Interestingly, Carter's most notable victories in 1980 came *after* his defeat in the general election. Following Reagan's landslide victory, Congress approved Carter's proposal for a $1.6 billion toxic waste cleanup bill and the Alaska Land Bill, which doubled the amount of land designated as national parks and tripled the amount deemed wilderness reserves.[87]

Table 19. Congressional Concurrence with the President, 1977–1980

Year	Total H&S Concurrence	House Concurrence	# of House Votes	Senate Concurrence	# of Senate Votes
1977	75.4	74.7	79	76.1	88
1978	78.3	69.9	112	84.8	151
Average	**76.9**	**72.3**		**80.5**	
Total			191		239
1979	76.8	71.7	145	81.4	161
1980	75.1	76.9	117	73.3	116
Average	**76.0**	**74.3**		**77.4**	
Total			262		277

Source. Compiled from data in *Vital Statistics on American Politics, 2007–2008* (p. 264) by Harold Stanley and Richard Niemi. Washington, DC: CQ Press, 2008.

Failed Attempts at Legislative Bargaining/Compromise

Although Carter's concurrence rates remained high, many of his major legislative proposals failed. Congress eventually gave in to Carter's gasoline rationing plan, but his original proposal lost by a 246–159 vote margin in the House in February 1979.[88] More embarrassment came when the House rejected his proposal to control hospital costs by a vote of 234–166, a bill Carter called his "top-priority anti-inflation measure of 1979."[89] The House further humiliated Carter as it voted down legislation to implement the Panama Canal treaties.[90] Furthermore, when Carter finally achieved success in the House by getting his welfare reform proposals passed, the Senate undercut his leadership by never taking action on the bill.[91] Likewise, neither the House nor Senate took action on Carter's national health insurance initiative.[92]

These defeats throughout 1979 foreshadowed the difficulties of 1980. One scholar stated that "the president's scorecard on Capitol Hill was nearly blank during the first half of 1980."[93] Congress ignored his proposal for increased health care benefits for poor children, his proposal to expand the Department of Commerce's Economic Development Association, and his lone new initiative, an employment program to assist minority youths. Yet, Kaufman noted, "these setbacks paled beside two crushing defeats for the White House: Congress's rejection of the president's proposal to establish an Energy Mobilization Board…and the peremptory override of his veto of a joint resolution that would have prevented him from imposing a ten-cents-per-gallon surcharge on imported oil."[94] This was the first override of a presidential veto under unified government since Truman.[95]

Other Efforts at Bargaining and Negotiation

Carter's most important nonlegislative bargaining strategy ended in failure because he could not keep Senator Kennedy from seeking the Democratic nomination for president in 1980, nor could he convince his challenger to abandon his insurgent candidacy prior to the national convention. Carter's March 1979 National Health Plan proposal was his first veiled attempt to appease Kennedy, given Kennedy's disdain for Senator Russell Long's existing proposal, which only provided catastrophic insurance.[96] In contrast, the president's plan not only provided for catastrophic health insurance but also provided comprehensive health coverage to 16 million poor Americans, merged Medicare and Medicaid, mandated employer-provided coverage for women and infants, and established what he deemed "the framework" for "a universal, comprehensive national health plan."[97] Instead of gaining Kennedy's support and preventing him from entering the presidential campaign, Kennedy announced his own proposal for national health insurance in May 1979.[98] A few months later, on September 20, Carter hosted Senator Kennedy at the White House, hoping to end the speculation that Kennedy may enter the presidential race. Six weeks later, Kennedy formally announced his candidacy.[99]

After a long and arduous primary process, on June 3, 1980, Carter successfully garnered enough delegates to ensure his renomination. The president once again invited his rival to the White House in an effort to promote party unity. Kennedy not only refused to endorse Carter but challenged him to a nationally televised debate.[100] As the convention commenced, Kennedy further defied the president as he sought to release all delegates from prior candidate commitments. When this motion failed, Kennedy remained insolent, refusing the typical hand-clasped display of public support following Carter's speech.[101]

Executive Actions

Even though President Carter maintained high levels of success in Congress throughout 1979 and 1980, he utilized his veto power twelve times during this period, two of which led to embarrassing defeats for the president. In addition to the vetoes, Carter recognized the significance of executive orders in the implementation of both domestic and foreign policy initiatives. Domestically, Carter issued executive orders to establish the President's Commission on the Accident at Three Mile Island (E.O. 12130), delegate authority to state governors to ration gasoline (E.O. 12140), and promote diversity within the federal bureaucracy (E.O. 12232). Regarding foreign policy, he issued executive orders to maintain unofficial relations with Taiwan (E.O. 12143), freeze Iranian assets within the United States (E.O. 12170), remove sanctions placed on Rhodesia (E.O. 12183), and establish new sanctions against Iran (E.O. 12211).

Arguably, Carter's most important unilateral executive action during his final two years in office was to issue Presidential Directive 59 (PD-59) on July 25, 1980. It declared,

> To continue to deter in an era of strategic nuclear, it is necessary to have nuclear (as well as conventional) forces such that in considering aggression against our interests any adversary would recognize that no plausible outcome would represent a victory or any plausible definition of victory…[W]e must be capable of fighting successfully so that the adversary would not achieve his war aims and would suffer costs that are unacceptable, or in any event greater than his gains, from having initiated the attack.[102]

Betty Glad explained its significance: "PD-59 countered the whole notion of Mutual Assured Destruction (MAD), which had been U.S. policy since the sixties," and consequently "provided the basis for a more assertive foreign policy."[103] Indeed, Kaufman noted that PD-59 authorized "the largest arms procurement program in thirty years."[104] As a result, the former CIA director Stansfield Turner argued that Carter's new policy "laid the whole foundation for Reagan's expansion of nuclear weapons, and war-fighting, and war-winning capabilities."[105]

Foreign Policy Initiatives and Actions
Although the final 444 days of the Carter presidency will forever be linked to the Iranian hostage crisis, his overall foreign policy record throughout 1979 and 1980 indicates high levels of success. In the year stretching from January 1979 through January 1980, Carter normalized diplomatic relations with the People's Republic of China; signed a series of science, technology, and cultural agreements with Chinese deputy prime minister Deng Xiaoping during his visit to the United States in late January and early February 1979; attended the G-7 Summit in Tokyo, where he convinced the other leaders to limit their oil imports; and placed a series of embargoes on the Soviet Union as a result of their actions in Afghanistan.[106] Overshadowing these accomplishments, however, were other developments.

When Israel and Egypt failed to reach an agreement prior to the December 17, 1978, deadline established at Camp David, Carter traveled to the Middle East in March 1979. In less than a month, he hosted Egyptian president Anwar Sadat and Israeli prime minister Menachim Begin at the White House, where they signed the Egyptian-Israeli Peace Treaty.[107]

Less than two months later, Carter himself was a key signatory to a historic treaty: the SALT II Treaty between the United States and the Soviet Union, signed on June 18. The treaty was the culmination of two years of negotiations between Carter and Leonid Brezhnev. Most notably, the treaty established that each side would be limited to 2,400 (later reduced to 2,250) bombers and missile launchers until 1985.[108]

Unfortunately, Carter could not obtain Senate approval. Carter called this "the most profound disappointment of my Presidency."[109] Interestingly, in response to the Soviet Union's deployment of 85,000 troops to Afghanistan in December 1979, Carter withdrew the treaty from Senate consideration.[110] Still, both countries abided by the terms of the treaty until 1986, when President Reagan withdrew from the arrangement.

In spite of the series of foreign policy successes, the Iranian hostage crisis consumed the Carter White House. The November 1979 embassy takeover was the result of several months of developments. In fact, the American embassy in Tehran had already been seized in February 1979. The most notable event connected to the second seizure, however, was the Carter administration's decision to allow the shah to visit the United States for cancer treatment in October.[111] Carter's immediate response to the crisis resulted in significant gains in popularity among the American people. Kaufman recalled, "According to a Gallup poll, in the four weeks since the hostages had been seized, public approval of Carter's presidency jumped from 30 percent to 61 percent, the sharpest gain ever in a Gallup survey of presidential popularity."[112] Perhaps more importantly, Senator Kennedy's lead over Carter in Democratic polls slipped from thirty to ten points, and Carter held a fourteen-point advantage over his likely Republican opponent, Ronald Reagan.[113] By December, Carter took the lead in national polls against Kennedy.[114]

President Carter remained committed to a diplomatic conclusion to the ordeal. On February 19, 1980, after weeks of negotiations in Paris led by Carter's chief of staff Hamilton Jordan, news reports indicated the end of the crisis seemed imminent.[115] Shortly thereafter, Ayatollah Khomeini gave a speech praising the embassy takeover and announced that the Iranian parliament (not yet elected) would determine the fate of the hostages.[116] Negotiations persisted, but the Iranians continually reneged on their promises. As a result, on April 7, Carter ended formal diplomatic relations with Iran and placed further restrictions on the already existing embargo against Iran.[117] Four days later, the president met with his National Security Council, whereupon he indicated his support for a previously discussed rescue mission. On April 24, six helicopters (along with two backup helicopters) proceeded with the mission. Within hours, three of the helicopters experienced mechanical problems and the rescue attempt was terminated.[118]

The hostage crisis remained at the forefront of the presidential campaign throughout the spring and summer of 1980. Finally, after the death of the shah in July and the invasion of Iran by Iraq in early September, negotiations proved promising. However, as a final punishment for President Carter's perceived support of the shah, Iranian officials determined not to release the hostages until January 20, 1981, less than an hour after Carter's presidency ended.[119]

Organizational Changes

Carter's approach to the organization and staffing of his administration during this period proved extremely important. On July 17, 1979, following his ten-day hiatus to Camp David and two days after his infamous "malaise" speech, Carter asked his entire cabinet to submit "pro forma resignations." Ultimately, Carter accepted the resignations of Treasury Secretary Michael Blumenthal, Attorney General Griffin Bell, HEW Secretary Joseph Califano, Energy Secretary James Schlesinger, and Transportation Secretary Brock Adams.[120] On July 27, the president announced their replacements. Carter moved G. William Miller from chairman of the Federal Reserve Board to treasury secretary; he asked Benjamin Civiletti, Bell's right-hand man in the Justice Department, to become attorney general; and he moved Patricia Harris from the Department of Housing and Urban Development (HUD) to the Department of Health and Human Services (HHS) (Education became its own department) and replaced her with former New Orleans mayor Moon Landrieu.[121] In addition, he called upon Charles Duncan, a former Coca-Cola executive and Pentagon official, to fill the void in the Department of Energy; and he asked Neil Goldschmidt, the mayor of Portland, Oregon, to oversee the Department of Transportation.[122] The president also named

Hamilton Jordan to the position of chief of staff, hoping to fill a void within his administration's hierarchy.[123] One scholar explained, "The effect of the changes was to tighten the political control of the White House over the executive Departments, to enhance Jordan's power, and generally to centralize authority in the White House."[124]

Reaction to the purging of top administration officials drew immediate criticism. Democratic congressman Charles Wilson exclaimed, "Good grief! They're cutting down the biggest trees and keeping the monkeys!"[125] Kaufman added, "By summarily firing four members of his cabinet and accepting the resignation of a fifth, the president destroyed both his administration's efforts to restore his image as a forceful leader and the goodwill created by his 15 July address."[126] To make matters worse, Carter kept Andrew Young in his position as UN ambassador, in spite of his continued embarrassing comments. However, he received his termination a few weeks later after he attended an unauthorized meeting with the Palestine Liberation Organization (PLO).[127]

The one bit of positive news that came out of the summer reorganization was Carter's decision to name Paul Volcker to the Federal Reserve Board. Volcker previously served as undersecretary of the Treasury during the Nixon administration and was the president of the Federal Reserve Bank of New York.[128] Because of his impeccable reputation among Wall Street insiders, the day after he received the appointment, the bond market and the Dow Jones Average both saw immediate positive increases and the value of the dollar instantly improved.[129]

Following his summer 1979 reorganization efforts, there were few additional organizational changes. In October 1979, Carter urged Kennedy supporters within his administration to resign, but this did not result in any high-level losses.[130] Thus, the only two remaining changes that occurred came in 1980, when the president asked Senator Edmund Muskie to replace Secretary of State Cyrus Vance and when Carter asked Hamilton Jordan to leave his position as chief of staff so that Jordan could manage Carter's reelection campaign.[131]

Going Public

In her book *All the Presidents' Words*, Carol Gelderman reported that President Carter spoke publicly more than any of his predecessors.[132] Throughout 1979 and 1980, he employed a "going public" strategy to promote himself as a strong leader and to establish emotional connections with the American people.

President Carter delivered his most well-known speech during his final two years in office on July 15, 1979, in what became known as "the malaise" speech. In this speech, Carter explained how he spent the previous ten days at Camp David, where he sought opinions from Americans from all walks of life and concluded that "a moral and a spiritual crisis" confronted the nation. Referencing Vietnam, Watergate, and the assassinations of John F. Kennedy, Robert Kennedy, and Martin Luther King, Jr., he argued that we faced "a crisis of confidence. It is a crisis that strikes at the very heart and soul and spirit of our national will."[133] Although the speech has acquired a reputation as a failure,[134] evidence suggests that at the time it was quite successful. House Speaker Tip O'Neill described it as "[o]ne of the strongest and best he [Carter] has made."[135] The American people seemed to agree, and Carter's approval rating shot up 11%.[136] Problems arose for the president because of his poor handling of organizational changes in the days following the speech. As Bourne explained, "In time the events of those two weeks would become fused together, with the speech increasingly derogated as the 'malaise speech,' although it was a term Carter never used."[137]

The president worked to promote his image as a leader in late December 1979, as he used his handling of the hostage situation to elevate himself above his opponents for the Democratic nomination; he suspended active campaigning and reneged on a commitment to debate Senator Kennedy and California governor Jerry Brown prior to the nominating caucuses in Iowa.[138] Instead, the president chose "to adopt the 'Rose Garden' strategy, enabling him to enhance his stature as president while avoiding getting mired in the fray of the primaries."[139]

Finally, he announced the "Carter Doctrine" in his 1980 State of the Union address. Carter proclaimed,

> Let our position be absolutely clear. An attempt by any outside force to gain control of the Persian Gulf region will be regarded as an assault on the vital interests of the United States of America, and such an assault will be repelled by any means necessary, including military force.[140]

He sought a 5% increase in real military spending, a boost in military and economic aid to Pakistan, and an expanded American military presence in the Indian Ocean.

Carter also used public appearances to establish emotional connections to the public. On April 1, 1979, a mere four days after the accident at Three Mile Island, Carter visited the town in an effort "to reassure local residents and the country as a whole of the absence of any residual radiation."[141] Then, in August, Carter sought to restore his populist image as he took a paddle steamboat down the Mississippi River from Saint Paul, Minnesota, to Saint Louis, Missouri, making forty-seven stops. Throughout the trip, he received favorable support among citizens, including a positive greeting from a crowd of 10,000 in Saint Louis.[142] Finally, in December 1979, Carter utilized the annual Christmas tree lighting ceremony effectively, surprising onlookers by only lighting the star at the top of the tree. In the meantime, he had his daughter Amy light fifty smaller trees. Carter announced that the fifty smaller trees symbolized the American hostages and the big tree would be fully lit when all of the hostages came home.[143]

Unconventional Actions

Carter carried out two noteworthy unconventional actions during his final two years in office. Interestingly, the events occurred weeks apart, but one significantly isolated the president, whereas the other exposed him to tens of thousands of Americans within a few days.

The first of these actions occurred in July 1979. Less than twenty-four hours before his fourth national speech regarding the energy crisis, he inexplicably retreated to Camp David. His decision to abandon the speech came so abruptly that rumors surfaced throughout the United States and Europe about a possible health difficulty. At a time when critics already questioned his leadership, it seemed quite odd to announce a national speech and then remain out of the public eye for over a week. Over a ten-day period at Camp David, Carter met with 134 prominent individuals, including members of Congress, mayor, governors, religious leaders, economists, union representatives, and individuals from previous presidential administrations.[144] The retreat proved vital for the Carter administration, because it was during this period of seclusion that Carter determined to ask for the resignations of his entire cabinet and decided to give his "crisis in confidence" speech.

In stark contrast to his Camp David isolation, where he met primarily with the political and business elites from across the United States, a few weeks later Carter boarded the *Delta Queen*, a paddle-wheel steamboat, for a forty-seven-stop trip along the Mississippi River. Carter hoped this display of political theater would illustrate him "as the leader of the nation, above partisan politics and controversy."[145]

Epilogue

Chief of Staff Jordan recalled that the president said to him, "1980 was pure hell—the Kennedy challenge, Afghanistan, having to put the SALT Treaty on the shelf, the recession, Ronald Reagan, and the hostages... always the hostages! It was one crisis after another."[146] Such developments led to a period of national division, which ultimately helped lead to one of the worst defeats in the United States for a sitting president, as Ronald Reagan defeated President Carter 51–41% in the popular vote and 489–49 in the electoral vote. In addition, Republicans attained a net gain of twelve seats in the Senate, which allowed the GOP to control the institution for the first time since 1954. To make matters worse for the Democrats, the electoral casualties included stalwarts such as George McGovern, Frank Church, Birch Bayh, and Gaylord Nelson.

Table 20a. Summarizing the President's Response to Adversity—National Division—Carter 1979–1980

Type of response	Summary data & significant examples
1. Bargaining & persuasion	*House & Senate concurrence with president— average for 1979-1980*: 76.0% *Legislative successes/compromises/concessions:* • Jun 1979: oil profits tax (compromise) • Oct 1979: Gas rationing plan • Jan 1980: Aid to Chrysler • Dec 1980: Toxic waste superfund *Failed attempts at legislative bargaining/compromise:* • 1979: Hospital Cost Control bill • 1979: Cong ignores natl health care plan • Jun 1980: Oil import fee veto overridden • Aug. 1980: VA Health Care veto overridden *Other:* • Kennedy challenges Carter's renomination • 1980 Olympics not moved from Moscow
2. Executive actions constitutional	*Vetoes:* 7 regular (71.4% sustained), 5 pocket *Pardons & clemency:* 316 (298 pardons, 18 commutations) *Proclamations:* 179 *Executive orders:* 150 • 12140 – Governors gas rationing power • 12170 – Froze Iranian assets in US • 12211 – Estd sanctions against Iran *Signing Statements:* 117 *Claims of executive privilege:* • Apr 1980: Energy Secy to withhold docs
other actions	N/A
3. Foreign policy initiatives & actions	*Presidential Directives:* 18 *Executive agreements:* 377
Outcome of case: Carter lost in a landslide (51%-41%, 489-49 electoral votes) & Republicans won 1ˢᵗ Senate majority since 1954	

Table 20b. Summarizing the President's Response to Adversity—National Division—Carter 1979–1980

Type of response	Summary data & significant examples
Foreign policy initiatives & actions *continued*	*Significant treaties:* (78 total) • 1979: SALT II Treaty *Uses of force:* • 1978: Logistical support to Zaire • April 1980: Failed hostage rescue mission *Other:* • Jan 1979: Normalize relations with PRC • Mar 1979: Israel-Egypt peace treaty • Dec 1979: End sanctions against Rhodesia • Jan 1980: Embargoes on Soviet Union • Jan 1980: Recalled ambdr from Moscow • Jan 1980: US withdrew from Olympics • April 1980: Cut ties w/Iran; tighter embargo
4. Organizational changes	• Jul 1979: Fired 5 Cabinet officials; named Hamilton Jordan chief of staff • Apr 1980: Muskie as Secy of State • Jun 1980: H Jordan to run reelection effort; Jack Watson as chief of staff
5. Going public	*Major speeches:* 7 (1979-4; 1980-3) *News conferences:* 18 (1979-12; 1980-6) *Key events/activities:* • Jan 1979: State of the Union • Apr 1979: Visit to "Three Mile Island" • Apr 1979: Third energy crisis speech • Jul 1979: "Crisis in Confidence" speech • Dec 1979 – Apr 1980: "Rose Garden Strategy" for reelection campaign • Jan 1980: State of Union/Carter Doctrine
6. Unconventional actions?	• July 1979: Seclusion at Camp David • Aug 1980: Trip down the Mississippi
Outcome of case: Carter lost in a landslide (51%-41%, 489-49 electoral votes) & Republicans won 1ˢᵗ Senate majority since 1954	

Table 20c. Comparing the President's Response to Non-Adverse Circumstances—Carter 1979–1980

Type of response	Comparison to non-adverse circumstances (1977-78)
1. Bargaining & persuasion	*House & Senate concurrence with president— average for 1977-1978*: 76.9% *Legislative successes/compromises/concessions:* • Aug. 1977: Clean Air Amendments • Aug 1977: Energy Dept • Nov 1977: Minimum Wage increase • Oct 1978: Civil Service Reform • Nov. 1978: energy bill (concession) *Failed attempts at legislative bargaining/compromise:* • May 1977: Crop subsidies • Jun 1977: Foreign aid appropriations • Nov 1977: Natural gas deregulation • 1977: Cong setbacks for energy plan • Feb 1978: House rejected proposal for consumer protection agency • Aug 1978: Weapons procurement (vetoed)
2. Executive actions constitutional	*Vetoes:* 6 reg. (100% sustained), 13 pocket *Pardons & clemency:* 168 (164 pardons, 4 commutations) • Amnesty for Vietnam draft evaders *Proclamations:* 150 *Executive orders:* 143 • 11967 – Pardon Vietnam War draft evaders • 12042 – Coal industry labor dispute board *Signing statements:* 110 *Claims of executive privilege:* None
other actions	N/A
3. Foreign policy initiatives & actions	*National security directives:* 43 *Executive agreements:* 644
Outcome of case: Carter lost in a landslide (51%-41%, 489-49 electoral votes) & Republicans won 1ˢᵗ Senate majority since 1954	

Table 20d. Comparing the President's Response to Non-Adverse Circumstances—Carter 1979–1980 (Cont.)

Type of response	Comparison to non-adverse circumstances (1977-78)
Foreign policy initiatives & actions *continued*	*Significant treaties:* (70 total) • Sept. 1977: Panama Canal Treaties *Uses of force:* None *Other:* • Mar 1977: Address United Nations • Mar 1977: arms-control proposals rejected by Soviet Union • Oct 1977: Signed International Covenants on Human Rights • Sept 1978: Camp David Accords
4. Organizational changes	• Sept 1977: Replaced OMB Director Bert Lance with James McIntyre
5. Going public	*Major speeches:* 9 (1977-5; 1978-4) *News conferences:* 41 (1977-22; 1978-19) *Key events/activities:* • Jan 1977: Inaugural Address • Feb 1977: Report to the nation • Apr 1977: Energy crisis • Apr 1977: Energy plan • Jan. 1978: State of the Union • Sept. 1978: Camp David Summit • Oct. 1978: Anti-Inflation Program
6. Unconventional actions?	• Mar 1977: "Ask President Carter" phone-in • Apr 1977: "Fireside Chat" concerning energy crisis
Outcome of case: **Carter lost in a landslide (51%-41%, 489-49 electoral votes) & Republicans won 1st Senate majority since 1954**	

GEORGE H. W. BUSH, 1992

Following the Persian Gulf War, George H. W. Bush received unprecedented public approval ratings; peaking at 89% in March 1991.[147] In fact,
Bush succeeded in being the only president since John F. Kennedy to

maintain an approval rating above 50% in every Gallup poll during his first three years of office.[148] The journalist Russell Baker commented that Bush held "a popularity and stature almost inconceivable for any president in his third year in office."[149] Such popularity prevented many leading Democrats, including New York governor Mario Cuomo and House majority leader Richard Gephardt, from entering the presidential race.[150] As Bush's approval rating held at 75% in May 1991, Timothy Naftali described, "Bush's reelection seemed as sure a thing as one could expect in American politics."[151]

Yet by year's end, a severe economic downturn and a highly volatile battle over Clarence Thomas's Supreme Court nomination in the fall of 1991 left Bush's approval at 46% as he entered into his fourth year in office, and it remained below 50% for the entire year.[152] To make matters worse, General Motors announced on February 24 that the company had lost a record $4.45 billion in 1991[153], and by June unemployment reached 7.8%.[154] Looking to the November election, one Republican pollster noted, "Our whole political problem is the recession…We face a twenty month recession, a 78 percent wrong track number, and (likely) a southern conservative Democrat. The situation is about as bad as it could be."[155]

Indeed, the economy became *the* issue of the 1992 campaign. Even prior to the general election, President Bush took fire from his own party, as political commentator Patrick Buchanan challenged the incumbent for the Republican nomination and received national attention for his strong showing (37%) in the New Hampshire primary. Buchanan attacked Bush for his failed "no new taxes" pledge and his intention to enter into the North American Free Trade Agreement (NAFTA). The historian John Robert Green explained that Buchanan, and later Independent candidate Ross Perot, argued that NAFTA "would result in the relocation of American industry and the loss of American jobs," and "[i]n the midst of a recession, their arguments struck home to a large number of voters, and opposition to NAFTA became an anti-Bush rallying cry."[156] Ultimately, Herbert Parmet described how Buchanan's candidacy "exposed a hard core of some 30 percent of Americans annoyed by what they regarded as Bush's indifference to the plight of ordinary Americans."[157]

Criticisms of Bush's detachment increased in the wake of the unrest in Los Angeles following the April 29 acquittal of the police officers involved in the infamous Rodney King beating. Rioting left 52 dead, 2,500 injured, and nearly $450 million worth of property damage. Critics described the president as "aloof" because it took him five days to visit the city.[158] Then, in late August, Hurricane Andrew, a category-five storm, demolished southern Florida and Louisiana, resulting in the deaths of 23 people and leaving 189,000 homeless. Naftali explained, "Although Bush wasted no time in declaring a state of emergency…it took many days for the U.S. government to respond adequately," which once again allowed his critics to raise questions of his detachment and his administration's competency.[159]

The economic downturn, NAFTA, and the ever-growing national debt led billionaire businessman Ross Perot to enter the presidential race as an Independent. National division became so bad that in June, Perot actually led Bush and the probable Democratic nominee Bill Clinton in several national polls. Parmet described that Perot "appeared as a fresh alternative for those disillusioned by Democratic and Republican politics."[160] Bush's approval plummeted to 29%, making him the fourth most unpopular president since polling began and on par with Nixon during Watergate (24%) and Carter during his crises (28%).[161]

Bargaining and Persuasion
Bush's leadership style has been described as one of a "guardianship," in which the president defines success as "holding the line against change in one way or another."[162] This strategy seemed ever-present in Bush's final year in office, as he faced a significantly partisan Congress and vetoed twenty-one bills. Consequently, 1992 became a year of limited legislative success for both the president and the Democrat-controlled Congress.

Legislative Successes/Compromises/Concessions

As shown in table 21, Bush's overall success score in Congress plummeted to 43% in 1992, which at the time was the lowest score ever recorded by *Congressional Quarterly*.[163] Though his success in the House had always been low, what made matters worse in 1992 was that Republican support for the president waned, especially in the Senate, which further limited his attempts at legislative leadership. Republican representative Tom DeLay criticized the president for lacking a clear legislative agenda.[164] Not surprisingly, there were no major legislative successes for Bush in 1992.

Table 21. Congressional Concurrence with the President, 1989–1992

Year	Total H&S Concurrence	House Concurrence	# of House Votes	Senate Concurrence	# of Senate Votes
1989	62.6	50.0	86	73.1	101
1990	46.8	32.4	108	63.4	93
1991	54.2	43.2	111	67.5	83
Average	**54.5**	**41.9**		**68.0**	
Total			305		277
1992	43.0	37.1	105	53.3	60

Source. Compiled from data in *Vital Statistics on American Politics, 2007–2008* (p. 265) by Harold Stanley and Richard Niemi. Washington, DC: CQ Press, 2008.

Failed Attempts at Legislative Bargaining/Compromise

The twenty-one vetoed bills during the 1992 session illustrate Bush's lack of bargaining throughout his final year in office. Among the vetoes were bills that stripped China of its most-favored-nation trade status, new campaign finance laws, family leave requirements, and "motor-voter" registration.[165] Importantly, the only veto override came on a bill established to place increased regulations on the cable television industry. But this event provides insight into President Bush's legislative difficulties throughout 1992, for it took a group of Senate Republicans to join the Democratic-majority to override the president's veto. The problem for President Bush was that this was not an isolated occurrence. As *Congressional Quarterly* reported, "For President Bush, 1992 was simply the worst of times. An administration that had always been dogged by meager congressional support saw its final redoubt—Senate Republicans—crack."[166] This included significant declines in support from key senators, including Alfonse D'Amato from 79% to 60% and Arlen Specter from 68% to 45%.[167]

In regard to Bush's specific legislative proposals, *Congressional Quarterly* reported, "None of the three major legislative requests he made in his State of the Union address—an economic stimulus package, school choice, and a healthcare plan—became law."[168] In addition, when the balanced budget amendment made it onto the congressional agenda, Bush announced his support for the popular measure, yet Senate majority leader George Mitchell refused to grant the president an election-year victory and actually convinced seven of the bill's cosponsors to vote against the amendment. In turn, the press reported it as another failure for the administration.[169] Because of such losses, *Congressional Quarterly* described, "Bush ran his re-election campaign as much against Congress as against Clinton. In his acceptance speech Aug. 20 in Houston, for instance, he chided 'the gridlock Democrat Congress.'"[170] Adding insult to injury, the Senate did not vote to ratify NAFTA until after Bush left office.[171]

Other Efforts at Bargaining and Negotiation
Like Johnson and Carter, Bush tried unsuccessfully to use his bargaining abilities to influence the election. Following Perot's announcement of withdrawal from the race, the president personally called his adversary, hoping to convince Perot that crucial elements of his agenda would be pursued by during a second Bush term, and thus sought his endorsement. Not only did Perot refuse to endorse the incumbent, but weeks later he reentered the race.[172]

Executive Actions

As previously indicated, the twenty-one vetoes issued by President Bush during his final year in office demonstrated his inability to effectively bargain. As a result, Bush relied heavily on unilateral executive actions, issuing 39 executive orders and 120 proclamations. Though the overwhelming majority of these actions were procedural or ceremonial, two executive orders responded to the ongoing conflict in Yugoslavia (E.O. 12808 and E.O. 12810); another executive order established a fetal tissue bank (E.O. 12806); and one proclamation extended most-favored-nation trade status to the Czech and Slovak Federal Republic and the Republic of Hungary (6419). Additionally, one executive order (E.O. 12804) and one proclamation (6427) dealt with the federal response to the riots in Los Angeles. The president's actions federalized 5,500 National Guardsmen, dispatched 2,000 federal law enforcement officials, and sent 4,500 members of the armed forces into the city.

More important than his use of executive orders and proclamations, however, was President Bush's determination to further institutionalize the presidential signing statement as a tool for circumventing Congress and shaping policies enacted by Congress. For example, when Bush signed the Torture Victim Protection Act on March 12, he included a statement, which read, "I must note that I am signing the bill based on my understanding that the Act does not permit suits for alleged human rights violations in the context of United States military operations abroad or law enforcement actions."[173] In fact, even on legislation that would seem minor in stature, Bush asserted his executive authority. For instance, when he signed a drought relief bill on March 5, he included a signing statement in which he described Congress's requirement that the secretary of the Interior provide drought contingency plans as "advisory and not mandatory" because the Constitution specifically grants the president (not other executive officials) the power to make recommendations to Congress. In addition, he determined that the legislation's allowance for the secretary of the Interior to approve of contingency plans submitted by governors could potentially give governors executive authority under the national Constitution, and thus, the president determined the role of governors would be "advisory."[174]

Finally, President Bush turned to his constitutional pardon power, as he issued twenty-five pardons in 1992 (all on December 24). Most notably, Bush pardoned six individuals indicted for their activities related to the Iran-Contra affair, including President Reagan's secretary of defense (Caspar Weinberger) and national security advisor (Robert McFarlane).

Foreign Policy Initiatives and Actions

President Bush remained quite effective in the foreign policy realm during his period of adversity. The president signed a major climate change agreement, signed an arms reduction agreement with Russian president Boris Yeltsin, launched a humanitarian mission in Somalia, and signed NAFTA with Mexico and Canada. In spite of these numerous accomplishments, the year did not start well for President Bush; on a tour of Asia, the president threw up on the lap of the Japanese prime minister, not the ideal news story for an incumbent president declining in the polls and gearing up for a primary challenge from his party's base.[175]

Nevertheless, the president bounced back from this embarrassing situation with several foreign policy accomplishments throughout the year. The first came in June when he attended the UN Conference on Environmental Development in Rio de Janeiro, referred to as the Earth Summit, and signed a treaty that sought to reduce carbon dioxide emissions, but he declined to sign an endangered species treaty that critics claimed surrendered American sovereignty.[176] Less than a week later, President Bush and Russian president Boris Yeltsin met for three days in Washington, DC, where they established a "joint understanding" that called for the elimination or significant reduction of several types of nuclear weapons.[177] Following these June successes, the campaign took precedence for several months. Consequently, prior to December, the only major foreign policy development that took place was the establishment of a second no-fly zone in Iraq in August 1992.[178]

Perhaps most importantly, the Bush case illustrates the importance of presidential actions during the most difficult of circumstances, even after a significant electoral loss. Weeks after losing the 1992 election, Bush launched Operation Restore Hope in Somalia and eventually toured the war-torn country on December 31.[179] Furthermore, the president signed NAFTA with his Canadian and Mexican counterparts.[180] Additionally, though not part of the 1992 calendar year, Bush successfully entered into the START II Treaty with Yeltsin on January 3, 1993, and ordered missile strikes against Saddam Hussein during his final days in office.[181]

Organizational Changes

Three organizational changes occurred during President Bush's last year in office. First, Bush asked James Baker to leave his post as secretary of state to fill the role of chief of staff, largely to help with campaign strategies.[182] Second, Bush named Transportation Secretary Andrew Card the new "czar" for emergency response in the wake of Hurricane Andrew (Card remained in his role as transportation secretary).[183] Finally, Bush removed Edward Derwinski from his post as secretary of veterans affairs because of his decision to proceed with a trial plan to allow public health clinics to refer patients to VA hospitals. The plan received immediate criticism from veterans' groups, and thus Derwinksi became a political liability for the president as the election loomed.[184]

Of the three changes, only the appointment of Baker to chief of staff proved substantial. Baker replaced Samuel Skinner, who had been appointed in December 1991 to replace John Sununu. Skinner's appointment became a disaster. Podhoretz described that Skinner "was chief of staff for eight months, and in all that time he never had a good day."[185] Secretary Derwinski further explained that with Skinner's appointment, "the White House bureaucracy collapsed."[186] Upon taking over for Skinner, Baker removed domestic policy czar Clayton Yeutter (Skinner's closest ally), relocated Skinner's deputy chief of staff Henson Moore to the Old Executive Office Building, and restructured the White House under four chief deputies.[187] In spite of Baker's political prowess, even he could not turn around the Bush candidacy.

Going Public

President Bush's "going public" strategy fit the description of a "guardian" president. Mervin described guardian presidents as "likely to be short on charisma and flamboyance, to be disinclined to resort to rhetorical appeals and to specialize in working quietly behind the scenes."[188] President Bush only made two major speeches during 1992: the State of the Union address and his national address during the Los Angeles riots. This fit the pattern of the Bush presidency. Podhoretz wrote, "Bush was uncomfortable serving as the tribune of the people."[189] Another scholar explained that President Bush "insisted on being a 'hands-on' chief executive rather than a salesman, or a mere mouthpiece for his administration."[190] Interestingly, Bush actually spoke often but in smaller gatherings. In fact, Podhoretz recounted,

> No president had ever spoken more frequently than Bush; no president had ever said less. By the end of his four years in office, Bush had given more speeches and made more public appearances than Ronald Reagan had in eight years' time. And yet if people were asked what memorable things Bush had ever said, they could think of only three: "Read my lips: no new taxes," "a kinder, gentler nation," and "a thousand points of light." All three came from his acceptance speech at the 1988 Republican convention. Once he was president, he never uttered a phrase worth remembering.[191]

But Bush's difficulties throughout 1992 went far beyond his frequency or style; his major problem was public perception. It took the administration until December 1991 to admit that the economy was in recession, and even then, the president feared giving speeches focused on economic distress because he believed that would lead to a worsening of consumer confidence and further deterioration of the economy. Yet he also refused optimistic rhetoric that would suggest he misunderstood the economic climate. Consequently, as David Demarest, Bush's communication director, described, Bush's message became "muddled."[192]

As a result, not only did Bush lose the public's support for breaking the "no new taxes" pledge; he also lost support because of his inability to effectively communicate about the economic downturn. When he finally hit the campaign trail in early 1992, the press focused on the embarrassing event when the president seemingly did not know how the price scanner worked at a grocery store.[193] Thus, President Bush, like President Carter, lost credibility with the American people. Mervin explained, "Bush's credibility suffered badly from his obvious lack of interest in domestic policy, and his unwillingness to act in response to the widely held belief that the economy was in trouble."[194]

Epilogue

The national division President Bush faced in 1992 ultimately led to the second worst electoral outcome for an incumbent president, as he garnered a mere 38% of the vote. *Congressional Quarterly* commented, "Only William Howard Taft, in 1912, did worse (with 23 percent). Like Taft, Bush was beset by a reinvigorated Democratic Party on one hand and by a tenacious, charismatic third candidate on the other."[195] Nevertheless, although 13 million more voters went to the polls in 1992 than in 1988, so Bush actually received 9 million fewer votes in 1992. As such, Naftali argued, "This was repudiation on par with that experienced by Barry Goldwater in 1964 and George McGovern in 1972. And one had to reach back eighty years to see as great a collapse of national support for an incumbent running for reelection."[196] The electorate disapproval was directed only at the president; Republicans actually gained nine seats in the House and maintained the status quo in the Senate.

Table 22a. Summarizing the President's Response to Adversity—National Division—George H.W. Bush, 1992

Type of response	Summary data & significant examples
1. Bargaining & persuasion	*House & Senate concurrence with president—* *1992:* 43.0% *Legislative successes/compromises/concessions:* N/A *Failed attempts at legislative bargaining/compromise:* • Jan: School Choice • Aug: Strategic Defense Initiative funding cut • Balanced Budget Amendment (No Senate vote) • Economic Stimulus Package (no action) • Health Care Proposal (no action) *Other:* • Sought Ross Perot's endorsement following Perot's withdrawal from 1992 presidential race
2. Executive actions constitutional	*Vetoes:* 11 regular (91% sustained), 10 pocket • Jun: Motor Voter • Sept: Family & Medical Leave • Oct: Cable Reregulation (overridden) • Oct: Abortion at Military Hospitals *Pardons & Clemency:* 25 (all pardons) • Dec. 1992: Six tied to Iran-contra affair *Proclamations:* 120 • 6419 –MFN status Hungary/Slovakia/Czech • 6427 – Natl Guard to suppess LA riots *Executive orders:* 39 • 12804 – Armed Forces to respond to LA riots • 12806 – Established fetal tissue bank • 12808 – Blocked property of govts of Yugoslavia, Serbia & Montenegro • 12810 – No financial transactions w/Yugoslavia
Outcome of case: ***Bush suffered the second worst defeat for an incumbent (only 38% of the popular vote)***	

Table 22b. Summarizing the President's Response to Adversity—National Division—George H.W. Bush, 1992

Type of response	Summary data & significant examples
	• Mar: Drought Relief – duties assigned to Sec of Inter "& state governors only advisory *Claims of executive privilege:* None
other actions	N/A
3. Foreign policy initiatives & actions	*National security directives:* 11 *International agreements:* 280 *Significant treaties:* • Jun: Carbon Emissions Treaty • Dec: NAFTA with Canada and Mexico • Jan 1993: START II Treaty with Russia *Uses of force:* • Dec: Operation Restore Hope in Somalia *Other:* • Jan: Embarrassing incident Japan state dinner • Jun: Refused to sign Endangered Species Treaty • Jun: understanding w/Russia on nucl weapons • Aug: Estd 2nd no-fly zone in Iraq
4. Organizational changes	Aug: Jas Baker to chief of staff; Treas Secy A Card as "czar" for Hurricane Andrew Sept: Ed Derwinski dismissed as VA Secy
5. Going public	*Major speeches:* 2 *News conferences:* 22 *Key Events:* • Jan: State of the Union Address • May: National Address concerning LA riots • Aug.: Acceptance of Republican nomination • Dec.: Address regarding mission in Somalia
6. Unconventional actions?	N/A
Outcome of case: Bush suffered the second worst defeat for an incumbent (only 38% of the popular vote)	

Table 22c. Comparing the President's Response to Non-Adverse Circumstances-—George H.W. Bush, 1992

Type of response	Comparison to non-adverse circumstances (1991)
1. Bargaining & persuasion	*House & Senate concurrence with pres—1991:* 54.2% *Legislative successes/compromises/concessions:* • Jan: Persian Gulf War authorization • Jun: Brady Bill (compromise) • Nov: Strategic Defense Initiative (compromise) • Oct: Civil Rights Act (concession) • Oct: Clarence Thomas confirmation *Failed attempts at legislative bargaining/compromise:* • Mar: Housing funding • Sept: Unemployment Benefits • Dept of Environment proposal
2. Executive actions constitutional	*Vetoes:* 3 reg. (100% sustained), 1 pocket *Pardons & clemency:* 29 (all pardons) *Proclamations:* 157 *Executive orders:* 45 • 12743 – Call-up of Ready Reserve • 12744 – Designated combat zones • 12750 – Est Desert Shield Zone • 12778 – Civil Justice Reform • 12779 – Certain transactions w/Haiti prohibited *Signing statements:* 35 • Jan: AUMF – noted that he was not adhering to War Powers Act • Apr: War Appropriations – interpret certain provisions in accordance with his understanding of presidential power *Claims of executive privilege:* 1 • Def Secy not give docs to Congress
Outcome of case: **Bush suffered the second worst defeat for an incumbent (only 38% of the popular vote)**	

Table 22d. Comparing the President's Response to Non-Adverse Circum-
stances-—George H.W. Bush, 1992 (Cont.)

Type of response	Comparison to non-adverse circumstances (1991)
other actions	N/A
3. Foreign policy initiatives & actions	*National security directives:* 11 *International agreements:* 274 *Significant treaties:* • Jul: START I, with Soviet Union *Uses of force:* • Persian Gulf War *Other:* • Sept: Recognized Estonia, Latvia, & Lithuania • Oct: Middle East Peace conference in Spain
4. Organizational changes	N/A
5. Going public	*Major speeches:* 6 *News conferences:* 47 *Key Events:* • Jan: Gulf War air strikes • Jan: State of the Union Address • Feb: Allied combat in Persian Gulf • Mar: Cessation of conflict in Persian Gulf
6. Unconventional actions?	N/A
Outcome of case: Bush suffered the second worst defeat for an incumbent (only 38% of the popular vote)	

OUTCOME AND ASSESSMENT

Periods of national division present presidents with unique challenges.
Each president examined in this chapter encountered significant division
within his own party, the rise of a third-party candidate, job approval
ratings below 40%, and a national electorate that eventually determined to
side with the opposition party. In spite of the differences among the particular cases analyzed, we can establish some initial conclusions about pres-

idential powers during periods of national division. In particular, factors other than bargaining and persuasion were most important.

Did the President's Actions Make Any Difference?

Although table 23 indicates that Johnson and Carter maintained high levels of concurrence in Congress, their successes largely came on minor issues and their major agenda items failed. With their persuasive influence minimized, all three presidents relied heavily on unilateral executive powers to respond to both domestic and international crises. In addition, perhaps because of the national division on the domestic front, all three chief executives maintained active leadership internationally, both through diplomacy and through use of additional unilateral actions. Unfortunately, for Johnson and Carter, their international successes were overshadowed by the continued hostilities in Vietnam and the hostage crisis in Iran, respectively.

How Did Adversity Limit What the President Could Do or Accomplish?

Not surprisingly, in all three cases the presidents seemed limited in their ability to implement successful bargaining and persuasion tactics, both inside and outside of Congress. As indicated earlier, though Johnson and Carter maintained high levels of success in Congress, their agendas remained significantly restricted, with their major proposals stalling on Capitol Hill. Bush, in contrast, saw his success in Congress plummet, largely because of the divided government that he faced. Furthermore, all three men signed major treaties that the Senate refused to ratify.

Table 23a. Assessing the President's Response to Adversity—National Division

President	Response types (and significance)
Johnson, 1967-68 *Outcome: Johnson chose not to seek reelection, Nixon wins presidency, and Republicans make small gains in Congress*	**1. Bargaining & persuasion:** With a large Democratic majority in Congress, Johnson had continued success. However, he had to limit his agenda and concede on several issues. Outside of Congress, his influence fell. **(Significance: Mixed)** **2. Executive actions:** Johnson utilized a variety of unilateral executive powers, with executive orders being most important. Executive orders provided an important tool to combat domestic crises. **(Significance: High)** **3. Foreign policy initiatives & actions** Johnson was very active in diplomatic efforts and relied heavily on unilateral executive actions to accomplish tasks. **(Significance: High)** **4. Organizational changes:** Limited in scope, with the two most significant changes due to disagreement over Vietnam policy. **(Significance: Low)** **5. Going public:** Johnson's lack of forthrightness with the public and his desire not to make many public appearances led to a "credibility gap." **(Significance: High)** **6. Unconventional actions:** Decided not run for reelection. **(Significance: High)**

Table 23b. Assessing the President's Response to Adversity—National Division (Cont.)

President	Response types (and significance)
Carter, 1979-80 _Outcome_: _Carter lost a landslide presidential election and Republicans won the Senate for the first time since 1954._	**1. Bargaining & persuasion:** Carter maintained high levels of success in Congress, but could not hold the Democratic-coalition together on key issues. Ultimately he alienated his own party's base, which led to the contentious nomination battle. **(Significance: Mixed)** **2. Executive actions:** Mixed success when it came to vetoes, but relied heavily on unilateral executive powers, especially executive orders, to respond to unanticipated circumstances **(Significance: High)** **3. Foreign policy initiatives & actions:** Carter used a combination of unilateral actions and intense diplomacy to maintain control over non-hostage issues. Unfortunately, for him, he could not overcome the most important issue; the hostages. **(Significance: High)** **4. Organizational changes:** Centralized White House decision-making with the appointment of Hamilton Jordan to Chief of Staff and forcing five Cabinet resignations. The Cabinet shake-up was a major blunder by Carter, as the American public perceived instability in the White House at a time when confidence was already low. **(Significance: High)** **5. Going public:** Maintained high level of public appearances, but most were in smaller settings. The combination of Carter's unannounced ten-day retreat to Camp David, the malaise speech, and the Cabinet upheaval led to a lack of confidence in the president. **(Significance: High)** **6. Unconventional actions:** Used unconventional actions as an extension of the public presidency, as he tried to re-make his public image, both as a strong leader and a populist. Instead, caused confusion among most Americans. **(Significance: Mixed)**

Table 23c. Assessing the President's Response to Adversity—National Division (Cont.)

Bush, 1992 *Outcome*: *Bush suffered the second worst defeat for an incumbent (only 38% of the popular vote)*	**1. Bargaining & persuasion:** Unable to exert legislative leadership in Congress or use office to exert influence outside of Washington, D.C. **(Significance: Low)** **2. Executive actions:** Veto was significant weapon. Also made extensive use of executive orders to respond to both domestic and international circumstances. Further institutionalized the presidential signing statement for shaping policies passed by Congress. **(Significance: High)** **3. Foreign policy initiatives & actions:** Bush maintained high level of diplomatic activity, helped lead military responses in Iraq and Somalia, and entered into three significant treaties. **(Significance: High)** **4. Organizational changes:** Limited in scope, the most important of which was naming James Baker Chief of Staff in an effort to bolster re-election campaign, which ultimately failed. **(Significance: Low)** **5. Going public:** Maintained high level of public appearances, but most were in smaller settings. Message became "muddled" and lost credibility on *the* key issue (the economy) with voters as the 1992 election neared. **(Significance: High)** **6. Unconventional actions:** N/A **(Significance: Low)**

But all three presidents saw their persuasive abilities limited outside of Congress as well. In each of the cases, the president tried to influence the upcoming election but failed in his efforts (this was especially true in the Carter and Bush cases, given that they both unsuccessfully tried to influence opponents to support them). Perhaps most important, however, was the public perception problems that all three presidents encountered. All three faced a credibility gap. Johnson lost credibility because of the secretiveness of his administration, as well as his unwillingness to make many public speeches. Carter lost credibility after his unannounced seclusion at Camp David, which triggered his "malaise speech" and the botched reorganization of his cabinet. Lastly, Bush lost his credibility first because he broke his "no new taxes" pledge, but also because he was uncomfortable speaking to the American people about the economy and the public's perception that he did not understand their struggles.

Did Adversity Open Opportunities in Any Way?

These cases show that the domestic difficulties presidents face during periods of national division enhance the likelihood that presidents seek to demonstrate international leadership. Lyndon Johnson helped manage the Six-Day War and signed two significant treaties (the Treaty of Outer Space and the Nuclear Non-Proliferation Treaty). Jimmy Carter normalized diplomatic relations with the People's Republic of China, helped finalize a treaty between Israel and Egypt, and signed the SALT II Treaty. George Bush signed a major climate change agreement, signed an arms reduction agreement with Russia, and signed NAFTA with Mexico and Canada. Unfortunately for Johnson and Carter, their international crises (the Vietnam War and the Iranian hostage crisis) overshadowed the successes just mentioned.

What Powers Did the President Retain Despite Adversity, and How Did the President Exercise Them in a Relevant Way?

Periods of national division once again draw attention to the vast arsenal of unilateral powers that presidents enjoy. All three presidents analyzed in this chapter pursued an effective veto strategy. In addition, all three used executive orders to respond to domestic crises. Most importantly, all three presidents used a specific unilateral executive power to leave a definable mark not only on the presidency as an institution but on the entire government. Johnson issued Executive Order 11375, which expanded federal affirmative action programs to women. Carter issued Presidential Directive 59, which former CIA director Stansfield Turner argued "laid the whole foundation for Reagan's expansion of nuclear weapons, and war-fighting, and war-winning capabilities."[197] Finally, George Bush expanded a precedent set by his predecessor as he institutionalized the use of signing statements to exert increased executive powers and did so with regard to state, national, and international issues.

Separation of powers, staggered terms, the dominance of two parties, and many other factors all help lead to the periods of national division analyzed in this chapter. The three significant periods of national division presented here occurred within a twenty-four-year time frame, yet each demonstrated the incredible obstacles presidents must face during these periods of adversity. Of particular significance in these three cases was the credibility gap found among all three presidents. Johnson chose not to make many public appearances, whereas Carter and Bush focused on smaller events, which limited their ability to overcome the public's perception of their ineptness as leaders. None of the men overcame their difficulties with the American people, and ultimately the consequences proved severe; Johnson chose not to run for reelection, and we have to go back to 1912 to find an incumbent president with fewer electoral votes than Carter and a smaller popular vote percentage than Bush. In spite of their weakened position during national division, the cases of Johnson, Carter, and Bush illustrate that even presidents who cannot electorally overcome the obstacles they face can effectively utilize unilateral executive actions, both domestically and internationally, to leave a definable mark on the institution and on the country.

Endnotes

1. Irving Bernstein, *Guns or Butter: The Presidency of Lyndon Johnson* (New York: Oxford University Press, 1996), 410.
2. George Reedy, *Lyndon Johnson: A Memoir* (New York: Andrews and McMeel, 1982), 142.
3. Irwin Unger and Debi Unger, *LBJ: A Life* (New York: John Wiley & Sons, 1999), 407.
4. Bernstein, *Guns or Butter*, 379.
5. Ibid., 417; Randall B. Woods, *LBJ: Architect of American Ambition* (New York: Free Press, 2006), 790; Joseph A. Califano, Jr., *The Triumph & Tragedy of Lyndon Johnson: The White House Years* (New York: Simon & Schuster, 1991), 209, 213, 220.
6. Thomas S. Langston, *Lyndon Baines Johnson* (Washington, DC: CQ Press, 2002), 77.
7. Lyndon Baines Johnson, *The Vantage Point* (New York: Hold, Rinehart & Winston, 1971), 243.
8. Vaughn Davis Bornet, *The Presidency of Lyndon B. Johnson* (Lawrence: University Press of Kansas, 1983), 254.
9. Langston, *Lyndon Baines Johnson*, 175.
10. Bornet, *Presidency of Lyndon B. Johnson*, 257, 272.
11. Ibid., 255.
12. Bernstein, *Guns or Butter*, 417.
13. Califano, *Triumph & Tragedy*, 248.
14. Bornet, *Presidency of Lyndon B. Johnson*, 259.
15. Califano, *Triumph & Tragedy*, 258.
16. Ibid., 251.
17. Bernstein, *Guns or Butter*, 372.
18. Unger and Unger, *LBJ*, 443.
19. Califano, *Triumph & Tragedy*, 258.
20. Merle Miller, *Lyndon: An Oral Biography* (New York: G. P. Putnam's Sons, 1980), 500.
21. Califano, *Triumph & Tragedy*, 257.
22. L. B. Johnson, *Vantage Point*, 384.
23. Langston, *Lyndon Baines Johnson*, 176.
24. Unger and Unger, *LBJ*, 448.
25. Ibid.

26. Bernstein, *Guns or Butter*, 477.

27. Langston, *Lyndon Baines Johnson*, 77.

28. Califano, *Triumph & Tragedy*, 265.

29. Langston, *Lyndon Baines Johnson*, 77.

30. Califano, *Triumph & Tragedy*, 270–271.

31. Ibid., 274.

32. Bruce J. Schulman, *Lyndon Johnson and American Liberalism: A Brief Biography with Documents* (New York: Bedford/St. Martins, 1995), 119; Bernstein, *Guns or Butter*, 497.

33. Woods, *LBJ*, 832.

34. Califano, *Triumph & Tragedy*, 319.

35. Bornet, *Presidency of Lyndon B. Johnson*, 313.

36. Califano, *Triumph & Tragedy*, 318.

37. Bernstein, *Guns or Butter*, 515.

38. Langston, *Lyndon Baines Johnson*, 218, 220.

39. Doris Kearns Goodwin, *Lyndon Johnson and the American Dream* (New York: St. Martin's Press, 1991), 226.

40. Bernstein, *Guns or Butter*, 457; Unger and Unger, *LBJ*, 435–436.

41. Califano, *Triumph & Tragedy*, 207.

42. Ibid., 282.

43. Unger and Unger, *LBJ*, 436.

44. Califano, *Triumph & Tragedy*, 305.

45. Congressional Quarterly, *CQ Almanac: 90th Congress 2nd Session, 1968* (Washington, DC: CQ Press, 1969), 70.

46. Unger and Unger, *LBJ*, 466.

47. Congressional Quarterly, *CQ Almanac 90th Congress 2nd Session*, 70.

48. Califano, *Triumph & Tragedy*, 206.

49. Burnet, 313–315.

50. Unger and Unger, *LBJ*, 465; Woods, *LBJ*, 845.

51. Unger and Unger, *LBJ*, 464; Woods, *LBJ*, 845.

52. Langston, *Lyndon Baines Johnson*, 167.

53. "The Presidential Timeline," accessed May 18, 2010, http://www.presidentialtimeline.org/timeline/bin/.

54. Miller, *Lyndon*, 469–470.

55. Califano, *Triumph & Tragedy*, 319; Langston, *Lyndon Baines Johnson*, 125.

56. Califano, *Triumph & Tragedy*, 319.

57. Ibid., 205.

58. Woods, *LBJ*, 810.

59. Bernstein, *Guns or Butter*, 471.
60. Califano, *Triumph & Tragedy*, 183.
61. Langston, *Lyndon Baines Johnson*, 235.
62. Ibid., 234.
63. Califano, *Triumph & Tragedy*, 172.
64. Langston, *Lyndon Baines Johnson*, 178.
65. Bernstein, *Guns or Butter*, 477.
66. Schulman, *Lyndon Johnson and American Liberalism*, 147.
67. Woods, *LBJ*, 837.
68. Ibid., 845.
69. Andrew E. Busch, "1978 GOP Sets Stage for Reagan," September 2006, accessed May 3, 2010, http://www.ashbrook.org/publicat/oped/busch/06 /1978.html.
70. Garland A. Haas, *Jimmy Carter and the Politics of Frustration* (Jefferson, NC: McFarland & Co., 1992), 79.
71. Burton I. Kaufman, *The Presidency of James Earl Carter, Jr.* (Lawrence: University Press of Kansas, 1993), 135.
72. Peter G. Bourne, *Jimmy Carter: A Comprehensive Biography from Plains to Postpresidency* (New York: Scribner, 1997), 431.
73. Ibid., 430–431.
74. Ibid., 437.
75. Haas, *Jimmy Carter*, 93.
76. Kaufman, *Presidency of James Earl Carter, Jr.*, 138.
77. Bourne, *Jimmy Carter*, 440.
78. Kaufman, *Presidency of James Earl Carter, Jr.*, 143.
79. Bourne, *Jimmy Carter*, 450.
80. Betty Glad, *Jimmy Carter: In Search of the Great White House* (New York: W. W. Norton & Company, 1980), 450.
81. Bourne, *Jimmy Carter*, 450–451.
82. Clifton McCleskey and Pierce McCleskey, "Jimmy Carter and the Democratic Party," in *The Carter Years: The President and Policy Making*, ed. M. Glenn Abernathy, Dilys M. Hill, and Phil Williams (New York: St. Martin's Press, 1984), 136.
83. Bourne, *Jimmy Carter*, 452.
84. Ibid., 449; Haas, *Jimmy Carter*, 86.
85. Haas, *Jimmy Carter*, 88; See also C. Jones, *Passages to the Presidency*, 1998, 184–188.
86. Haas, *Jimmy Carter*, 86, 87.

87. Rosalynn Carter, *First Lady from Plains* (Boston: Houghton Mifflin, 1984), 305.
88. Haas, *Jimmy Carter*, 83.
89. Kaufman, *Presidency of James Earl Carter, Jr.*, 142; Haas, *Jimmy Carter*, 81.
90. Glad, *In Search of the Great White House*, 454.
91. Haas, *Jimmy Carter*, 80.
92. Ibid., 82.
93. Kaufman, *Presidency of James Earl Carter, Jr.*, 177.
94. Ibid.
95. Ibid., 178.
96. Ibid., 140.
97. Jimmy Carter, "National Health Plan Message to the Congress on Proposed Legislation," June 12, 1979, accessed May 7, 2010, http://www.presidency.ucsb.edu/ws/index.php?pid = 32466.
98. Haas, *Jimmy Carter*, 82; Kaufman, *Presidency of James Earl Carter, Jr.*, 140.
99. Bourne, *Jimmy Carter*, 450–451.
100. Ibid., 461.
101. Kaufman, *Presidency of James Earl Carter, Jr.*, 193–195.
102. Jimmy Carter, "PD-59: Nuclear Weapons Employment Policy," Januart 19, 1981.accessed May 7, 2010, http://www.fas.org/irp/offdocs/pd/pd59.pdf.
103. Betty Glad, *Jimmy Carter, His Advisors, and the Making of American Foreign Policy* (Ithaca, NY: Cornell University Press, 2009), 220, 222.
104. Kaufman, *Presidency of James Earl Carter, Jr.*, 192.
105. Glad, *Making of American Foreign Policy*, 219.
106. Glad, *In Search of the Great White House*, 434; Haas, *Jimmy Carter*, 103–104; Bourne, *Jimmy Carter*, 441, 457.
107. Kaufman, *Presidency of James Earl Carter, Jr.*, 122–123.
108. Glad, *In Search of the Great White House*, 430.
109. Raymond A. Moore, "The Carter Presidency and Foreign Policy," in *The Carter Years: The President and Policy Making*, ed. M. Glenn Abernathy, Dilys M. Hill, and Phil Williams (New York: St. Martin's Press, 1984), 70.
110. Glad, *Making of American Foreign Policy*, 111–116.
111. Kaufman, *Presidency of James Earl Carter, Jr.*, 158–160.
112. Ibid., 160.
113. Bourne, *Jimmy Carter*, 456.

114. Kaufman, 161.

115. Mark Bowden, *Guests of the Ayatollah: The First Battle in America's War with Militant Islam* (New York: Atlantic Monthly Press, 2006), 363.

116. Ibid., 365.

117. Bourne, *Jimmy Carter*, 460.

118. Kaufman, *Presidency of James Earl Carter, Jr.*, 174–175.

119. Bowden, *Guests of the Ayatollah*, 577.

120. Kaufman, *Presidency of James Earl Carter, Jr.*, 145–146.

121. Glad, *In Search of the Great White House*, 447; Kaufman, *Presidency of James Earl Carter, Jr.*, 147.

122. Kaufman, *Presidency of James Earl Carter, Jr.*, 147.

123. Bourne, *Jimmy Carter*, 446.

124. Dilys M. Hill, "Domestic Policy," in *The Carter Years: The President and Policy Making*, ed. M. Glenn Abernathy, Dilys M. Hill, and Phil Williams (New York: St. Martin's Press, 1984), 29.

125. Haas, *Jimmy Carter*, 85.

126. Kaufman, *Presidency of James Earl Carter, Jr.*, 147.

127. Glad, *In Search of the Great White House*, 448–449.

128. Kaufman, *Presidency of James Earl Carter, Jr.*, 142.

129. Bourne, *Jimmy Carter*, 448–449.

130. Ibid., 450.

131. Ibid., 461.

132. Carol Gelderman, *All the Presidents' Words: The Bully Pulpit and the Creation of the Virtual Presidency* (New York: Walker Publishing, 1997), 117.

133. Jimmy Carter, "Address to the Nation on Energy and National Goals: 'The Malaise Speech,'" July 15, 1979, accessed March 22, 2011, http://www.presidency.ucsb.edu/ws/index.php?pid = 32596&st = &st1 = #axzz1HLZCip00.

134. Public Broadcasting Service, "People & Events: Carter's 'Crisis in Confidence' Speech," accessed May 6, 2010, http://www.pbs.org/wgbh/amex/carter/peopleevents/e_malaise.html.

135. Bourne, *Jimmy Carter*, 445.

136. Ibid.

137. Ibid., 446.

138. C. Jones (1998), *Passages to the Presidency*, 184-188.

139. Bourne, *Jimmy Carter*, 456.

140. Jimmy Carter, "The State of the Union Address Delivered Before a Joint Session of Congress," January 23, 1980, accessed March 22, 2011,

http://www.presidency.ucsb.edu/ws/index.php?pid = 33079&st = &st1
= #axzz1HLZCip00.

141. Bourne, *Jimmy Carter*, 439.

142. Glad, *In Search of the Great White House*, 449.

143. Ibid., 462.

144. Ibid., 444.

145. Ibid., 449.

146. Hamilton Jordan, *Crisis: The Last Year of the Carter Presidency* (New York: G. P. Putnam's Sons, 1982), 7.

147. Timothy Naftali, *George H. W. Bush* (New York: Times Books, 2007), 131.

148. American Presidency Project, "Presidential Job Approval." Interestingly, George W. Bush came closest to pulling off this feat as well, given that he only fell below 50% once during his first three years in office.

149. Herbert S. Parmet, *George Bush: The Life of a Lone Star Yankee* (New York: Scribner, 1997), 490.

150. Naftali, *George H. W. Bush*, 131.

151. Ibid.

152. American Presidency Project, "Presidential Job Approval."

153. Peter B. Levy, *Encyclopedia of the Reagan-Bush Years* (Westport, CT: Greenwood Press, 1996), 413

154. *George H. W. Bush*, 145.

155. John Robert Greene, *The Presidency of George Bush* (Lawrence: University Press of Kansas, 2000), 164.

156. Ibid., 171.

157. Parmet, *George Bush*, 503.

158. Greene, *Presidency of George Bush*, 169.

159. Naftali, *George H. W. Bush*, 147.

160. Parmet, *George Bush*, 501.

161. Naftali, *George H. W. Bush*, 145.

162. David Mervin, *George Bush and the Guardianship Presidency* (New York: St. Martin's Press, 1996), 8.

163. Congressional Quarterly, *CQ Almanac: 102nd Congress 2nd Session, 1992* (Washington, DC: CQ Press, 1993), 5B.

164. Congressional Quarterly, *CQ Almanac 102nd Congress 2nd Session*, 3–4B.

165. Levy, *Encyclopedia*, 413–414.

166. Congressional Quarterly, *CQ Almanac* Vol. XLVIII, 3B.

167. Ibid., 4B.

168. Ibid., 3B.
169. John Podhoretz, *Hell of a Ride: Backstage at the White House Follies, 1989–1993* (New York: Simon & Schuster, 1993), 101.
170. Congressional Quarterly, *CQ Almanac* Vol. XLVIII, 5.
171. Parmet, *George Bush*, 498.
172. Ibid., 502.
173. George H. W. Bush, "Statement on Signing the Torture Victim Protection Act of 1991," March 12, 1992, accessed July 23, 2010, http://www.presidency.ucsb.edu/ws/index.php?pid = 20715.
174. George H. W. Bush, "Statement on Signing the Reclamation States Emergency Drought Relief Act of 1991," March 5, 1992, accessed July 23, 2010, http://www.presidency.ucsb.edu/ws/index.php?pid = 20689.
175. Barbara Bush, *Barbara Bush: A Memoir* (New York: Charles Scribner's Sons, 1994), 446–451.
176. Ibid., 462; Schulman, 93.
177. Physicians for Social Responsibility, "Arms Control Summits," accessed June 11, 2010, http://www.psr.org/nuclear-weapons/arms-control-summits.html.
178. Naftali, *George H. W. Bush*, 146.
179. Levy, *Encyclopedia*, 415.
180. Parmet, *George Bush*, 498.
181. Ibid., 509.
182. Naftali, *George H. W. Bush*, 146.
183. Ibid., 147.
184. Greene, *Presidency of George Bush*, 155.
185. Podhoretz, *Hell of a Ride*, 74.
186. Edward J. Derwinski, "Organizing for Policymaking," in *Portraits of American Presidents*, vol. 10, *The Bush Presidency*, ed. Kenneth Thompson (Lanham, MD: University Press of America, 1997), 23.
187. Podhoretz, *Hell of a Ride*, 76.
188. Mervin, *George Bush and the Guardianship Presidency*, 9.
189. Podhoretz, *Hell of a Ride*, 111.
190. Mervin, *George Bush*, 47.
191. Podhoretz, *Hell of a Ride*, 197.
192. Greene, *Presidency of George Bush*, 161; Mervin, *George Bush*, 49.
193. Greene, *Presidency of George Bush*, 143.
194. Mervin, *George Bush*, 223.
195. Congressional Quarterly, *CQ Almanac 102nd Congress 2nd Session*, CQ 6A.

196. Naftali, *George H. W. Bush*, 149.
197. Glad, *Making of American Foreign Policy*, 219.

CHAPTER 5

ADVERSITY AND POWER
IN THE FORD PRESIDENCY

Gerald Ford's presidency was marked by a rare degree of political adversity. He came to office as the successor to the disgraced Richard Nixon, who was forced to resign in the face of threatened impeachment over the Watergate scandal. Ford had been an unelected vice president, the first appointed to that office under the provisions of the Twenty-fifth Amendment. He faced a Congress controlled by Democratic majorities, which were enlarged in the 1974 midterm elections only a few months after he assumed office. Following his pardon of Richard Nixon in September 1974, Ford's approval ratings plummeted and he faced cries of outrage over the pardon. He even faced dissension within his own party as conservatives led by Ronald Reagan challenged his policies and leadership. It would be difficult to construct a more difficult set of circumstances under which to be president.

Ford barely enjoyed a honeymoon as president. When he assumed office on August 9, 1974, there was an outpouring of relief across the nation that Richard Nixon had left office quietly and that Ford had moved confidently to replace him. The words he spoke that day captured the mood of the time: "My fellow Americans, our long national nightmare is over. Our Constitution works; our great Republic is a government of laws and not of men. Here the people rule."[1]

For the next month, Ford enjoyed a sort of honeymoon. He experienced "bipartisan goodwill, the trust and affection of a divided nation that didn't know him but was willing to extend him the benefit of the doubt."[2] He sought to repair relations with Congress, reassure allies about continuity in American foreign policy, put his administration in order, and restore public trust. A Gallup poll released shortly after he took office showed Ford leading Senator Ted Kennedy (D-Massachusetts), the presumed front-runner for the 1976 Democratic presidential nomination, by a margin of almost two-to-one.[3] Although he had no electoral base, Ford appeared to be winning support for his presidency.

He also spent a considerable amount of time considering what to do about Richard Nixon. There was no doubt that Nixon would be prosecuted for his participation in Watergate, and Ford faced repeated questions about whether he would pardon Nixon. After consulting his staff about the legal and political issues of a pardon, on September 8, Ford granted a "full, free and absolute pardon unto Richard Nixon."[4]

Reaction to Ford's decision was overwhelmingly negative. "His month-long honeymoon, which he and the Republicans hoped would propel them through the fall elections, crumpled overnight. The next day in Pittsburgh, protestors booed and chanted 'Jail Ford!' as he arrived downtown for a speech on inflation."[5] Editorial opinion and most members of Congress denounced the pardon. Almost overnight, Ford's job approval rating dropped from 71% to 49%, and within days the Senate voted 55–24 for a resolution opposing any further Watergate pardons until defendants had been tried and found guilty and exhausted all appeals.[6] Some Democrats in Congress questioned whether Ford had made a deal to pardon Nixon in exchange for becoming president. In November, Republicans suffered significant setbacks in the midterm elections, despite Ford's energetic campaigning for his party's candidates. Democrats gained forty-three House seats and three Senate seats, giving them powerful majorities in both chambers.

The honeymoon was over. Consequently, Ford's entire tenure as president can be regarded as one of tough times. Yet he nearly won the presidential election of 1976. The transformation of Ford's political fortunes lay in his response to the political adversity he faced.

BARGAINING AND PERSUASION

Gerald Ford made several efforts at bargaining and persuasion, from friendly overtures to his former colleagues on Capitol Hill to dealing with revelations about controversial activities of the CIA. Ford could claim several key successes and demonstrated a willingness to concede to political reality in order to maintain his opportunities for future influence.

Legislative Successes/Compromises/Concessions

Gerald Ford had spent nearly his entire political career in the House of Representatives and was devoted to Congress as an institution. In his first address to Congress, he told the legislators that "my heart will always be here on Capitol Hill...I love the House of Representatives. I revere the traditions of the Senate...As President, within the limits of basic principles, my motto toward the Congress is communication, conciliation, compromise, and cooperation."[7] To emphasize his commitment to working with Congress, he told his former colleagues, "I do not want a honeymoon with you. I want a good marriage."[8] For the remainder of his presidency, he sought to work with Congress despite significant disagreements with its Democratic majorities over policy and national priorities.

Overall, Ford's legislative record reflects his disagreements with Congress. By the measure of average vote concurrence,[9] Ford's position on votes before Congress was supported by a majority of House and Senate members on 58.3% of votes.[10] This record, though showing that Ford was supported by majorities in both chambers slightly more than half of the time, was the lowest average vote concurrence rate for all presidents from Eisenhower through Reagan (Eisenhower 69.9%, Kennedy 84.6%, LBJ 82.2%, Nixon 64.3%, Carter 76.6%, Reagan 62.2%).[11] Table 24 gives the record of congressional vote concurrence with the president during this period.

Table 24. Congressional Vote Conurrence with the President, 1974-1976

Year	Total H&S Concurrence	House Concurrence	# of House Votes	Senate Concurrence	# of Senate Votes
1974	58.2	59.3	54	57.4	68
1975	61.0	50.6	89	71.0	93
1976	53.8	43.1	51	64.2	53
Average	**58.3**	**51.0**		**65.0**	
Total			194		214

Source. Compiled from data in *Vital Statistics on American Politics, 2009–2010* (p. 244) by Harold Stanley and Richard Niemi. Washington, DC: CQ Press, 2010.

Ford achieved some outright successes with Congress, such as the Railroad Act of 1976, which created the Consolidated Rail Corporation (ConRail) to operate the properties of Penn Central and other bankrupt railroads in the Northeast and Midwest. When railroad interests tried to have key deregulation provisions of Ford's plan removed from the bill, he threatened a veto and ultimately won passage of his proposal. In his memoir, Ford pointed to this act as an example of both legislative success and the effectiveness of veto threats for helping the president shape policy.[12]

On several other legislative issues, Ford made concessions to political reality or found a way to compromise on legislation.[13] In December 1974, Congress attached the Jackson-Vanik Amendment to a trade bill; this measure denied most-favored-nation[14] trading status to the Soviet Union unless it allowed a certain quota of Jews to emigrate (mostly to Israel). Ford had tried to convince legislators that the provision would decrease—

rather than increase—Jewish emigration from the Soviet Union (as Soviet retaliation against what it regarded as American meddling in an internal matter) and even pointed to Soviet statements that there would likely be fewer Jews emigrating in 1975 than 1974. But when Congress sent him the amended bill, Ford signed it. As Ford explained his decision in his memoir, "A veto would have been overridden by an overwhelming majority."[15]

In the case of the 1975 Energy Policy and Conservation Act, Ford chose compromise. The bill included a provision for gradually phasing out federal price controls on domestic oil and other price-control measures contrary to Ford's energy policies.[16] Ford was caught between his economic advisors, who wanted those controls lifted immediately, and his political aides, who saw an opportunity for Ford to take the lead in creating a national energy policy. Ford ultimately signed it into law, although he said it was only "half a loaf"[17] and included less reform of energy policy than he had wanted.

Failed Attempts at Legislative Bargaining/Compromise

The focus of Ford's domestic policy agenda was fighting inflation. Faced with the problem of "stagflation" (simultaneous recession and inflation), Ford and his advisors concluded that inflation was a more serious threat to the nation's economic health than the recession that was underway.[18] In his first address to Congress, he declared, "Inflation is domestic enemy number one."[19] In October 1974, he addressed legislators again, calling for a one-year tax surcharge and spending cuts to meet his target budget ceiling. He also called on citizens to join a volunteer effort to "Whip Inflation Now" (or WIN), and he wore a "WIN button" on his lapel as he spoke.[20] Members of Congress from both parties were skeptical of Ford's plan for tax increases and spending cuts, and critics reacted scornfully to WIN. Citizens were more positive about the WIN campaign, requesting thousands of WIN buttons, but it was widely dismissed as a meaningless stunt that would have little real effect on inflation.

Ford's commitment to fighting inflation by budgetary restraint brought him into continuing conflict with Congress over spending, and he used the veto frequently in an effort to force the legislature to cut the budget (more on that strategy later). As the recession wore on, Ford reversed himself on taxes and called in January 1975 for a tax rebate, which again brought conflict with Congress over the appropriate size of a tax cut.

Those early disagreements set the tone for Ford's relations with Congress on the budget. He would clash frequently with legislators over the size of the deficit and chastise them for not exercising necessary fiscal discipline. The results of this veto strategy were largely—but not completely—successful: 75% of his vetoes were sustained. As the historian John Robert Greene summarized the results, "Ford's veto was sustained mainly on spending bills, including Democratic plans for higher farm-price supports, large housing subsidies, and more public-service jobs."[21]

One key failure occurred over the issue of common situs picketing (the practice of picketing an entire construction site even if a union had a disagreement with only one contractor on the site). The Supreme Court had found common situs picketing to be illegal in 1951, and organized labor wanted that decision reversed. Intense conflict between labor and business interests had prevented any resolution. Ford was willing to support limited approval of common situs picketing but not the unrestricted type sought by unions and many Democrats. Responding to a bill introduced in the House in April 1975, Labor Secretary John Dunlop told Ford he could draft an alternative that would satisfy both labor and the construction industry. Ford replied, "If you can do that...I'll support the bill openly."[22] Dunlop produced a workable compromise, and it passed both chambers that fall. But the deal began to unravel when a contractors' group reversed its position and opposed the bill. An intense grassroots lobbying campaign began, and the White House received more letters, telegrams, and phone calls on that issue than any other of Ford's presidency.[23] Ford was caught between rejecting a compromise he had encouraged and signing a bill that could have dangerous political consequences for him in the 1976 Republican primary campaign. He vetoed the bill in January 1976 and Dunlop resigned in protest.

Ford also encountered failure in bargaining with Congress in 1975 over American intervention in the civil war in the African nation of Angola.[24] One faction in that conflict was the Marxist MPLA (*Movimento Popular de Libertação de Angola* [People's Movement for the Liberation of Angola]), which was supported by Cuba. The Ford administration had supported the anti-MPLA factions with limited funds and—according to some sources—collaborated with South African intervention. When the situation reached a crisis point in November 1975, Ford sought greater American assistance for the non-Marxist factions. He requested the smallest appropriation that his advisors told him would be helpful. But the previous covert American support of the anti-MPLA factions had become public knowledge and the resulting controversy led to denunciations of U.S. involvement in the civil war. Consequently, Democratic critics of the administration succeeded in amending a defense bill to prohibit all funding for Angola. In December 1975, American involvement ended, and Ford publicly criticized the Senate's action as a "deep tragedy" for nations who depend on American support.[25]

Other Efforts at Bargaining and Negotiation

In describing presidential power as the power to persuade, Richard Neustadt focused on actions by the chief executive to maximize personal power and influence, to conserve political capital, and to keep open options for the future. By that standard, Gerald Ford made one significant effort to maximize his personal influence and conserve political capital: he appointed a presidential commission to investigate charges of CIA wrongdoing in an effort to forestall a congressional investigation. As we shall see, this effort was unsuccessful.

Revelations about controversial CIA activities had surfaced in 1973 before Ford became president, but by the fall of 1974, so much information about the intelligence agency's activities—domestic intelligence gathering, surveillance of journalists, plans to assassinate foreign heads of state, and spying on the antiwar movement—had been made public that it could not be ignored. The turning point was publication of a story in the *New York Times* in December 1974 that charged that the CIA had engaged in a massive spying operation during the Nixon administration against antiwar protesters and other dissident groups. The story made the issue of the CIA as a "rogue elephant" a national issue.[26]

Ford's reaction was to seek information from the CIA, but he also wanted to forestall a congressional investigation that would remove the issue from the hands of the executive and could be politically damaging as well.[27] He issued Executive Order 11828, establishing a blue-ribbon commission, chaired by Vice President Nelson Rockefeller,[28] to investigate CIA activities.[29]

Despite the president's hopes, the commission did not forestall congressional action. It was bipartisan and included labor leader Lane Kirkland, Ronald Reagan, and other respected figures Ford thought would quiet potential critics. But the commission's report (June 1975) was regarded as too protective of the CIA. The Senate soon voted to conduct its own investigation, headed by Senator Frank Church (D-Idaho), and this inquiry became all that Ford had hoped to avoid: a kind of "witch-hunt" aimed at advancing Church's presidential ambitions and making headlines.[30] The House of Representatives conducted its own investigation,[31] but most of its work was overshadowed by conflict with the White House over leaks of classified information.[32] Ford's efforts to make investigation of the CIA more constructive than sensational had failed.

Ford expended considerable efforts at bargaining and persuasion, but his record was a mixed one. He made several concessions to political reality in dealing with Congress, but he failed to forestall an embarrassing and leaky congressional investigation of the CIA. It is not surprising that throughout his presidency Ford relied on other means for advancing his goals.

EXECUTIVE ACTIONS

Faced with an opposition Congress that was in no mood to appear to be following the lead of an unelected minority president, Ford turned to a range of executive actions to advance his policy goals. These included standard presidential tools such as the veto, pardons and clemency, and executive orders but also came to encompass more controversial actions, such as signing statements, claims of executive privilege, and other assertions of unilateral presidential power.[33]

Constitutional Actions

Ford used the constitutional powers of the presidency in a variety of ways. Most famous, of course, was his pardon of Richard Nixon, but he also deployed the veto in an effort to restrain spending and eventually used signing statements to defy Congress over legislative provisions he believed violated the powers of the presidency.

Vetoes

Several years after leaving office, Gerald Ford reflected on his presidency and observed,

> I set a record for the number of vetoes while I was in the White House…One thing that most people don't realize is—a veto is not a negative action…it is an affirmative action by the president to reflect views of all the people in the country…The veto is action taken by the chief executive to reflect views of the public as a whole.[34]

Ford vetoed sixty-six measures passed by Congress—forty-eight by conventional veto and another eighteen by pocket veto. As his remarks make clear, he viewed the veto as an instrument of presidential power.

Ford's most well-known use of the veto was as a weapon wielded to force Congress to restrain federal spending. His use of the veto as a budget weapon was explicitly a strategic move, employed on the advice of Alan

Greenspan, the chairman of the Council of Economic Advisers.[35] As Ford assistant James Cannon recalled, "Ford was not in office long enough to stop the nation's headlong plunge into national debt, but he did show that a president could slow it down."[36] Ford defended his veto strategy, telling Cannon, "I felt it was the constitutional mandate for the President of the United States, as *the* person who represented everybody, that this executive tool had to be used to prevent the Congress from making unwise judgments."[37] In his memoir, Ford argued that his use of the veto brought policy results. In several cases, he believed, his veto forced Congress to make improvements in legislation.[38]

Pardons and Clemency

Gerald Ford employed the president's broad pardon and clemency power in two high-profile areas while president. The first and most controversial was Ford's "full, free and absolute pardon" of Richard Nixon for "all offenses against the United States" during his tenure as president.[39] This action was a definitively unilateral use of presidential power, exercised over the objections of many members of Congress Ford informed of his decision before its public announcement, as well as contrary recommendations from some of his staff.[40]

Ford granted the pardon only a month after assuming office. According to Ford's own account in his memoir, it took him only a few days after taking office to conclude that he would grant Nixon a pardon; as he explained it, he decided that the nation would be served best by putting Watergate behind it (which a pardon of Nixon would facilitate), and Ford sensed that the disgrace of resignation had caused Nixon to suffer enough.[41] The only remaining question was one of timing, and Ford discussed this subject extensively with his staff—although not with congressional leaders. When he ultimately decided to pardon Nixon immediately and thus avoid a protracted trial and appeals, on September 8, 1974, Ford informed his staff and former colleagues in Congress before making an address to the nation. His press secretary, Jerald terHorst, objected so strongly that he resigned shortly after Ford announced his decision.[42] Congressional leaders vehemently opposed the timing: Senator Barry Goldwater (R-Arizona), House Majority Leader Tip O'Neill (D-Massachusetts), and others suggested that he delay the pardon until a more politically auspicious time (even after the 1976 presidential election) or until Nixon was indicted or even convicted.[43] Nevertheless, Ford announced his decision as soon as his mind was made up, and he paid a high price for it—his job approval rating plummeted, Republicans thought it only made their job in the midterm elections harder (it did), and anti-Nixon Democrats in Congress protested loudly.

Ford also used his power to create and conduct a program of earned clemency for Vietnam-era draft resisters and deserters. Not long after assuming office, he announced his plan for "earned reentry...into an atmosphere of hope, hard work, and mutual trust" for draft evaders and called on the veterans to assist him.[44] Employing his constitutional authority, he established a system whereby those who had fled to Canada to avoid the military draft, or even deserted the military to avoid serving in Vietnam, could earn clemency. Despite criticisms from the right (that he was coddling cowards and turncoats) and from many on the left and among draft evaders (that he was hypocritical for pardoning Nixon but not draft evaders), Ford stuck to his plan.

Gerald Ford saw the primary purpose of his presidency as working to heal the nation in the wake of Watergate and Vietnam. To highlight that purpose, he even entitled his memoir *A Time to Heal*. But to advance these twin goals, he turned to unilateral actions of presidential clemency that neither Congress nor public opinion could undo.

Executive Orders

Ford issued 169 executive orders, covering a range of policy and management issues. Two examples illustrate how he employed orders as instruments of unilateral power. Executive Order 11821 (November 27, 1974) required all legislative proposals, regulations, and rules emanating from the executive branch to include a statement certifying the inflationary impact of the proposed action. But the most visible of his orders was Executive Order 11905 (February 18, 1976), which specifically provided that "No employee of the United States Government shall engage in, or conspire to engage in, political assassination."[45] The order on inflation-impact statements followed a precedent set by Richard Nixon in requiring "Quality of Life Reviews" for proposed federal regulations, and Ford's action would serve as a further precedent for the administrative clearance process instituted by Ronald Reagan and maintained by his successors.[46] The order against assassinations, though somewhat modified after September 11, 2001, has affected American foreign policy—especially antiterrorist operations—since it was signed.

Signing Statements

Ford issued 130 signing statements. Although most of these were rhetorical in nature, he also used them to make statements of policy; in many cases he admonished Congress to show restraint in spending or government regulation. Significantly, he also used signing statements to declare how he would implement a law. The issue that moved him to assert executive authority was the legislative veto.

Before the summer of 1975, Ford's policy-oriented remarks in signing statements tended to be calls for better legislation and reflected his desire for a cooperative working relationship with Congress. After about a year in office, Ford began issuing signing statements that stated he would ignore unconstitutional provisions or instruct his administration to treat them as advisory. In August 1975, upon signing a Social Security bill, Ford declared the legislative veto unconstitutional and instructed the secretary of HEW to "treat this provision of H.R. 7710 simply as a request for information" rather than a binding requirement on his administration.[47] He issued similar instructions in response to other bills with legislative veto provisions.

By February 1976, Ford had had enough of legislative vetoes in bills. Responding to yet another legislative veto imposed by Congress—in this case, the Defense Appropriation Act sought to give the Appropriations and Armed Services Committees in each chamber a veto over the army's procurement of ammunition—the president proclaimed that he would treat it as "a complete nullity. I cannot concur in this legislative encroachment upon the constitutional powers of the executive branch."[48] He no longer couched his unilateralism in the language of cooperation. He had arrived at a use of the signing statement that has come to be associated with later presidents.

Claims of Executive Privilege

Ford invoked executive privilege on several occasions to withhold information from Congress for purposes of national security. In one case, he refused to allow Secretary of State Henry Kissinger to comply with a November 1975 subpoena from the House Select Committee on Intelligence.[49] In another, Ford went even farther. In 1976, a House subcommittee requested information from the American Telephone and Telegraph Company (AT&T) regarding a program of warrantless wiretaps of citizens for reasons of national security. Not only did the president tell the subcommittee chair that divulging such information was contrary to national security, but he acted to prevent AT&T from complying with the subcommittee's request on its own.[50]

Other Actions

Ford undertook other actions that invoked executive power to shape policy. Two significant ones occurred in the fall of 1975. In September, he declared an embargo against sales of American wheat to the Soviet Union. The move was prompted not by Soviet conduct but by domestic concerns: Ford believed that a large grain sale would drive up the cost of food inside the United States, thus exacerbating inflation; he was also responding to union pressures to try to get the Soviet Union to ship grain on American vessels. But the embargo did little more than anger farmers, a key political constituency, and part of Ford's response was to choose a farm-state senator who had opposed the embargo (Bob Dole, R-Kansas) as his running mate for the 1976 presidential election.[51]

His other executive action occurred in October 1975, when he decided to oppose a federal bailout of the financially troubled New York City. The city was nearly bankrupt, and municipal officials and New York's governor met with administration officials that May to discuss the possibility of a federal loan of $1 billion.[52] Treasury Secretary William Simon, believing that bankruptcy was a better course for the city, turned them down, and they sought a meeting with the president. At the meeting a week later, Ford asked for a detailed request in writing. Again, Ford turned down the request. The State of New York intervened, and Vice President Nelson Rockefeller broke with administration policy to advocate federal relief for New York City. Nevertheless, Ford held firm against a bailout. On October 29, he announced that he would veto any federal bailout of New York City.[53] Ford was embarrassed by the furor, which included a newspaper headline accusing him of telling New York to "drop dead."[54]

Eventually, Ford reversed himself and supported the federal plan that involved short-term loans and required more aggressive action by both New York City and State to address the city's financial problems. The reversal seems to have been motivated—at least in part—by a desire to appease New York's Republican senator James Buckley. Buckley, who Ford's advisers feared might support Reagan for the 1976 Republican nomination, was willing to endorse Ford if the president could support some kind of federal help for the city. This concession aided Ford's chances in 1976 but only up to a point—like other actions he took, it could not stop Reagan's challenge to Ford in the nomination race.

Ford employed a range of executive powers to advance his policy and political goals. Although not all of these actions achieved their intended results, Ford was nevertheless able to exercise the power of his office in the face of adversity.

FOREIGN POLICY INITIATIVES AND ACTIONS

Despite frustration in the domestic sphere, Gerald Ford acted to shape American foreign policy. By and large he continued the foreign policy of Richard Nixon. This approach engendered criticism from conservatives, led by Ronald Reagan, but it did not prevent Ford from continuing along the line that he set out with Secretary of State Henry Kissinger.

National Security Directives

President Ford made many decisions in the area of national security policy, and eighty-four of these were formally recorded in National Security Decision Memoranda (NSDM). These instruments were used to set out American foreign policy regarding a particular issue or region of the world, to record presidential approval of security-related research programs, or to order changes in official national security policy. For example, NSDM 280 (signed November 28, 1974) authorized underground nuclear testing for fiscal year 1975 (subsequent NSDMs would cover later years) and declared it to be "Highest National Priority" that testing be accomplished before the Threshold Test Ban Treaty took effect in 1976.[55] Other memoranda demonstrate even more clearly President Ford's willingness to act unilaterally in national security affairs. NSDM 286 (signed February 7, 1975) ordered long-term reductions in American troop levels in Thailand,[56] whereas through NSDM 305 (signed September 15, 1975) the president unilaterally terminated U.S. restrictions on other countries trading with Cuba.[57]

Significant Treaties

As president, Gerald Ford maintained the policy of détente that had been part of Richard Nixon's strategy for creating an architecture of international stability through engagement with the People's Republic of China and arms-control agreements with the Soviet Union. One part of this overall strategy—and less controversial than other aspects of détente—was the conclusion of treaties intended to reduce the threat of nuclear conflict. Ford signed two such treaties. The first was the Protocol to the Anti-Ballistic Missile (ABM) Treaty. This agreement, which had been signed by Richard Nixon in July 1974, was submitted to the Senate by Ford that September (it was approved by the Senate the following year).[58] Its purpose was to reduce the number of ABM sites the United States and Soviet Union could possess from two to one, and it received favorable action by the Senate. The second was the Peaceful Nuclear Explosions Treaty,[59] which governed nuclear tests (the Senate held hearings but did not act on this treaty until Ronald Reagan was president). These agreements continued the overall policy of seeking to reduce nuclear tensions that had characterized American foreign policy since the 1960s.

Executive Agreements

Gerald Ford signed a total of 677 executive agreements. The most famous of these was the Final Act of the Conference on Security and Cooperation in Europe, better known as the "Helsinki Accord." Concluded in 1975, it has been seen as a *"critical contribution to the development of human rights movements in Eastern Europe and the Soviet Union."*[60] It contained language committing its signatories to observe human rights but was dismissed by critics as lacking in enforcement mechanisms. Nevertheless, dissidents in the Soviet Union and elsewhere used the Accord as a shield beneath which they could establish committees to monitor implementation of the agreement, thus beginning the human rights movements that would eventually contribute to the fall of communism.[61]

Uses of Force

Ford became president as opposition to presidential war was peaking. In 1973, Congress had passed the War Powers Resolution over Richard Nixon's veto, with the intention of preventing future military commitments like the one in Vietnam. By December 1974, Congress also proceeded to legislate an end to American participation in the war. Ford complied with the restrictions imposed by Congress but only up to a point —he deployed American military force five times while in office. Three of these instances were to evacuate American personnel from dangerous situations (in Vietnam, Cambodia, and Lebanon), one was to rescue the crew of the USS *Mayaguez* in 1975, and one was to bolster U.S. troops in South Korea following the deaths of two Americans in 1976. Ford never requested congressional approval in any of these cases. He made a general attempt to comply with the reporting provisions of the War Powers Resolution but pointed out after the *Mayaguez* incident (which occurred during a congressional recess) that it was physically impossible to inform all relevant members of Congress of military action as prescribed by the resolution. In fact, he thought it "naive" for some members of Congress to insist on presidential consultation before almost any military action.[62]

The rescue of the *Mayaguez* crew engendered the most controversy. Democrats and liberal critics denounced Ford for ignoring the War Powers Resolution and being too quick to employ force.[63] Ford himself admitted that he was "disturbed a lot" by the number of casualties sustained in accomplishing the rescue (forty-one Americans—more lost than were rescued), as well as the operational problems that almost undid the mission.[64] Ford himself took pride in the incident and believed that it helped to boost national confidence. His approval ratings rose by eleven points.[65] Since that time, however, the *Mayaguez* incident has come to be seen as a military failure even if a political victory for Ford.

Other Foreign Policy Initiatives and Actions

Ford undertook an array of initiatives and actions in foreign policy. These actions included appointing General Alexander Haig (holdover White House chief of staff when Ford took office) to the position of supreme commander of NATO (September 1974), attending a summit meeting with Soviet leader Leonid Brezhnev in Vladivostok (November 1974) at which an accord outlining a future arms-control agreement was signed, sponsoring an agreement on the Sinai peninsula between Egypt and Israel (September 1975), and taking four foreign trips while in office.

Although he acquiesced to Congress in ending American military involvement in Southeast Asia and the Jackson-Vanik Amendment and was frustrated by congressional resistance to U.S. intervention in the Angolan civil war, Ford's conduct of his office demonstrated the chief executive's constitutional preeminence in foreign affairs. He was limited (but not paralyzed) by the assertiveness of the legislature in the post-Watergate period and managed to retain the leading (even if not commanding) role in orchestrating U.S. relations with the world.

ORGANIZATIONAL CHANGES

Upon taking office, Ford inherited Richard Nixon's administration and with it a challenge. Although he thought it would be disruptive to engage in a wholesale restructuring of his administration, he also wanted to signal a change in the government and put together his own team. He named a small transition team, headed by Donald Rumsfeld, to assist him in taking over the White House. Ford and Rumsfeld set January 1975 as the deadline for completing cabinet and staff changes, and most of these were accomplished through voluntary resignations or appointments to different positions.[66]

Ford's approach to assembling an administration took into account his political situation and his desire to build an effective team and restore government integrity, all while avoiding unnecessary fights over controversial appointments. He brought in new staff members to make the White House his own, including Rumsfeld as chief of staff (although without that title), and set about constructing a cabinet. To that end, he kept some Nixon appointees; in particular, he persuaded Treasury Secretary William Simon and Agriculture Secretary Earl Butz to remain in their posts.[67] But he also chose new cabinet officers with an eye toward enhancing administration credibility with Congress and the public.

The key position in this regard was that of attorney general; the Justice Department had—as Ford himself put it—"lasting scars" from Watergate.[68] He moved the incumbent attorney general, William Saxbe, to an ambassadorship,[69] giving himself an opportunity to depoliticize the Justice Department and restore its morale and integrity. He found his candidate in Edward H. Levi, president of the University of Chicago and a widely respected legal scholar. After convincing Levi that he would respect Levi's independence in that job, Ford then turned to selling the nomination to the Senate. To accomplish this task, he met privately with members of the Senate Judiciary Committee. Acknowledging the fear of some senators that Levi was a liberal academician, Ford argued, "He is not a liberal academic who is going to give the store away. I want both of you to know that when we asked, 'What's wrong with Levi?' we were told, 'He's too tough. He's too hard-headed.'"[70] Ford thus got the endorsement of the committee's Democratic chair and ranking Republican, and Levi became attorney general.

Ford made other changes that helped accomplish his goals. He moved James Lynn from the post of secretary of Housing and Urban Development to serve as director of the Office of Management and Budget, naming Carla Hills to replace him at HUD. He nominated William Coleman, a prominent African American Republican, to serve as transportation secretary. And he named John Dunlop, an economist and veteran of the Nixon administration, to be secretary of labor. Ford was now satisfied that "the Cabinet took on a new, more independent look."[71]

Ford's reshaped his administration in early November 1975. Under mounting criticism from conservatives and facing a challenge for the 1976 Republican nomination from Ronald Reagan, Ford made a number of personnel changes that came to be known as the "Halloween Massacre." He asked Vice President Nelson Rockefeller (a stalwart of the Republican Party's liberal wing) to withdraw as his running mate for 1976, then fired Defense Secretary James Schlesinger, CIA director William Colby, and Commerce Secretary Rogers Morton. Henry Kissinger, who was both secretary of state and national security advisor, was relieved of the security advisor's job. The new team included Rumsfeld as defense secretary,

George H. W. Bush as CIA director, Elliot Richardson (a moderate) as commerce secretary, General Brent Scowcroft as national security advisor, and Dick Cheney as chief of staff.[72]

The shakeup did little to help Ford politically. Conservatives disliked the dismissal of Schlesinger, while Reagan said of Kissinger's loss of one job, "I am not appeased."[73] The sweeping changes seemed to backfire and create the appearance of an administration in trouble. Reaction from commentators was almost uniformly fierce,[74] and the Gallup poll showed Ford falling behind in the 1976 nomination race after the "Halloween Massacre" was announced.[75]

GOING PUBLIC

Like his predecessor, Gerald Ford employed public politics to announce decisions to the nation and to cultivate public support for his policies. With the 1976 election drawing near, he stepped up his public appearances as he sought the Republican presidential nomination and then the presidency itself.

Several of Ford's addresses to the nation were announcements of decisions, with the secondary intention of justifying them. In September 1974, he made a national address to announce his decision to pardon Richard Nixon and to explain it, but the speech was tremendously unsuccessful. Later that month, he announced his clemency plan for Vietnam-era draft evaders, which conservatives regarded as too lenient and antiwar critics considered too stingy. In May 1975, Ford addressed the nation on the recovery of the USS *Mayaguez*, which was received with widespread approval. Except for this last appearance, these announcements did little to improve Ford's standing or support for controversial decisions.

Other incidences of going public were intended to make direct appeals for public and congressional support for Ford's policies. In October 1974, he appeared before Congress to announce his WIN program and call for a national campaign against inflation. Though Ford was heartened by a positive public reaction to the WIN program, there was little substance to the WIN campaign and it was dismissed as little more than a gimmick. Ford made other national addresses—one in January 1975 on energy and the economy, a State of the Union address that same month, and an address to Congress on foreign policy in April 1975—but these had mostly modest or mixed results.

Ford's efforts at going public accelerated in 1976, as he campaigned to win the White House in his own right. These activities included the usual campaign speeches and rallies, as well as appearances on CBS's *Face the Nation* and NBC's *Today* show and three radio addresses. Ford's campaign activities can be characterized as largely successful: after falling behind Reagan in November 1975 in polling for the 1976 Republican nomination, he managed over the next nine months to fight his way back and win his party's endorsement in August 1976. Then he went on to close a thirty-three-point lead by Democratic nominee Jimmy Carter. On the eve of the election, pollsters saw the race as effectively even. In the end, Ford lost to Carter by two percentage points (50.1% for Carter, 48% for Ford).[76] Considering the low point Ford had reached—his public approval rating had been only 39% at the end of 1975[77]—Ford was a successful campaigner.

UNCONVENTIONAL ACTIONS

Ford engaged in one noteworthy unconventional action while president. In the wake of his pardon of Richard Nixon, Democrats in Congress introduced resolutions calling for an investigation of the pardon. Many raised questions about whether Nixon and Ford had made some kind of "deal"[78] by which Nixon would step aside so Ford could become president, in exchange for which Ford would pardon his predecessor. The ensuing controversy threatened to paralyze Ford's presidency, and he volunteered to "go up to Capitol Hill, testify and spell it all out."[79] On

October 17, 1974, Ford appeared before a subcommittee of the House Judiciary Committee to make a statement and answer questions on the pardon. He was the first president since Abraham Lincoln to appear before a congressional committee in this fashion. He denied making any kind of deal with Nixon or his aides and responded—sometimes testily—to intense questioning from committee members. "There was no deal, period, under no circumstances," he told them.[80] Ford's appearance did little to satisfy critics angry about the Nixon pardon, but it did manage to avert a crippling debate on the question of a deal.[81]

OUTCOME AND ASSESSMENT

Beginning with his pardon of Richard Nixon, Gerald Ford experienced some of the toughest times that a president can face. Yet, over the next two-and-a-half years, he managed to shape policy, deal with a sometimes hostile Congress, engender public support, and go on to win his party's nomination and close a gap of more than thirty percentage points to narrowly lose the 1976 election. Moreover, as time passed, Ford's presidency would come to be remembered in a more positive light than it was regarded at the time.

Did the President's Actions Make Any Difference?

The evidence from the Ford presidency suggests that his conduct of office did make a difference. He achieved some success with bargaining and persuasion. His use of executive power, especially the veto, made him much more than a caretaker in office. He asserted the power of the presidency to act, whether in executive orders, signing statements, or claims of executive privilege.

Table 25 summarizes the president's response to adversity.

Table 25a. Summarizing the President's Response to Adversity—Ford Presidency

Type of response	Summary data & significant examples
1. **Bargaining & persuasion**	*House & Senate concurrence with president—average for Ford presidency:* 58.3% *Legislative successes/compromises/concessions:* • Jackson-Vanik Amendment (1974, concession) • Revenue Adjustment Act of 1975 (concession) • Energy Policy & Conservation Act of 1975 (concession) • 1976 defense budget (compromise) • ConRail (1976) (success, after veto threat) *Failed attempts at legislative bargaining/compromise:* • 1974: Restraint on spending (led to veto strategy) • 1975: Energy & economy program • 1975: Common situs picketing bill • 1975: Congress prohibits intervention in civil war in Angola *Other:* • Rockefeller Commission on CIA (failed to forestall congressional investigation) • Cabinet: Assembling Cabinet in early months of administration (successful) versus "Halloween Massacre" reorganization of Cabinet & senior staff (Nov 1975, unsuccessful)
Outcome of case: *Ford narrowly lost the 1976 election; he left office with a 53% job approval rating and over time he came to be admired even by former political adversaries*		

Table 25b. Summarizing the President's Response to Adversity—Ford Presidency (Cont.)

2. Executive actions **-constitutional**	*Vetoes:* 48 regular (75% sustained), 18 pocket *Pardons & clemency:* 409 • Sept 1974: Nixon pardon • Sept 1974-Sept 1975: Clemency program for Vietnam era draft evaders *Executive orders*: 169 • 11905—Clarified authority and responsibilities of US intelligence agencies and prohibited them from participating in any assassination plots *Proclamations:* 175 *Signing statements:* 130 • Feb 1976: Dept. of Defense Appropriation Act—declared that president would treat provision he regarded as unconstitutional as "complete nullity" *Claims of executive privilege:* • Nov 1975: Refused to allow State Dept to turn over to House Intelligence Committee documents on covert actions since 1961 • Feb 1976: Refused to allow AT&T to give House Commerce Comm info on warrantless wiretaps
-other actions	Sept 1975: Grain embargo against Soviet Union Oct 1975: Opposed (thus effectively blocking) federal bailout of New York City
Outcome of case: *Ford narrowly lost the 1976 election; he left office with a 53% job approval rating and over time he came to be admired even by former political adversaries*	

Table 25c. Summarizing the President's Response to Adversity—Ford Presidency (Cont.)

Type of response	Summary data & significant examples
3. **Foreign policy initiatives & actions**	*National security directives:* 84 • NSDM 305—Terminated US restrictions on 3rd countries trading with Cuba (Sept 1975) • NSDM 345—Authorized US development and acquisition of "non-nuclear anti-satellite capability" to "nullify certain militarily important Soviet space systems" (January 18, 1977—two days before leaving office) *Significant treaties:* • September 1974: Protocol to ABM Treaty • July 1976: Peaceful Nuclear Explosions Treaty *Executive agreements:* 677 • Aug 1975: Final Act of the Conference on Security and Cooperation in Europe—aka, "Helsinki Accord" on human rights in Eastern Europe and the Soviet Union *Uses of force:* 5 • Evacuations of US personnel—Vietnam (1975), Cambodia (1975), & Lebanon (1976) • *Mayaguez* incident, 1975 • Korea—US forces dispatched after two Americans killed, 1976

Outcome of case: Ford narrowly lost the 1976 election; he left office with a 53% job approval rating and over time he came to be admired even by former political adversaries

Table 25d. Summarizing the President's Response to Adversity—Ford Presidency (Cont.)

Type of response	Summary data & significant examples
3. Foreign policy initiatives & actions (Cont.)	*Other:* • Sept 1974: Appd Alexander Haig as NATO Supreme Commander • Nov 1974: US-Soviet summit & accord on nuclear arms control, Vladivostok • 1974-76: 4 foreign trips • Sept 1975: US negotiated Egypt-Israel accord on Sinai peninsula
4. Organizational changes	Sept 1974: Donald Rumsfeld as staff coordinator, job of staff chief downgraded Fall 1974-early 1975: Assembling Cabinet Nov 1975: "Halloween Massacre" of Cabinet/senior staff, VP Rockefeller dropped from 1976 from 1976 Republican ticket
5. Going public	Sept 1974: Announce Nixon pardon Sept 1974: Announce clemency program for Vietnam era draft evaders Oct 1974: Address to Congress on WIN (Whip Inflation Now) program Jan 1975: Address to nation on energy & economic programs Jan 1975: State of the Union Address Apr 1975: Address to Congress on foreign policy May 1975: Remarks to nation on recovery of USS *Mayaguez*

Outcome of case: Ford narrowly lost the 1976 election; he left office with a 53% job approval rating and over time he came to be admired even by former political adversaries

Table 25e. Summarizing the President's Response to Adversity—Ford Presidency (Cont.)

5. Going public **(Cont.)**	Sept 1974: Announcement of Nixon pardon Sept 1974: Announcement of clemency program for Vietnam era draft evaders Oct 1974: Address to Congress July 1975: Announcement of candidacy for 1976 Republican nomination for president Jan 1976: Briefing for reporters on FY 1977 budget Feb-Aug 1976: campaign activities for Republican nomination, including appearance on "Face the Nation" & nomination acceptance speech Sept-Nov 1976: campaign activities for presidential election, including appearance on "Today" & 3 radio addresses (on peace, crime, & future goals for America)
6. Unconventional actions?	Oct 17, 1974: Ford appeared before House Judiciary Committee to answer questions about Nixon pardon

Outcome of case: Ford narrowly lost the 1976 election; he left office with a 53% job approval rating and over time he came to be admired even by former political adversaries

Despite the setback of the 1975 Angolan civil war, Ford was able to conduct foreign policy along the lines he wanted to pursue, even in the face of criticism from conservatives. His engagement in "going public" was not always successful, but it paid off for him in 1976 when it was really needed. And his unconventional appearance before the House Judiciary Committee in October 1974 squelched charges of a deal with Nixon over the pardon. In short, Ford's actions improved his situation and addressed the political adversity he faced.

How Did Adversity Limit What the President Could Do or Accomplish?

Of course adversity limited Ford's presidency. This fact is especially apparent in his efforts to address the faltering economy through budgetary restraint. Had Ford been blessed with a Republican-controlled Congress (and maybe an electoral base), he would not have had to rely on a veto strategy to shape domestic policy. He might not have been limited in dealing with the civil war in Angola in 1975. He probably would not have had to endure the spectacle of the two congressional investigations of the CIA. And had Ford begun his presidency through election, he would have had a preexisting political base that might have forestalled Ronald Reagan's nearly successful challenge for the 1976 Republican nomination. Ford's presidency would certainly have benefited from a different set of political conditions.

Did Adversity Open Opportunities in Any Way?

Adversity did open opportunities for Gerald Ford. Because of the unusual circumstances that made him president—and denied him the usual political base for being president—Ford faced both the challenge and the opportunity to deal with Nixon and Watergate in a way that might not have been possible had he come to office after a campaign in which a Nixon pardon was an issue. Ford saw the issue of the Nixon pardon as one that he alone needed to address, and he thought that it was his responsibility to do the right thing despite any political fallout.[82]

What Powers Did the President Retain Despite Adversity, and How Did the President Exercise Them in a Relevant Way?

Despite his adverse political circumstances, Gerald Ford retained a range of presidential powers: the veto, the pardon and clemency power, executive orders, proclamations, the ability to issue signing statements, and executive privilege. His vetoes were sustained three-fourths of the time, but he also used the veto threats to pressure Congress to shape legislation in a way that would make it more acceptable to him. He also retained a large measure of control over the personnel of his cabinet and at least the opportunity to use the presidency as a "bully pulpit." He held the president's constitutional preeminence in foreign policy and used it to continue a policy he thought was in the nation's best interest. Ford used the prominence of the presidency and the political resources of the Republican Party to grasp the nomination of his party, even in the face of a serious challenge. He was not a passive president.

Assessment

Table 26 presents an assessment of how significant the various factors examined in this case were to its outcome. Of the six factors under review, only two can be said to have been highly significant to Ford's conduct of his presidency or his political fortune. Ford's use of unilateral executive powers and control over foreign policy had the greatest significance for influencing this case. Had he not used those powers and been a passive, caretaker president, then it is unlikely he would have been a serious contender for the 1976 Republican nomination or nearly won the election that year. But Ford was able to mount a serious campaign because he had been a serious and active president.

Ford's efforts at bargaining and persuasion met with limited success. Nevertheless, whereas his efforts were especially important for helping him assemble a cabinet at the outset of his presidency, bargaining and persuasion were ultimately less significant to Ford's presidency than his use of executive power and his conduct of foreign policy. Despite Richard Neustadt's claim about presidential power being the power to persuade, Ford was more persuasive with Congress because he was willing to use the veto and could make his vetoes stick.

Table 26. Assessing the President's Response to Adversity—Ford Presidency

Outcome	Response types (and significance)
Ford narrowly lost the 1976 election; he left office with a 53% job approval rating and over time he came to be admired even by former political adversaries	1. **Bargaining & persuasion:** As a former legislator, Ford wanted to have a productive relationship with Congress—he was frustrated by congressional resistance to his attempts to hold down spending and to conduct foreign policy **(Significance: Low)**
	2. **Executive actions:** Ford found that unilateral executive powers were important to his conduct of office in several areas **(Significance: High)**
	3. **Foreign policy initiatives & actions:** Like other presidents, Ford found that foreign policy demanded time and attention, and that unilateral executive powers were significant to his conduct of it **(Significance: High)**
	4. **Organizational changes:** Reorganization in Nov 1975 politically costly **(Significance: Mixed)**
	5. **Going public:** Ford made a limited number of public addresses and they were of limited value; campaign activities in 1976 were more effective **(Significance: Mixed)**
	6. **Unconventional actions:** Appearance before House committee helped quell rumors of a pardon deal, but did little to dampen furor over pardon itself **(Significance: Low)**

Faced with serious political adversity, Ford managed to keep his presidency from being a cipher or an asterisk. He conducted it in a fashion that employed the power of the office despite the political limitations that might have hobbled him. None of this is to suggest that Gerald Ford dominated politics and policy during his presidency as Franklin Roosevelt or Ronald Reagan had done, but he conducted himself forcefully despite the tough times that he faced.

ENDNOTES

1. Gerald Ford, "Gerald Ford's Remarks on Taking the Oath of Office as President," August 9, 1974, accessed January 14, 2010, http://www.ford.utexas.edu/LIBRARY/speeches/740001.htm.
2. Barry Werth, *31 Days* (New York: Doubleday, 2006), 331.
3. Ibid., 308.
4. Quoted in Gerald Ford, *A Time to Heal* (New York: Harper and Row, 1979), 178.
5. Werth, *31 Days*, 331.
6. Ford, *Time to Heal*, 180.
7. Gerald Ford, "Address to a Joint Session of the Congress," August 12, 1974, accessed January 14, 2010, http://www.presidency.ucsb.edu/ws/index.php?pid = 4694&st = &st1 = .
8. Ibid.
9. "Vote concurrence is measured by the number of times a majority of members of Congress vote with the president's position on roll call votes. Member concurrence is the percentage of members who agree with the president's position on a roll call vote." Ragsdale, *Vital Statistics*, 362.
10. Ibid., 383.
11. Ibid., 383–384.
12. Ford, *Time to Heal*, 366.
13. This paragraph is drawn mostly from Ford, *Time to Heal*, 225.
14. "Most-favored-nation" trading status means that the United States gives to a country with this status the most favorable trade arrangements (e.g., a lower tariff on imports) it extends to any other country.
15. Ford, *Time to Heal*, 225.
16. This paragraph is drawn mostly from Ford, *Time to Heal*, 340–342.
17. Ford, *Time to Heal*, 341.
18. John Robert Greene, *The Presidency of Gerald R. Ford* (Lawrence: University Press of Kansas, 1995), 71.
19. Ford, "Address to a Joint Session."
20. Greene, *Presidency of Gerald R. Ford*, 72.
21. Ibid., 77.
22. Ford, *Time to Heal*, 342.
23. Greene, *Presidency of Gerald R. Ford*, 97. See also Ford, *Time to Heal*, 342.

24. This paragraph draws mostly from Graeme S. Mount, with Mark Gauthier, *895 Days that Changed the World: The Presidency of Gerald R. Ford* (Montreal: Black Rose Books, 2006), 45–53.
25. Gerald Ford, "Remarks on Senate Action to Prohibit United States Assistance to Angola," December 19, 1975, accessed January 15, 2010, http://www.presidency.ucsb.edu/ws/index.php?pid = 5447&st = &st1 = .
26. Greene, *Presidency of Gerald R. Ford*, 103–104.
27. Ford, *Time to Heal*, 230.
28. Ibid.
29. Exec. Ord. 11828, January 4, 1975. http://www.presidency.ucsb.edu/ws/index.php?pid = 23910. Accessed August 20, 2012.
30. Greene, *Presidency of Gerald R. Ford*, 110.
31. This paragraph draws mostly from Gerald K. Haines, "The Pike Committee Investigations and the CIA: Looking for a Rogue Elephant," *Studies in Intelligence* (Winter 1998–1999), Center for the Study of Intelligence, Central Intelligence Agency, accessed January 19, 2010, https://www.cia.gov/library/center-for-the-study-of-intelligence/csi-publications/csi-studies/studies/winter98_99/art07.html.
32. Andrew Downer Crain, *The Ford Presidency: A History* (Jefferson, NC: McFarland & Co., 2009), 126–127.
33. This section draws heavily from Ryan J. Barilleaux and David Zellers, "Executive Unilateralism in the Ford and Carter Presidencies," in *The Unitary Executive and the Modern Presidency*, ed. Ryan J. Barilleaux and Christopher S. Kelley (College Station: Texas A&M University Press, 2010).
34. Gerald Ford, "Presidential Conversations on the Constitution," accessed January 21, 2010, http://www.whyy.org/tv12/presidents/issues.html#vp.
35. Greene, *Presidency of Gerald R. Ford*, 77.
36. James Cannon, *Time and Chance* (New York: HarperCollins, 1994), 403.
37. Quoted in ibid., 403. Emphasis in original.
38. Ford, *Time to Heal*, 339.
39. Werth, *31 Days*, 221. See also Ford, *Time to Heal*, 179.
40. Werth, *31 Days*, 316–319.
41. Ford, *Time to Heal*, 160.
42. Werth, *31 Days*, 328.
43. Ibid., 317–318.
44. Ford, *Time to Heal*, 142.

45. Gerald Ford, "Executive Order 11905," February 18, 1976, accessed February 15, 2007, http://www.presidency.ucsb.edu/ws/index.php?pid = 59348.

46. See Barilleaux, *Post-Modern Presidency*, 85–86.

47. Gerald Ford, "Statement on Signing a Bill Amending Child Support Provisions of the Social Security Act," August 11, 1975, accessed February 6, 2007, http://www.presidency.ucsb.edu/ws/index.php?pid = 5 168&st = &st1 =

48. Gerald Ford, "Statement on Signing the Department of Defense Appropriation Act, 1976," February 10, 1976, accessed February 13, 2007, http://www.presidency.ucsb.edu/ws/index.php?pid = 6277.

49. Fisher, *Politics of Executive Privilege*, 247–248.

50. Ibid., 246–247.

51. Crain, *Ford Presidency*, 112. See also Ford, *Time to Heal*, 312–313.

52. Greene, *Presidency of Gerald R. Ford*, 91.

53. Ibid., 93.

54. Ibid., 94.

55. National Security Decision Memorandum 280, November 28, 1974, accessed February 15, 2007, http://www.fordlibrarymuseum.gov/library/document/0310/nsdm280.pdf.

56. National Security Decision Memorandum 286, February 7, 1975, accessed February 15, 2007, http://www.fordlibrarymuseum.gov/library/document/0310/nsdm286.pdf.

57. National Security Decision Memorandum 305, September 15, 2007, accessed February 15, 2007, http://www.fordlibrarymuseum.gov/library/document/0310/nsdm305.pdf.

58. Gerald Ford, "Message to the Senate Transmitting the Protocol to the United States–Soviet Antiballistic Missile Treaty," September 19, 1974, accessed January 25, 2010, http://www.presidency.ucsb.edu/ws/index.php?pid = 4722&st = ABM+treaty&st1 = .

59. Gerald Ford, "Message to the Senate Transmitting United States–Soviet Treaty and Protocol on the Limitation of Underground Nuclear Explosions," July 29, 1976, accessed January 25, 2010, http://www.presidency.ucsb.edu/ws/index.php?pid = 6245&st = treaty&st1 = .

60. Anthony Clark Arend, "Gerald Ford and the Helsinki Accord," December 27, 2006, accessed February 15, 2007, http://explore.georgetown.edu/blogs/?id = 21610. Emphasis in original.

61. See, for example, "Moscow Helsinki Group's 30th Anniversary," accessed February 15, 2007, http://2001-2009.state.gov/r/pa/prs/ps/2006/66134.htm.

62. Ford, *Time to Heal*, 283.

63. See ibid., 283.

64. Ibid.

65. Ibid., 283. See also Richard Pious, *Why Presidents Fail* (Lanham, MD: Rowman & Littlefield, 2008), ch. 4. Pious examines in detail the problems that made the *Mayaguez* incident a military failure. But the bottom-line outcome of the affair—the recovery of the *Mayaguez* crew—crowded out the heavy costs of the action in the public's mind. Military officers, determined to conduct missions effectively and efficiently—and with a minimal loss of life—study the incident as an operational failure.

66. Ford, *Time to Heal*, 234.

67. Ibid., 238.

68. Ibid., 237.

69. Ibid., 238.

70. Ibid., 237.

71. Ibid., 241.

72. See Greene, *Presidency of Gerald R. Ford*, 161. See also Ford, *Time to Heal*, 320–331.

73. Quoted in Greene, *Presidency of Gerald R. Ford*, 161.

74. Quoted in Ford, *Time to Heal*, 330–331.

75. Ford, *Time to Heal*, 331.

76. Crain, *Ford Presidency*, 281.

77. Ragsdale, *Vital Statistics*, 201.

78. Ford, *Time to Heal*, 196.

79. Ibid., 197.

80. Gerald Ford, "Statement and Responses to Questions from Members of the House Judiciary Committee Concerning the Pardon of Richard Nixon," October 17, 1974, accessed January 26, 2010, http://www.presidency.ucsb.edu/ws/index.php?pid = 4471&st = &st1 = .

81. See Crain, *Ford Presidency*, 67.

82. Although the fallout at the time was enormous, over time Ford's decision was vindicated and many of his former critics came to praise the decision. Senator Ted Kennedy, D-Massachusetts, who had been an especially fierce critic of the pardon in 1974, in 2001 personally presented to Gerald Ford the John F. Kennedy Library and Museum's "Profiles in Courage" Award for making the pardon. At the award ceremony, Kennedy said,

"[T]ime has a way of clarifying past events, and now we see that President Ford was right. His courage and dedication to our country made it possible for us to begin the process of healing and put the tragedy of Watergate behind us." "Remarks by Senator Edward M. Kennedy," John F. Kennedy Presidential Library and Museum, May 21, 2001, accessed January 26, 2010, http://www.jfklibrary.org/Education+and+Public+Programs/ Profile+in+Courage+Award/Award+Recipients/Gerald+Ford/Remarks +by+Senator+Edward+M.+Kennedy.htm.

Chapter 6

Tough Times Point to a New View of Presidential Power

As the case studies have shown, tough times are a common situation for presidents. Since the end of World War II, every chief executive except John Kennedy has experienced at least one period of political adversity while in office. In consequence, our investigation of how presidents responded to tough times has implications beyond these specific cases; adversity is a frequent companion of the president, perhaps more so than the political dominance that we so often associate with heroic presidents. Chief executives are often called upon to respond to those situations in which they lack key elements (or most elements) of political capital and persuasive influence. What powers does the president retain? What resources can the chief executive draw on? Is it the case, as George W. Bush told Bob Woodward, that "[t]here's always another card?"

Results of the Case Studies

Table 27 brings together the results of the eleven case studies. It summarizes how each of the factors explored in these cases affected their outcomes. Although we explored only eleven cases of White House experience, they provide interesting and significant evidence about the sources of presidential power and its exercise. Several points stand out.

Table 27a. Comparing Cases of Presidential Response to Political Adversity

Case	Persuas	Exec	Foreign Policy	Outcome
Unmandate				
Truman 1947-48	mixed	high	high	Won 1948 election; Dems won control of House & Senate
Eisenhower 1955-56	mixed	low	high	Won 1956 election
Clinton 1995-96	mixed	high	high	Won 1996 election
GW Bush 2007-08	mixed	high	high	33% approval at end of term; foreign policy largely intact
Scandal				
Nixon/ Watergate	mixed	high	high	Resigned—impeachment threat; 24% approval Aug 1974
Reagan/ Iran-Contra	low	high	high	Survived; 58% approval in Jan 1988; his VP won 1988 presidential election
Clinton/ Lewinsky	mixed	high	high	Survived impeachment; high approval throughout period
National Division				
Johnson 1967-68	mixed	high	high	Did not run in 1968; 35% job approval in Aug 1968
Carter 1979-80	mixed	high	high	Lost 1980 election; 31% job approval in Nov 1980
GHW Bush 1992	low	high	high	Lost 1992 election; 37% job approval in Nov 1992
Ford	low	high	high	Narrowly lost 1976 election

"Significance" refers to importance, not level of activity. For example, George H.W. Bush made little effort at public politics during the period of division in 1992, and this inactivity was significant for affecting public attitudes toward him.

First, in six of these cases the president recovered from tough times. In five cases (Truman, Eisenhower, Clinton/1995–1996, Reagan, and

Clinton/Lewinsky) the president triumphed over adversity, and Ford recovered from the deep low of late 1974 to nearly win the 1976 election.

Table 27b. Comparing Cases of Presidential Response to Political Adversity

Case	Organiz	Public	Unconv	Outcome
Unmandate				
Truman 1947-48	low	high	high	Won 1948 election; Dems won control of House & Senate
Eisenhower 1955-56	N/A	high	N/A	Won 1956 election
Clinton 1995-96	high	high	high	Won 1996 election
GW Bush 2007-08	mixed	low	N/A	33% approval at end of term; foreign policy largely intact
Scandal				
Nixon/ Watergate	high	high	high	Resigned—impeachment threat; 24% approval Aug 1974
Reagan/ Iran-Contra	high	high	high	Survived; 58% approval in Jan 1988; his VP won 1988 presidential election
Clinton/ Lewinsky	low	high	low	Survived impeachment; high approval throughout period
National Division				
Johnson 1967-68	low	high	high	Did not run in 1968; 35% job approval in Aug 1968
Carter 1979-80	high	high	mixed	Lost 1980 election; 31% job approval in Nov 1980
GHW Bush 1992	low	high	low	Lost 1992 election; 37% job approval in Nov 1992
Ford	low	mixed	low	Narrowly lost 1976 election

"Significance" refers to importance, not level of activity. For example, George H.W. Bush made little effort at public politics during the period of division in 1992, and this inactivity was significant for affecting public attitudes toward him.

Bill Clinton also demonstrated again that he was the "Comeback Kid," recovering from the unmandate of 1994 to win reelection in 1996, then surviving impeachment in the Lewinsky scandal and maintaining strong job approval ratings. In all of these recoveries, bargaining and persuasion played at best a mixed role in the outcome. More important were executive actions, foreign policy, going public, and (in two cases) unconventional presidential actions.

The cases suggest other patterns. Three of the unmandate presidents won reelection, whereas George W. Bush was in the last two years of his tenure. He left office with low approval ratings but his foreign policy largely intact. Because he was the only one of these presidents ineligible for reelection, his case raises the tantalizing question of how a reelection bid might have affected his actions or his political fortunes. Nevertheless, it is not inevitable that a president will recover from an unmandate—a fact relevant to the unfinished Obama case—but it is also not the case that an unmandate is a final judgment on a presidency.

In the scandal cases, two chief executives (Reagan and Clinton) survived, whereas Nixon was driven from office under the threat of impeachment. Reagan and Clinton both employed unilateral presidential powers to govern during these scandals, and Reagan created the Special Review Board. The board did not prevent a congressional investigation, but it—along with a decision not to invoke executive privilege—helped diffuse any charges of a cover-up. Clinton also used unilateral powers and like Reagan continued active engagement in foreign affairs. Three cases are too few from which to make significant generalizations, but it also true that scandal does not necessarily finish a presidency.

The presidents facing national division did not recover. LBJ decided not to run in 1968 after being embarrassed in the New Hampshire primary, and Carter and George H. W. Bush lost their bids for reelection. Perhaps the problem facing each president was that national division ran so deep, even into the president's own party, that it was impossible to recover. Or it could be that other factors were at work: the relative political skills of the presidents involved, stubbornness on the part of the president, or even the difficulty of the policy problems each faced. In any event, three cases are too few on which to base significant generalizations, so it is not necessarily the case that national division dooms a presidency. But it presented some of the most difficult circumstances faced by the ten presidents in these cases.

Gerald Ford's experience also involved some of the most adverse circumstances a president has encountered. Despite the lack of an electoral base, a strong reaction against the Nixon pardon, and significant Republican losses in the 1974 elections (almost to the point of being seen as an unmandate), Ford was able to direct foreign policy and to put his imprint on domestic policy. Certainly, Ford had to make concessions to Congress and often clashed with it, but he was a significant force in the politics of the time and nearly won the presidency in his own right. Ford engaged in bargaining and persuasion, but when that failed him, he employed unilateral presidential powers to advance his policy and political goals.

The cases of Gerald Ford and these other presidents provide evidence of the powers and limitations that accompany residence in the White House. Eleven cases do not represent the entire experience of the post–World War II presidency, but they cover ten of the twelve chief executives in this period. Moreover, these cases offer examples of presidents drawing on sources of power beyond bargaining and persuasion; they were able both to revive their political fortunes and to advance their goals through actions that Neustadt dismissed as "command." In short, these cases suggest that a better understanding of presidential power is in order.

TOWARD A NEW VIEW OF PRESIDENTIAL POWER

Traditionally, scholars (and presidents) talked of the "president's powers,"[1] focusing on the veto power, the message power, the power as commander in chief, the treaty power, and other specific powers vested by the Constitution. Later, Richard Neustadt taught generations of analysts to view "presidential power" not only as the "power to persuade" but as a single thing that depended primarily on the president's "professional reputation" and skill at bargaining and persuasion. Each of these approaches had its limits for illuminating political reality: the legalistic approach tended to view the exercise of the president's powers in an apolitical fashion, underemphasizing or even ignoring the political context in which presidents act (consider Lincoln's care in timing the use of his powers), whereas the Neustadt "power to persuade" approach tended to underemphasize the constitutional and ethical context of presidential actions (a point that led to criticisms of Neustadt in the 1970s, to which he felt compelled to respond in a chapter added to *Presidential Power*[2]), and Neustadt's dismissal of "command" leads to a distorted understanding of how presidents operate and the bases of their influence.

In all of the cases, adversity made it difficult for the chief executive to engage in the kind of persuasion that Neustadt prescribed. But adversity did not prevent the president from employing other powers that fit the category of "command"—even to the point of overcoming that adversity. Foreign policy was particularly significant in several cases and involved chief executives taking advantage of their constitutional and institutional advantages in this area. In addition, most of these presidents also engaged in unilateral actions and going public. The six cases of recovery featured a chief executive who used what Neustadt called "command" to revive his political fortunes, to advance his goals, and to govern in some respect. These powers were not just personal powers of persuasion but powers rooted in the Constitution, law, and the institution of the presidency, as well as in political and personal factors.

What was going on in these cases, if not just power through persuasion? The answer is that presidents have other power resources than just persuasion and implicit powers of the office. Persuasion is one source of presidential power, but it is not the only one. In the case studies, we explored situations in which the chief executives were able to gain leverage by applying various power resources toward their goals. Harry Truman, Gerald Ford, and others all gained leverage by using the powers of "command." Indeed, it was only through an exercise of "command" (shutting down the government through the veto) that Bill Clinton revived his presidency.

If persuasion is not the sole basis of presidential power, then what is? As we suggested previously, the power of the chief executive is more a matter of leverage in particular situations than a general form of personal power or prestige. A better understanding of White House power ought to be centered on the leverage that presidents possess and apply in different circumstances.

PRESIDENTIAL POWER AS SITUATIONAL LEVERAGE

Leverage is the key to understanding presidential power, and it is related to the circumstances in which the chief executive is operating. Power in the White House is not a seamless whole, nor is it exercised in a vacuum; presidents have more power in some situations than in others, and they use their powers and resources to promote certain ends. *Presidential power is a matter of situational leverage.* The chief executive's leverage in any situation is a function of constitutional/legal, institutional, political, and personal resources that can be applied toward the advancement of the president's goals, taking into account the risks, obstacles, and opportunities presented by the situation. In some cases, the president's leverage may be great, in others quite limited; but in all cases it is a result of how the power resources of the presidency can be applied in a specific set of circumstances.

Seeing presidential power as *situational leverage* helps us to gain a more accurate understanding of the office and those who have occupied it. It helps to explain why some presidents have been able to revive their political fortunes despite adversity. It also helps to highlight the role that unilateral powers play in undergirding presidential efforts to persuade or even compel others to cooperate. And situational leverage reminds us that the circumstances in which presidents operate affect which resources they can employ and why chief executives may hesitate to use powers they clearly possess. The components of presidential situational leverage are summarized in figure 3 and are then considered in turn.

Presidents have several potential sources of power, so call them *power resources*. Depending on the situation, a president may be able to draw on all or only a few of them. There are four major types of power resources available to the chief executive.

Figure 3. Components of the President's Situational Leverage

RESOURCES (examples)		PRES GOALS weighed against	RISKS
Constitutional, legal, & prerogative *veto *appointments *war powers *pardon *others by law *prerogative powers	**Institutional** *staff *OMB, NSC *Cabinet & agencies *secrecy *intelligence		*Risks of inaction *Risk of negative reaction *Risk of court challenge *Possibility of failure
Political *electoral margin *party in Congress *interest groups *public opinion *consensus and/or deference to pres *sense of crisis	**Personal** *rhetorical skills *bargaining skills *media relations *reputation *timing, surprise		**OBSTACLES** *Opposition (who, how strong, how effective) *Bureaucratic resistance *Constitutional/legal obstacles *Economic constraints *Other situational obstacles

RESULT OF THIS CALCULATION:

OPPORTUNITIES
*Achieve policy goals
*Achieve political goals (reelection, etc)
*Meet responsibilities
*Advance other goals

LEVERAGE APPLIED TOWARD ADVANCING PRESIDENTIAL GOALS

*Obviously, this figure vastly oversimplifies what is in reality a complex and subtle political calculation. We are under no illusion that political reality can be captured adequately with a few boxes and arrows.

Presidential Power Resources: The Constitution, Laws, and Prerogative

Constitutional Power Resources

At its most basic level, the presidential power is rooted in the Constitution. The president's powers include the veto, the appointment power, diplomatic powers (recognition of governments, negotiating treaties, concluding executive agreements), and the power of commander in chief.

Presidents use these powers to give them leverage in pursuing their goals, and their resources are greater in some areas than in others (e.g., foreign versus domestic policy). As our cases illustrate, skillful use of constitutional powers can even help to revive a president's political fortunes. Truman used his Article II authority to call the 80th Congress back into session, then campaigned in 1948 against the "do-nothing Congress" for its failure to act on important issues. Clinton vetoed two continuing resolutions in 1995, leading to a government shutdown and reversing the onslaught of the Republican majority on Capitol Hill.

The Constitution establishes the bedrock of presidential powers, as any chief executive who has threatened or wielded the veto knows. Ultimately, the chief executive's place and influence in the American political system rests on these powers. Moreover, the president's constitutional powers have been expanded over the course of American history, primarily through a dynamic that can be described as *venture constitutionalism*.[3]

Venture constitutionalism is an assertion of constitutional legitimacy for presidential actions that do not conform to settled understandings of the president's constitutional authority. It is a form of constitutional risk-taking. It is a gamble by the president that his action will be accepted, or at least acquiesced to, by other key actors in the political system. Venture constitutionalism usually occurs when the president takes an action (including negative actions, such as claims of executive privilege or immunity, impoundment, etc.) that "stake out" a claim to authority not already accepted as within the chief executive's constitutional orbit. It has occurred throughout American history and in a wide range of cases, but it has been especially common in foreign affairs, and it results in "pushing back the frontiers" of presidential constitutional authority

Presidents engage in three general types of venture constitutionalism, according to the purpose for which greater executive power is claimed. Type I venture constitutionalism consists of actions to protect the institutional interests of the presidency; this type includes assertions of executive privilege, invoking immunity from lawsuits, and proclaiming broad authority to control executive subordinates. Type II venture constitutionalism is aimed at promoting American security and advancing the national interest; this type includes assertions of broadly defined war powers, invoking the doctrine of state secrets, various emergency powers, and control over the nation's foreign relations. Type III venture constitutionalism includes actions aimed at enhancing the president's influence in shaping policy; this type includes assertions of presidential control over budget-making in the executive branch, the use of executive orders and proclamations to make policy, and oversight and review of administrative rule-making.

Presidents typically engage in venture constitutionalism to increase their leverage in particular circumstances. Faced with a situation in which the accepted understanding of constitutional authority does not conform to what the president believes he needs to achieve his goals and meet his responsibilities, the chief executive asserts broader constitutional power and claims legitimacy for an expanded definition of authority. The president takes a risk; if Congress or the courts or the public acquiesce in this claim, the reward is that the president's assertion is legitimated and a new precedent is set. If the president is rebuffed—say, by the Supreme Court (as occurred in the steel seizure case)—then the president must back down.

Much of the history of venture constitutionalism has been a story of success—the Louisiana Purchase, the Civil War, the acceptance of the removal power (after a long struggle), and executive agreements. Nevertheless, it has also included many failures—the steel seizure case, Clinton's three defeats in the Supreme Court on claims of immunity and executive privilege, and the outlawing of impoundment. There have also been many ambiguous instances, some of which are still unresolved—presidential signing statements, for example. It is a history that dates at least as far back as Washington's Neutrality Proclamation and is as current as the war on terrorism.

Legislative Power Resources

Congress also gives the chief executive power through legislation. These legal grants of power have enabled chief executives to undertake a wide range of actions, including establishing military commissions to try terrorism suspects, declaring national emergencies that authorize broader federal government powers (a favorite target of conspiracy theorists on both the left and right), issuing wage and price controls (now defunct but used by Nixon in 1971), intervening in labor disputes, producing an annual budget proposal, implementing a multitude of programs, and enforcing federal laws.

Prerogative Powers

Beyond the grants of Article II and the laws enacted by Congress, the president also has recourse to prerogative power. John Locke wrote, "This power to act according to discretion, for the public good, without the prescription of the law, and sometimes even against it, is that which is called prerogative."[4] This third category is controversial, but it has been exercised by chief executives throughout the history of the republic. The most impressive case was Lincoln's conduct of the Civil War, from his enlargement of the army and spending funds without appropriation to his suspension of habeas corpus, but other presidents have taken extraordinary actions to defend against threats to the public interest. Prerogative is a source of presidential leverage in extraordinary situations.[5]

For the purposes of the constitutional system, prerogative refers to the president's capacity to take extraordinary actions in defense of core national interests, actions that are justified because constitutional grants of authority are insufficient to meet the threat. Prerogative power flows from the president's responsibility to preserve, protect, and defend the Constitution *as a whole*. As Lincoln said in defense of his suspension of habeas corpus in 1861, "Are all the laws *but one* to go unexecuted, and the Government itself go to pieces lest that one be violated?"[6] Prerogative does not flow from ambition, convenience, or desire; it cannot be justified as an expedient means of achieving the president's political or policy goals. Rather, it flows from necessity: the president takes extraordinary actions because the core public interest is threatened and cannot be defended by ordinary constitutional means. Prerogative, as Lincoln understood it and as we should as well, is an extraordinary defense of the Constitution; in exercising it, the president must be accountable for extraordinary actions through such means as impeachment and the electoral process (as Lincoln was).[7]

Some analysts, such as Gene Healy in *The Cult of the Presidency*, reject nearly every action that expands presidential power.[8] But although Healy pointed out (as have others) several excesses of executive power and a national tendency to look to the president as a savior for all ills, he imagined a world in which there are no threats to the public interest graver than a more powerful president. For example, his discussion of Lincoln—surprisingly brief in a book on the expansion of presidential power—tends to emphasize the president's actions that compromised civil liberties (e.g., suspension of habeas corpus) rather than the threat to the nation posed by secession. This kind of analysis is dreamlike in its unreality: presidents must confront threats to the national interest, even if we wish those threats did not occur. It is not the case that presidential action is always the worst threat to the public interest; it may be a cliché to say that the Constitution is not a suicide pact, but clichés—including this one—are often true. Presidential action—whether based in the Constitution or prerogative—is necessary to secure the nation's interest.

That is why presidential prerogative must be understood as a defensive measure within the constitutional system. Does this mean that all assertions of presidential prerogative are legitimate? Of course not, but neither are all unilateral exercises of power forebodings of tyranny. Legitimate use of prerogative power is limited by its purpose (which must be to preserve the constitutional system and protect core national interests) and by requiring the president to be accountable for extraordinary actions. If the president's action is specific and appropriate to the situation, then the chief executive should be prepared to defend it. Healy might

protest that Americans are too willing to look to the president for salva-
tion, but his solution to that problem is to reject all assertions of presidential prerogative. That approach leaves the nation vulnerable to the fate that
Lincoln worked to avoid: "[A]ll the laws *but one* to go unexecuted, and
the Government itself go to pieces lest that one be violated."

Presidential Power Resources: Executive Institutions
The president can also draw on institutional power resources, including
the White House staff, the Office of Management and Budget, the
National Security Council, the cabinet, and executive agencies. As Harry
McPherson once said of the chief executive, "[H]e has a staff around him
of people who have big ears and listen and meet with people all the time
and will send him memoranda and will talk to him on the phone and tell
him what they think is going on."[9] These institutions provide the president
with information, intelligence, analysis, and contacts with other parts of
the political system.

The president also possesses the ability to employ and manage secrecy
as an institutional resource, giving presidents the opportunity (for good or
ill) to shield many of their actions and policies—from covert operations
to trading arms for hostages to planning a diplomatic opening to China
—from Congress, the public, and others. The president does not exercise
absolute control over the executive branch; nevertheless, the chief executive has access to a wide array of resources based in the institution.

Presidential Power Resources: Political Capital
The political resources of the president are more variable than constitutional and institutional ones. These resources correspond to what is usually
termed "political capital"—their presence or absence can be important factors in influencing the dynamics of a political situation. These
resources include the president's electoral margin, support in Congress,
public support and approval, and interest groups (which can assist the
president in promoting administration goals).

Beyond these resources, presidents are also able to draw on two other intangible factors that can and have been significant at many points in the history of the office: deference and crisis. The president is the beneficiary of deference, usually in foreign policy. Half a century ago, Aaron Wildavsky noted in "The Two Presidencies" that presidents are more likely to get their way from Congress in foreign affairs than in domestic policy,[10] and that deference continues to apply and appeared throughout our case studies. Even in the midst of tough times, Congress tended to defer to the chief executive on international issues, even controversial wars. Of course, this deference was not absolute—as several presidents also found—but it was a significant resource for the president. This deference also enhances presidential influence in times of national crisis, when the ordinary pulling and hauling of politics gives way to consensus and rallying around the nation's leader. This has been the situation in Cold War crises, in the aftermath of September 11, 2001, and in the 2008 financial crisis.

Presidential Power Resources: Personal Skills
Presidents are also politicians and possess a variety of personal skills. These skills are the sorts that Neustadt focused on in his description of presidential power and include the chief executive's rhetorical skills, bargaining and negotiation skills, and ability to communicate through the media and relations with journalists. Personal resources include even the president's reputation—both professional and public—which can affect the likelihood of others to cooperate with the chief executive. Some presidents, such as Ronald Reagan and Bill Clinton, possessed an ability to connect with the public that helped each man survive a crisis that could have destroyed his presidency (Iran-Contra for Reagan, the Lewinsky scandal for Clinton); other presidents do not have such a rapport with the public and, like Jimmy Carter and George H. W. Bush, suffer for it. Finally, the president often has the ability to control timing and surprise to influence events; for example, Nixon used both to manage the diplomatic opening to China in 1972, thus contributing to his success in that endeavor.

Of course, presidents do not possess all of these personal resources in equal amount. Also, these personal resources are not uniform even in the same person. Even gifted politicians can find their personal skills failing them in certain circumstances (as happened to LBJ in the matter of Vietnam), whereas those who seem politically unskilled in one domain can be successful in another (as happened with Jimmy Carter and the Camp David Accords).

Weighing Risks, Obstacles, and Opportunities
Presidents must decide when and how to apply their power resources to gain leverage in specific contexts, and those decisions are made by weighing the risks, obstacles, and opportunities of action or inaction. Lyndon Johnson famously commented in frustration about his office, "Power? The only power I've got is nuclear—and I can't use that."[11] Whereas the legalistic approach to presidential powers tended to view the veto, pardons, and treaty power in isolation from the political circumstances in which they are exercised, presidents must employ their power resources in the real world of politics. That was the insight of LBJ's remark: the president's leverage is a matter of *leverage in context*.

The first contextual factor that a president must weigh are the *risks* of the situation: the risk of inaction, the risk of failure, the risk of a court challenge (especially in cases of venture constitutionalism) or other negative reaction, the risk of bad timing, and other risks. Weighing these risks is an eminently political decision, and consciousness of them has led chief executives to proceed with caution (e.g., Lincoln and the timing of the Emancipation Proclamation, Kennedy and civil rights legislation) or with boldness (e.g., Nixon's opening to China, Reagan's firing of striking air traffic controllers, or Clinton's willingness to shut down the government).

A second contextual factor that presidents must weigh is the *obstacles* that stand in their way. These include opposition to the president's goals: who opposes them, how numerous and how powerful the opposition is, what resources the opposition possesses, and other considerations. Other obstacles include constitutional and legal barriers to the president's plan and goals, bureaucratic resistance, economic constraints, and other obstacles imposed by the particular situation. For example, Barack Obama was able to overcome the obstacles that stood in the way of the health care reform plan (although some remained after the bill's passage that raised questions about its implementation), whereas Bill Clinton in 1994 was unable to overcome opposition to his plan and George W. Bush in 2005 could not attract support for his call for Social Security reform.

Obstacles also include the intensity of opposition to the president's goals, which can make the president's job even more difficult: in the cases of Truman and MacArthur, Eisenhower and Orville Faubus in Little Rock, or Kennedy confronting George Wallace at the University of Alabama in 1963, each chief executive had to contend with a highly motivated adversary. This fact is a key reason why each of these presidents had to rely on executive power (Neustadt's "command") in order to act as he believed the situation required.

Third, specific situations also present opportunities. These include opportunities to advance the president's policy goals (e.g., change environmental policy, support democracy abroad), promote their political goals (such as reelection), meet their responsibilities (which often motivates forays into venture constitutionalism),[12] or seize other opportunities.

Of course, obstacles, risks, and opportunities must be weighed in relation to one another. These calculations may be simple and obvious or complex and subtle, depending on the situation. Presidents must determine what power resources can be applied to advance their goals and how these contextual factors will affect the likelihood of success. Conversely, a president may believe that the situation requires action, even if the risks are very high and the obstacles to success are formidable (e.g., the Cuban Missile Crisis).

In any situation, the president's power resources, weighed against the risks, obstacles, and opportunities presented by circumstances, are applied as leverage toward advancing the president's goals. Obviously, the consequent leverage will not be the same in all circumstances but will vary according to the situation.

A Continuum of Presidential Leverage

The president's situational leverage can be thought of as existing on a continuum that ranges from occasions when it is minimal or even nonexistent to situations when it is absolute or nearly so. (See figure 4.) The broad realm between these extremes is where presidents live and work the vast majority of the time, with more or less leverage according to circumstances. Situations closer to the left side of the continuum (which terminates at leverage = 0) are those in which the chief executive depends more on bargaining and persuasion. Situations closer to the right side of the continuum (which terminates at leverage = 1) are those in which the president is in a position to command or compel others' cooperation.

Figure 4. A Continuum of Presidential Leverage

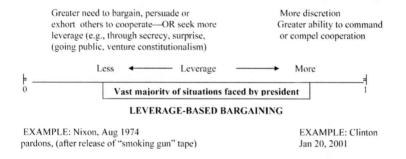

Greater need to bargain, persuade or
exhort others to cooperate—OR seek more
leverage (e.g., through secrecy, surprise,
(going public, venture constitutionalism)

More discretion
Greater ability to command
or compel cooperation

Less ◄―――― Leverage ――――► More

0   1

Vast majority of situations faced by president

LEVERAGE-BASED BARGAINING

EXAMPLE: Nixon, Aug 1974
pardons, (after release of "smoking gun" tape)

EXAMPLE: Clinton
Jan 20, 2001

Of course, this continuum is conceptual and its extreme ends are mostly hypothetical. Presidents rarely have unlimited discretion, although there is at least one example that might fit: the pardons issued by an outgoing president in the final days of office. On January 20, 2001, Bill Clinton issued several controversial pardons, most notoriously pardoning fugitive financier Marc Rich (Rich's former wife had made large contributions to Clinton's library and to Hillary Clinton's Senate campaign, eliciting charges of bribery); the outcry against the pardons was irrelevant because such actions are unilateral and absolute decisions of the president, and any political fallout was limited by Clinton's departure from office. On the other end, one must turn to political thrillers or fantasy to imagine a situation in which the president has lost all leverage; even in the two cases of presidential impeachment in our history, partisan ties (and, in Clinton's case, public opinion) provided leverage for the president. One might imagine a case in which a president is impeached for an offense so heinous that even fellow partisans abandon their chief executive—thus stripping the president of any constitutional, institutional, political, or personal resources—but such a case is unlikely to occur in political reality.

The broad middle ground is the realm of bargaining. It is leverage-based bargaining in which presidents not only are supported by implicit threats of power but can and do use unilateral actions, going public, and even unconventional actions to press others to comply or compromise with the president's purpose. Neustadt argued that presidential recourse to "command" always means failure to persuade; on the contrary, our cases (and other evidence from the history of the office) indicate that employing power resources—including and especially unilateral actions—can increase the president's leverage. It is precisely because unilateralism increases presidential leverage that chief executives—especially in the period since Watergate—have devoted so much time and effort to expanding their unilateral powers (e.g., signing statements and war powers) through venture constitutionalism.

Leverage and Presidential Power

Presidential power is, as we have said, a function of situational leverage. Leverage explains why presidents seem weak in certain circumstances and dominant in others. This variation is more than just a matter of persuasion; indeed, acting decisively can give a president the ability to achieve political and policy goals and even recover amid adverse circumstances.

Richard Neustadt may have overstated the case in defining presidential power as no more or less than persuasion, but he did see that power can be gained or lost and can be exercised in different ways. The problem in Neustadt's analysis was in deciding a priori that only one type of presidential action is legitimate, not because it conformed to constitutional government or democratic theory but because he had concluded (without demonstrating) that decisive unilateral actions (instances of "command") were self-defeating. In chapter 1, we discussed the limitations of this analysis, but it is only fair to also give Neustadt his due. By focusing on what he called "three cases of command," he saw that situational factors do matter. What was missing from his analysis was a more comprehensive understanding of the nature and sources of presidential power, as well as how presidents apply those power resources as leverage.

Seeing presidential power as situational leverage highlights the ways in which power resources and contextual factors interact to shape the president's influence in particular situations. It takes into account both prerogative and persuasion as elements of presidential power. It also helps to explain why adversity does not necessarily doom a presidency, in addition to why presidents can fail even in the best of times.

WHAT NEXT?

This study of political adversity has drawn out the roots of presidential power, but it leaves much more to be done. We have identified power as situational leverage, but that suggests a better view of presidential power without fully exploring the implications of this new view. Our discussion of situational leverage suggests several avenues for additional research.

First, there needs to be more research into the components of presidential leverage. This work would draw together the large body of research that already exists on presidential powers in a way that is consistent with our notion of power resources. Likewise, scholars should explore further the contextual factors that affect presidential decisions regarding when and how to employ power resources.

Both power resources and contextual factors can and ought to be explored through case studies of presidents in action. Case studies make it possible for scholars to see how resources, risks, obstacles, and opportunities interact in specific cases. A body of case studies, drawing on existing research and primary sources, will make it possible to develop a body of evidence on which to propose generalizations about the nature and exercise of presidential power.

To make case studies most useful for making generalizations, they should be conducted along similar lines. For example, case studies could focus on highlighting the power resources that presidents draw on in different situations, or on how contextual factors make a difference, or even on how different cases in a specific policy area highlight differences in presidential leverage. Our case studies provide one model of how to compare different instances of presidential action; other approaches can be employed to examine different aspects of situational leverage. However the case studies are conducted, they should be directed toward illuminating the sources of power and its exercise.

Beyond studying the roots of power, case studies hold particular promise for exploring the exercise of that power. One area that needs particular attention is the ends to which presidents apply leverage and their means for doing so. At one time, analysts tended to assume that presidents always had the national interest at heart. Certainly, American presidents have acted to preserve the national interest, but over the past half-century there have been several cases of chief executives pursuing questionable ends (and using questionable means). As noted earlier, Neustadt was criticized in the 1970s for taking a strictly instrumental view of power and for failing to address ethics and the ends to which presidents apply their power.[13] Indeed, as Ethan Fishman and others have pointed out, Neustadt was not unique in overlooking the ends of presidential power while focusing on its means.[14]

It is well beyond the scope of this project to explore the ends and means of presidential power, but it is a topic that warrants attention. As scholars embark on this exploration, however, one caution is in order: too often, commentators and scholars have judged presidential ends and means according to their own preferences. This kind of partisanship in evaluating presidents has served mostly to suggest that the legitimacy of presidential action is a function of ideology—if the analyst is a liberal, one set of goals is seen as worthy of support and therefore certain actions laudable, whereas a conservative will find a different set of ends and means to be acceptable. For example, Terry Eastland's widely read *Energy in the Executive* criticized Neustadt's *Presidential Power* for embodying the perspective of a liberal Democrat (which Neustadt certainly was);[15] in response, Eastland proposed to give what he called a "constitutional corrective" to Neustadt but ended up substituting his own conservative Republican preferences for Neustadt's liberal ones.[16]

As analysts consider presidential ends and means, they need to develop a kind of "golden rule" for understanding the presidency: one that they are willing to grant to their enemies as well as their heroes. The best place to begin that understanding is the Constitution. Of course, there is considerable debate about constitutional interpretation, but that is a fact of politics and does not mean that there is no ground for agreement about most constitutional issues. Debates about the fringes of the Constitution—certain actions that both George W. Bush and Barack Obama have taken in the war on terrorism, for example—obscure the fact that there is a broad consensus on what is constitutional presidential action.

It is possible to start from this beginning and engage in reflection—informed by cases from history—on presidential ends and means. One need not be Pollyannaish to do so: it is not necessary to assume that chief executives always have the nation's best interests at heart when they act, but neither is it reasonable to move to the other extreme and assume that all presidents are knaves.

Presidential power is more than just persuasion. Of course, in a democratic system, persuasion is important, but chief executives must also take decisive action to promote the public interest. This study has shown that, even in tough times, presidents usually do have "another card" to play and are not always victims of fate. Presidential power is complex, and understanding it requires more than just prescribing one type of conduct. Viewing presidential power as leverage will make it possible to better understand the nature and use of that power and the chief executive's place in the American political system.

ENDNOTES

1. William Howard Taft, *Our Chief Magistrate and His Powers* (New York: Columbia University Press, 1916).
2. See "Reappraising Power," ch. 10 in Neustadt, *Presidential Power*, 183–229.
3. The following discussion is drawn from Barilleaux, "Venture Constitutionalism."
4. John Locke, "Of Prerogative," *Second Treatise of Civil Government*, accessed March 14, 2011, http://www.constitution.org/jl/2ndtr14.htm.
5. There is an extensive literature on presidential prerogative, and it is beyond the scope of this work to enter into an extended discussion of the debates over it. Indeed, as Tatalovich and Engeman have pointed out, we need more discussion of prerogative. To begin, see George Thomas, "As Far as Republican Principles Will Admit: Presidential Prerogative and Constitutional Government," *Presidential Studies Quarterly* 30 (September 2000): 534–552; Daniel P. Franklin, *Extraordinary Measures* (Pittsburgh: University of Pittsburgh Press, 1991); Robert Scigliano, "The President's 'Prerogative Power,'" in *Inventing the American Presidency*, ed. Thomas Cronin (Lawrence: University Press of Kansas, 1989), 236–258; Thomas S. Langston and Michael E. Lind, "John Locke and the Limits of Presidential Prerogative," *Polity* 24 (Autumn 1991): 49–68; and Herman Belz, "Abraham Lincoln and American Constitutionalism," *Review of Politics* 50 (Spring 1988): 159–197.
6. Abraham Lincoln, "Special Session Message," July 4, 1861, accessed March 14, 2011, http://www.presidency.ucsb.edu/ws/index.php?pid = 69 802&st = &st1 = #axzz1GaB1DBTn.
7. On this point, see Thomas, "As Far as Republican Principles Will Admit," 548–550. See also Belz, "Abraham Lincoln," 186.
8. Gene Healy, *The Cult of the Presidency* (Washington, DC: Cato Institute, 2009). This paragraph draws on discussion at various points in Healy's book.
9. Harry McPherson, quoted in Samuel Kernell and Samuel L. Popkin, eds., *Chief of Staff* (Berkeley: University of California Press, 1986), 80.
10. Aaron Wildavsky, "The Two Presidencies," *Society* 4 (December 1966): 7–14.

11. Lyndon Johnson, quoted in "Lyndon B. Johnson, Man of the Year, 1967," *Time*, January 5, 1968, accessed February 14, 2011, http://www.time.com/time/subscriber/personoftheyear/archive/stories/1967.html.
12. See Barilleaux, "Venture Constitutionalism."
13. See discussion in Ethan M. Fishman, *The Prudential Presidency* (Westport, CT: Praeger, 2001), 2–3.
14. Ibid.
15. Terry Eastland, *Energy in the Executive: The Case for the Strong Presidency* (New York: Macmillan, 1992).
16. See Ryan J. Barilleaux, "Liberals, Conservatives, and the Presidency," *Congress & the Presidency* 20 (Spring 1993): 75–82, especially 79–80.

BIBLIOGRAPHY

Abshire, David. *Saving the Reagan Presidency*. College Station: Texas A&M Press, 2005.

Alarkon, Walter. "Patraeus Says Obama Told Him Iraq Surge Was a Success." *The Hill*, December 6, 2009. Accessed February 28, 2011. http://thehill.com/homenews/administration/7078 7-petraeus-says-obama-told-him-iraq-surge-was-a-success.

Ambrose, Stephen. *Eisenhower*, vol. 2, *The President*. New York: Simon & Schuster, 1984.

———. *Nixon*, vol. 3, *Ruin and Recovery 1973–1990*. New York: Simon & Schuster, 1991.

Arnold, Peri E. "Clinton and the Institutionalized Presidency," in *The Post Modern Presidency: Bill Clinton's Legacy in U.S. Politics*, edited by Steven E. Schier, 19-40 (Pittsburgh: University of Pittsburgh Press, 2000).

Baker, Peter. *The Breach: Inside the Impeachment and Trial of William Jefferson Clinton*. New York: Berkley Books, 2001.

Barilleaux, Ryan J. "Liberals, Conservatives, and the Presidency." *Congress & the Presidency* 20 (Spring 1993): 75–82.

———. *The Post-Modern Presidency*. New York: Praeger, 1988.

———. "The Presidency in the Twenty-first Century." In *Thinking About the Presidency*, edited by Gary L. Gregg II, 496–506. Lanham, MD: Rowman & Littlefield, 2005.

———. "Venture Constitutionalism and the Enlargement of the Presidency." In *Executing the Constitution: Putting the Presidency Back into the Constitution*, edited by Christopher S. Kelley, 137–152. Albany: SUNY Press, 2006.

Barilleaux, Ryan J., and David Zellers. "Executive Unilateralism in the Ford and Carter Presidencies." In *The Unitary Executive and the*

Modern Presidency, edited by Ryan J. Barilleaux and Christopher S. Kelley, 41–76. College Station: Texas A&M University Press, 2010.

Behar, Richard. "Rummy's North Korean Connection." *Fortune* [online], May 12, 2003. Accessed February 23, 2011. http://money.cnn.com/ magazines/fortune/fortune_archive/2003/05/12/342316/.

Belz, Herman. "Abraham Lincoln and American Constitutionalism." *Review of Politics* 50 (Spring 1988): 159–197.

Bennett, James. "Impeachment: Beyond the Vote President Maps Out a Strategy for Governing While on Trial." *New York Times*, December 20, 1998.

Berman, William C. *From the Center to the Edge: The Politics and Policies of the Clinton Presidency*. Lanham, MD: Rowman & Littlefield, 2001.

Bernstein, Irving. *Guns or Butter: The Presidency of Lyndon Johnson*. New York: Oxford University Press, 1996.

Billington, Monroe. "Civil Rights, President Truman, and the South." *Journal of Negro History* 58 (April 1973): 132.

Bornet, Vaughn Davis. *The Presidency of Lyndon B. Johnson*. Lawrence: University Press of Kansas, 1983.

Bourne, Peter G. *Jimmy Carter: A Comprehensive Biography from Plains to Postpresidency*. New York: Scribner, 1997.

Bowden, Mark. *Guests of the Ayatollah: The First Battle in America's War with Militant Islam*. New York: Atlantic Monthly Press, 2006.

Burns, James Macgregor. *Running Alone: Presidential Leadership from JFK to Bush II*. New York: Basic Books, 2007.

Busch, Andrew E. "1978 GOP Sets Stage for Reagan." September 2006. Accessed May 3, 2010. http://www.ashbrook.org/publicat/oped/ busch/06/1978.html.

Bush, Barbara. *Barbara Bush: A Memoir*. New York: Charles Scribner's Sons, 1994.

Bush, George H. W. "Statement on Signing the Reclamation States Emergency Drought Relief Act of 1991." March 5, 1992. Accessed July 23, 2010. http://www.presidency.ucsb.edu/ws/index.php?pid = 20689.

———. "Statement on Signing the Torture Victim Protection Act of 1991." March 12, 1992. Accessed July 23, 2010. http://www.presidency.ucsb.edu/ws/index.php?pid = 20715.

Bush, George W. "Address to the Nation on the National Economy." September 24, 2008. Accessed March 1, 2011. http://www.presidency.ucsb.edu/ws/index.php?pid = 84355&st = &st1 = .

———. "Address to the Nation on Military Operations in Iraq." January 10, 2007. Accessed March 1, 2011. http://www.presidency.ucsb.edu/ws/index.php?pid = 24432&st = &st1 = .

———. *Decision Points*. New York: Crown, 2010.

———. "Farewell Address to the Nation." January 15, 2009. Accessed March 1, 2011. http://www.presidency.ucsb.edu/ws/index.php?pid = 85423&st = &st1 = .

———. "The President's News Conference." November 8, 2006. Accessed February 24, 2011. http://www.presidency.ucsb.edu/ws/index.php?pid = 24269&st = &st1 = .

_____. Interview. "Decision Points." November 2010, accessed February 24, 2011, http://www.msnbc.msn.com/id/40076644/ns/politics-decision_points/

———. "Remarks on Returning Without Approval to the House of Representatives the 'U.S. Troop Readiness, Veterans' Care, Katrina Recovery, and Iraq Accountability Appropriations Act, 2007.'" May 1, 2007. Accessed March 1, 2011. http://www.presidency.ucsb.edu/ws/index.php?pid = 73974&st = &st1 = .

———. "Statement on Signing the National Defense Authorization Act for Fiscal Year 2008." January 28, 2008. Accessed February 25, 2011. http://www.presidency.ucsb.edu/ws/index.php?pid = 76389.

Busby, Robert. *Ronald Reagan and the Iran-Contra Affair: The Politics of Presidential Recovery*. New York: Macmillan, 1999.

Califano, Joseph A., Jr. *The Triumph & Tragedy of Lyndon Johnson: The White House Years*. New York: Simon & Schuster, 1991.

Cannon, James. *Time and Chance*. New York: HarperCollins, 1994.

Carter, Jimmy. "Address to the Nation on Energy and National Goals: 'The Malaise Speech.'" July 15, 1979. Accessed March 22, 2011. http://www.presidency.ucsb.edu/ws/index.php?pid = 32596&st = &st1 = #axzz1HLZCip00.

———. "National Health Plan Message to the Congress on Proposed Legislation." June 12, 1979. Accessed May 7, 2010. http://www.presidency.ucsb.edu/ws/index.php?pid = 32466.

———. "PD-59: Nuclear Weapons Employment Policy." Accessed May 7, 2010. http://www.fas.org/irp/offdocs/pd/pd59.pdf.

———. "The State of the Union Address Delivered Before a Joint Session of Congress." January 23, 1979.. Accessed March 22, 2011. http://www.presidency.ucsb.edu/ws/index.php?pid = 32657.

Carter, Rosalynn. *First Lady from Plains*. Boston: Houghton Mifflin, 1984.

Ceaser, James. "The Great Repudiation." *Claremont Review of Books* 10 (Fall 2010): 6.

———. "The Reagan Presidency and American Public Opinion." In *The Reagan Presidency: Promise and Performance*, edited by Charles O. Jones, 172–210. Chatham, NJ: Chatham House, 1988.

Clinton, William J. "Address Before a Joint Session of Congress on the State of the Union." January 19, 1999. Accessed January 28, 2010. http://www.presidency.ucsb.edu/ws/index.php?pid = 57577&st = & st1.

———. "Address to the Nation on Testimony Before the Independent Counsel's Grand Jury." August 17, 1998. Accessed January 24, 2010. http://www.presidency.ucsb.edu/ws/index.php?pid = 54794&st = & st1.

———. "The President's Radio Address." February 13, 1999. Accessed January 28, 2010. http://www.presidency.ucsb.edu/ws/index.php?pid = 56982.

———. "Remarks at the Kisowera School in Mukono, Uganda." March 24, 1998. Accessed January 20, 2010. http://www.presidency.ucsb. edu/ws/index.php?pid = 55672&st = &st1.

———. "Remarks to Genocide Survivors in Kigali, Rwanda." March 25, 1998. Accessed January 20, 2010. http://www.presidency.ucsb.edu/ ws/index.php?pid = 55677&st = &st1.

———. "Remarks on the After-School Child Care Initiative." January 26, 1998. Accessed January 23, 2010. http://www.presidency.ucsb.edu/ ws/index.php?pid = 56257&st = &st1.

———. "Remarks on the Conclusion of the Senate Impeachment Trial and an Exchange with Reporters." February 12, 1999. Accessed February 9, 2010. http://www.presidency.ucsb.edu/ws/index.php?pid = 56912&st = &st1.

———. "Statement on Signing the Cuban Liberty and Democratic Solidarity (LIBERTAD) Act of 1996." March 12, 1996. Accessed February 23, 2011. http://www.presidency.ucsb.edu/ws/index.php?pid = 52532 &st = &st1 = .

———. "Statement on Signing the Fisheries Act of 1995." November 3, 1995. Accessed February 23, 2011. http://www.presidency.ucsb.edu/ ws/index.php?pid = 50735&st = Fisheries+Act+of+1995&st1 = .

Cohen, Daniel. *The Impeachment of William Jefferson Clinton.* Brookfield, CT: Twenty-first Century Books.

Congressional Quarterly, *CQ Almanac: 100th Congress 1st Session, 1987.* Washington, DC: CQ Press 1988.

———. *CQ Almanac: 102nd Congress 2nd Session, 1992.* Washington, DC: CQ Press, 1993.

———. *CQ Almanac: 105th Congress 2nd Session, 1998.* Washington, DC: CQ Press, 1999.

———. *CQ Almanac: 106th Congress 1st Session, 1999.* Washington, DC: CQ Press, 2000.

———. *CQ Almanac: 90th Congress 2nd Session, 1968.* Washington, DC: CQ Press, 1969.

———. *CQ Almanac: 93rd Congress 1st Session, 1973*. Washington, DC: CQ Press, 1974.

———. *CQ Almanac: 93rd Congress 2nd Session, 1974*. Washington, DC: CQ Press, 1975.

———. *CQ Almanac: 99th Congress 2nd Session, 1986*. Washington, DC: CQ Press, 1987.

Conley, Richard S. "President Clinton and the Republican Congress, 1995–2000: Vetoes, Veto Threats, and Legislative Strategy." Paper presented at the Annual Meeting of the American Political Science Association, San Francisco, CA, August 30–September 2, 2001.

Conley, Richard S., and Annie Krepel. "Presidential Influence: The Success of Vetoes and Veto Overrides." Paper presented at the Annual Meeting of the American Political Science Association, Atlanta, GA, August 1999. Accessed March 1, 2011. http://web.clas.ufl.edu/users/kreppel/types.PDF.

Cooper, Philip. *By Order of the President*. Lawrence: University Press of Kansas, 2002.

Crain, Andrew Downer. *The Ford Presidency: A History*. Jefferson, NC: McFarland & Co., 2009.

Derwinski, Edward J. "Organizing for Policymaking." In *Portraits of American Presidents*, vol. 10, *The Bush Presidency*, edited by Kenneth Thompson 23–44. Lanham, MD: University Press of America, 1997.

Dickinson, Matthew. "We All Want a Revolution: Neustadt, New Institutionalism, and the Future of Presidency Research." *Presidential Studies Quarterly* 39 (December 2009): 736–770.

Divine, Robert A. *Eisenhower and the Cold War*. New York: Oxford University Press, 1981.

Draper, Theodore. *A Very Thin Line: The Iran-Contra Affair*. New York: Hill and Wang, 1991.

Drew, Elizabeth. *Richard M. Nixon*. Large print ed. Detroit: Thomson Gale, 2007.

———. *Showdown: The Struggle Between the Gingrich Congress and the Clinton White House*. New York: Simon & Schuster, 1996.

Exec. Order No. 13422. January 18, 2007. Accessed February 25, 2011. http://www.presidency.ucsb.edu/ws/index.php?pid = 24456

Eastland, Terry. *Energy in the Executive: The Case for the Strong Presidency*. New York: Macmillan, 1992.

"Economic rescue swiftly signed into law." AFP, October 3, 2008.

Edwards, George C., and Stephen J. Wayne. *Presidential Leadership*. 8th ed. New York: Wadsworth, 2009.

Ehrman, John, and Michael W. Flamm. *Debating the Reagan Presidency*. Lanham, MD: Rowman and Littlefield, 2009.

Eisenhower, Dwight. "The President's News Conference." March 16, 1955. Accessed January 7, 2011. http://www.presidency.ucsb.edu/ws/index.php?pid = 10434&st = &st1 = .

———. "Radio and Television Broadcast: 'The Women Ask the President.'" October 24, 1956. Accessed January 7, 2011. http://www.presidency.ucsb.edu/ws/index.php?pid = 10669&st = &st1 = .

———. "Television Broadcast: 'The People Ask the President.'" October 12, 1956. Accessed January 7, 2011. http://www.presidency.ucsb.edu/ws/index.php?pid = 10640&st = &st1 = .

Federal Highway Administration. "President Ronald Reagan and the Surface Transportation and Uniform Relocation Assistance Act of 1987." Accessed March 1, 2011. http://www.fhwa.dot.gov/infrastructure/rw01e.htm.

Feldman, Linda. "Bush Makes First Veto on Stem Cells." *Christian Science Monitor* [online], July 20, 2006. Accessed November 13, 2009. http://www.csmonitor.com/2006/0720/p02s02-uspo.html.

Felton, John. "Iran Arms and 'Contras': A Reagan Bombshell." *Congressional Quarterly Weekly Report*, November 29, 1986: 2971.

Fisher, Louis. *Constitutional Conflicts Between Congress and the President*. 5th rev. ed. Lawrence: University Press of Kansas, 2007.

———. *The Politics of Executive Privilege*. Durham, NC: Carolina Academic Press, 2004.

———. *Presidential War Power*. 2nd ed. Lawrence: University Press of Kansas, 2004.

Fishman, Ethan M. *The Prudential Presidency*. Westport, CT: Praeger, 2001.

Ford, Gerald. "Address to a Joint Session of the Congress." August 12, 1974. Accessed January 14, 2010. http://www.presidency.ucsb.edu/ws/index.php?pid = 4694&st = &st1 = .

———. "Executive Order 11905." February 18, 1976. Accessed February 15, 2007. http://www.presidency.ucsb.edu/ws/index.php?pid = 59348.

———. "Gerald Ford's Remarks on Taking the Oath of Office as President." August 9, 1974. Accessed January 14, 2010. http://www.ford.utexas.edu/LIBRARY/speeches/740001.htm.

———. "Message to the Senate Transmitting the Protocol to the United States–Soviet Antiballistic Missile Treaty." September 19, 1974. Accessed January 25, 2010. http://www.presidency.ucsb.edu/ws/index.php?pid = 4722&st = ABM+treaty&st1 = .

———. "Message to the Senate Transmitting United States–Soviet Treaty and Protocol on the Limitation of Underground Nuclear Explosions." July 29, 1976. Accessed January 25, 2010. http://www.presidency.ucsb.edu/ws/index.php?pid = 6245&st = treaty&st1 = .

———. "Presidential Conversations on the Constitution." Accessed January 21, 2010. http://www.whyy.org/tv12/presidents/issues.html#vp.

———. "Remarks on Senate Action to Prohibit United States Assistance to Angola." December 19, 1975. Accessed January 15, 2010. http://www.presidency.ucsb.edu/ws/index.php?pid = 5447&st = &st1 = .

———. "Statement on Signing a Bill Amending Child Support Provisions of the Social Security Act." August 11, 1975. Accessed February 6, 2007. http://www.presidency.ucsb.edu/ws/index.php?pid = 5168&st = &st1 =

———. "Statement on Signing the Department of Defense Appropriation Act, 1976." February 10, 1976. Accessed February 13, 2007. http://www.presidency.ucsb.edu/ws/index.php?pid = 6277.

———. "Statement and Responses to Questions from Members of the House Judiciary Committee Concerning the Pardon of Richard Nixon." October 17, 1974. Accessed January 26, 2010. http://www.presidency.ucsb.edu/ws/index.php?pid = 4471&st = &st1 = .

———. *A Time to Heal*. New York: Harper and Row, 1979.

Franklin, Daniel P. *Extraordinary Measures*. Pittsburgh: University of Pittsburgh Press, 1991.

"Gallup Daily: Obama Job Approval." Data for November 1–3, 2010. Accessed January 13, 2011. http://www.gallup.com/poll/113980/gallup-daily-obama-job-approval.aspx.

Garthoff, Raymond L. *Détente and Confrontation: American-Soviet Relations from Nixon to Reagan*. Washington, DC: The Brookings Institution, 1994.

Gelderman, Carol. *All the Presidents' Words: The Bully Pulpit and the Creation of the Virtual Presidency*. New York: Walker Publishing, 1997.

Gergen, David. *Eyewitness to Power*. New York: Simon & Schuster, 2000.

Glad, Betty. *Jimmy Carter, His Advisors, and the Making of American Foreign Policy*. Ithaca, NY: Cornell University Press, 2009.

———. *Jimmy Carter: In Search of the Great White House*. New York: W. W. Norton & Company, 1980.

Goodwin, Doris Kearns. *Lyndon Johnson and the American Dream*. New York: St. Martin's Press, 1991.

Gordon, Michael. "Troop 'Surge' Took Place Amid Doubt and Debate." *New York Times*, August 30, 2008. Accessed February 28, 2011. http://www.nytimes.com/2008/08/31/washington/31military.html?_r = 1.

Greene, John Robert. *The Presidency of George Bush*. Lawrence: University Press of Kansas, 2000.

———. *The Presidency of Gerald R. Ford*. Lawrence: University Press of Kansas, 1995.

Greenstein, Fred. *The Presidential Difference: Leadership Style from FDR to George W. Bush*. Princeton, NJ: Princeton University Press, 2004.

Haas, Garland A. *Jimmy Carter and the Politics of Frustration*. Jefferson, NC: McFarland & Co., 1992.

Haines, Gerald K. "The Pike Committee Investigations and the CIA: Looking for a Rogue Elephant." *Studies in Intelligence* (Winter 1998–1999), Center for the Study of Intelligence, Central Intelligence Agency. Accessed January 19, 2010. https://www.cia.gov/library/center-for-the-study-of-intelligence/csi-publications/csi-studies/studies/winter98_99/art07.html.

Hamby, Alonzo. *Man of the People: A Life of Harry S Truman*. New York: Oxford University Press, 1995.

Hamilton, Nigel. *Bill Clinton: Mastering the Presidency*. New York: Public Affairs, 2007.

Hargrove, Erwin. "Presidential Power and Political Science." *Presidential Studies Quarterly* 31 (June 2001): 245–261.

Harris, John F. *The Survivor: Bill Clinton in the White House*. New York: Random House, 2005.

Harvey, Diane Hollern. "The Public's View of Clinton." In *The Postmodern Presidency: Bill Clinton's Legacy in U.S. Politics*, edited by Steven E. Schier, 124–142. Pittsburgh: University of Pittsburgh Press, 2000.

Healy, Gene. *The Cult of the Presidency, Updated: America's Dangerous Devotion to Executive Power*. Washington, DC: Cato Institute, 2009.

Hill, Dilys M. "Domestic Policy." In *The Carter Years: The President and Policy Making*, edited by M. Glenn Abernathy, Dilys M. Hill, and Phil Williams, 13–34. New York: St. Martin's Press, 1984.

Hosansky, David, ed. *Eyewitnesses to Watergate: A Documentary History for Students*. Washington, DC: CQ Press, 2007.

Howell, William. *Power Without Persuasion: The Politics of Direct Presidential Action*. Princeton, NJ: Princeton University Press, 2003.

Hyland, William G. *Clinton's World: Remaking American Foreign Policy*. Westport, CT: Praeger, 1999.

The Iraq Study Group Report. December 6, 2006. Accessed February 28, 2011. http://media.usip.org/reports/iraq_study_group_report.pdf.

Jacobson, Gary C. "The War, the President, and the 2006 Midterm Congressional Elections." Paper presented at the Annual Meeting of the Midwest Political Science Association, Chicago, IL, April 12–15, 2007.

Johnson, Caitlin. "What Ben Stein Thinks Bush Should Do." *CBS Sunday Morning*, October 29, 2006. Accessed February 28, 2011. http://www.cbsnews.com/stories/2006/10/29/sunday/main2135739.shtml.

Johnson, Haynes. *The Best of Times: America in the Clinton Years*. New York: Harcourt, 2001.

Johnson, Lyndon Baines. *The Vantage Point*. New York: Holt, Rinehart & Winston, 1971.

Jones, Charles O. *The American Presidency: A Very Short Introduction*. New York: Oxford University Press, 2007.

———. *Passages to the Presidency*. Washington, DC: Brookings, 1998.

———. *The Presidency in a Separated System*. 2nd ed. Washington, DC: Brookings Institution, 2005.

Jones, Joseph M. *The Fifteen Weeks*. New York: Viking, 1955.

Jordan, Hamilton. *Crisis: The Last Year of the Carter Presidency*. New York: G. P. Putnam's Sons, 1982.

Kalb, Marvin. *One Scandalous Story: Clinton, Lewinsky, and Thirteen Days that Tarnished American Journalism*. New York: The Free Press, 2001.

Kaufman, Burton I. *The Presidency of James Earl Carter, Jr*. Lawrence: University Press of Kansas, 1993.

Kelley, Christopher S. "The Significance of the Presidential Signing Statement." In *Executing the Constitution: Putting the President Back into the Constitution*, edited by Christopher S. Kelley, 78–90. Albany: SUNY Press, 2006.

Kernell, Samuel. *Going Public: New Strategies of Presidential Leadership*. 4th ed. Washington, DC: CQ Press, 2007.

————. "The Truman Doctrine Speech: A Case Study of the Dynamics of Presidential Opinion Leadership." *Social Science History* 1 (Autumn 1976): 23.

Kernell, Samuel, and Samuel L. Popkin, eds. *Chief of Staff.* Berkeley: University of California Press, 1986.

Kilpatrick, Carroll. "Nixon Forces Firing of Cox; Richardson, Ruckelshaus Quit President Abolishes Prosecutor's Office; FBI Seals Records." *Washington Post*, October 21, 1973. Accessed March 1, 2011. http://www.washingtonpost.com/wp-srv/national/longterm/watergate/articles/102173-2.htm

Kissinger, Henry. *Years of Upheaval.* Boston: Little & Brown, 1982.

Krauthammer, Charles. "But He Never Asked for a Mandate." *Washington Post*, January 11, 1988, A23.

Kyvig, David E. *Reagan and the World.* New York: Praeger, 1990.

Landy, Marc, and Sidney M. Milkis. *Presidential Greatness.* Lawrence: University Press of Kansas, 2001.

Langston, Thomas S. *Lyndon Baines Johnson.* Washington, DC: CQ Press, 2002.

Langston, Thomas S., and Michael E. Lind. "John Locke and the Limits of Presidential Prerogative." *Polity* 24 (Autumn 1991): 49–68.

Levy, Peter B. *Encyclopedia of the Reagan-Bush Years.* Westport, CT: Greenwood Press, 1996.

Lewis, Alfred. "5 Held in Plot to Bug Democrats' Office Here." *Washington Post*, June 18, 1972. Accessed March 1, 2011. http://www.washingtonpost.com/wp-srv/national/longterm/watergate/articles/061872-1.htm

Lincoln, Abraham. "Special Session Message." July 4, 1861. Accessed March 14, 2011. http://www.presidency.ucsb.edu/ws/index.php?pid = 69802&st = &stl = #axzz1GaB1DBTn.

Locke, John. "Of Prerogative." *Second Treatise of Civil Government.* 1690. Accessed March 14, 2011. http://www.constitution.org/jl/2ndtr1 4.htm.

Lowry, Rich. *Legacy: Paying the Price for the Clinton Years*. Washington, DC: Regnery, 2003.

"Lyndon B. Johnson, Man of the Year, 1967." *Time*, January 5, 1968. Accessed February 14, 2011. http://www.time.com/time/subscriber/personoftheyear/archive/stories/1967.html.

Mayer, Jane, and Donald McManus. *Landslide: The Unmaking of the President, 1984–1988*. Boston: Houghton Mifflin, 1988.

Mayer, Kenneth. *With the Stroke of a Pen: Executive Orders and Presidential Power*. Princeton, NJ: Princeton University Press, 2002.

McCleskey, Clifton, and Pierce McCleskey. "Jimmy Carter and the Democratic Party." In *The Carter Years: The President and Policy Making*, edited by M. Glenn Abernathy, Dilys M. Hill, and Phil Williams, 125–143. New York: St. Martin's Press, 1984.

McCullough, David. *Truman*. New York: Simon & Schuster, 1992.

McMahon, Robert, ed. "The 110th Congress and Immigration Reform. February 13, 2007. Accessed February 25, 2011. http://www.cfr.org/population-and-demography/110th-congress-immigration-reform/p12628.

Mervin, David. *George Bush and the Guardianship Presidency*. New York: St. Martin's Press, 1996.

———. *Ronald Reagan and the American Presidency*. New York: Longman, 1990.

"Military Surge in Iraq Ends; 150,000 Troops Remain." *USA Today*, July 16, 2008. Accessed February 28, 2011. http://www.usatoday.com/news/world/iraq/2008-07-16-iraq-surge_N.htm.

Miller, Merle. *Lyndon: An Oral Biography*. New York: G. P. Putnam's Sons, 1980.

Bruce Miroff, "Moral Character in the White House: From Republican to Democratic," *Presidential Studies Quarterly* 29 (September 1999): 708–712.

Moore, Raymond A. "The Carter Presidency and Foreign Policy." In *The Carter Years: The President and Policy Making*, edited by M. Glenn

Abernathy, Dilys M. Hill, and Phil Williams, 54–83. New York: St. Martin's Press, 1984.

Mount, Graeme S., with Mark Gauthier. *895 Days that Changed the World: The Presidency of Gerald R. Ford*. Montreal: Black Rose Books, 2006.

Naftali, Timothy. *George H. W. Bush*. New York: Times Books, 2007.

National Security Decision Memorandum 280. November 28, 1974. Accessed February 15, 2007. http://www.fordlibrarymuseum.gov/library/document/0310/nsdm280.pdf.

National Security Decision Memorandum 286. February 7, 1975. Accessed February 15, 2007. http://www.fordlibrarymuseum.gov/library/document/0310/nsdm286.pdf

National Security Decision Memorandum 305. September 15, 2007. Accessed February 15, 2007. http://www.fordlibrarymuseum.gov/library/document/0310/nsdm305.pdf

Nelson, Michael. "Neustadt's 'Presidential Power' at 50." *Chronicle Review*, March 28, 2010. Accessed September 9, 2010. http://chronicle.com/article/Neustadts-Presidential/64816/.

Neustadt, Richard. *Presidential Power and the Modern Presidents*. Rev. ed. New York: Free Press, 1991.

Newell, Walker. *The Soul of a Leader*. New York: Harper, 2009.

Nichols, David A. *A Matter of Justice: Eisenhower and the Beginning of the Civil Rights Revolution*. New York: Simon & Schuster, 2007.

Nichols, David K. *The Myth of the Modern Presidency*. State College: Pennsylvania State University Press, 1994.

Nixon, Richard. "Address to the Nation About National Energy Policy." November 25, 1973. Accessed December 7, 2009. http://www.presidency.ucsb.edu/ws/index.php?pid = 4051&st = &st1.

———. "Address to the Nation About Policies to Deal with the Energy Shortages." November 5, 1973. Accessed December 7, 2009. http://www.presidency.ucsb.edu/ws/index.php?pid = 4034&st = &st1.

————. "Address to the Nation About the Watergate Investigations." April 30, 1973. Accessed December 5, 2009. http://www.presidency. ucsb.edu/ws/index.php?pid = 3824&st = &st1.

————. "Address to the Nation about Vietnam and Domestic Problems." March 29, 1973. Accessed December 7, 2009. http://www.presidency. ucsb.edu/ws/index.php?pid = 4161&st = &st1.

————. "Address to the Nation Announcing Answer to the House Judiciary Committee Subpoena for Additional Presidential Tape Recordings." April 29, 1974. Accessed December 7, 2009. http://www.presidency.ucsb.edu/ws/index.php?pid = 4189&st = &st1.

————. "Address to the Nation Announcing Price Control Measures." June 13, 1973. Accessed December 5, 2009. http://www.presidency. ucsb.edu/ws/index.php?pid = 3868&st = &st1.

————. "Radio Address About the Nation's Economy." July 1, 1973. Accessed December 5, 2009. http://www.presidency.ucsb.edu/ws/ index.php?pid = 3890&st = &st1.

————. "Remarks at a Reception for Returned Prisoners of War." May 24, 1973. Accessed December 7, 2009. http://www.presidency.ucsb. edu/ws/index.php?pid = 3856&st = &st1.

————. "The President's News Conference." June 22, 1972. Accessed December 5, 2009. http://www.presidency.ucsb.edu/ws/index.php?pid = 3472&st = &st1.

————. "The President's News Conference." September 5, 1973. Accessed December 7, 2009. http://www.presidency.ucsb.edu/ws/ index.php?pid = 3948&st = &st1.

————. *RN: The Memoirs of Richard Nixon.* New York: Gosset & Dunlap, 1978.

————. "Veto of the War Powers Resolution." October 24, 1973. Accessed December 7, 2009. http://www.presidency.ucsb.edu/ws/ index.php?pid = 4021&st = &st1.

Parmet, Herbert S. *George Bush: The Life of a Lone Star Yankee.* New York: Scribner, 1997.

Pemberton, William. *Exit with Honor: The Life and Presidency of Ronald Reagan*. Armonk, NY: M. E. Sharpe, 1998.

"Pentagon: Violence Down in Iraq Since 'Surge.'" *CNN*, June 23, 2008. Accessed February 28, 2011. http://www.cnn.com/2008/WORLD/meast/06/23/iraq.security/.

"People and the Power Game." Transcript. 1996. Accessed February 22, 2011. http://hedricksmith.com/site_powergame/files/panetta.html.

Physicians for Social Responsibility. "Arms Control Summits." Accessed June 11, 2010. http://www.psr.org/nuclear-weapons/arms-control-summits.html.

Pious, Richard. *The American Presidency*. New York: Basic Books, 1979.

———. *Why Presidents Fail*. Lanham, MD: Rowman & Littlefield, 2008.

Podhoretz, John. *Hell of a Ride: Backstage at the White House Follies, 1989–1993*. New York: Simon & Schuster, 1993.

"Presidential Job Approval: William J. Clinton." Accessed January 22, 2010. http://www.presidency.ucsb.edu/data/popularity.php?pres = 42 &sort = time&direct = DESC&Submit = DISPLAY.

"The Presidential Timeline." Accessed May 18, 2010. http://www.presidentialtimeline.org/timeline/bin/.

Public Broadcasting Service. "People & Events: Carter's 'Crisis in Confidence' Speech." Accessed May 6, 2010. http://www.pbs.org/wgbh/amex/carter/peopleevents/e_malaise.html.

Ragsdale, Lyn. *Vital Statistics on the Presidency: Washington to Clinton*. Washington, DC: CQ Press.

Reagan, Ronald. "Address to the Nation on the Iran Arms and Contra Aid Controversy." November 13, 1986. Accessed January 5, 2010. http://www.presidency.ucsb.edu/ws/index.php?pid = 36728&st = &st1.

———. *An American Life*. New York: Simon & Schuster, 1990.

———. "Appointment of Frank C. Carlucci as Assistant to the President for National Security Affairs." December 2, 1986. Accessed January 5, 2010. http://www.presidency.ucsb.edu/ws/index.php?pid = 36773&st = &st1.

———. "Appointment of Three Members of the Special Review Board for the National Security Council." November 26, 1986. Accessed January 5, 2010. http://www.presidency.ucsb.edu/ws/index.php?pid = 36763&st = &st1.

———. "Proclamation 5595—Imposition of Temporary Surcharge on Imports of Certain Softwood Lumber Products from Canada." December 30, 1986. Accessed January 5, 2010. http://www.presidency.ucsb.edu/ws/index.php?pid = 36843&st = &st1.

———. "Remarks Announcing the Review of the National Security Council's Role in the Iran Arms and Contra Aid Controversy." November 25, 1986. Accessed January 5, 2010. http://www.presidency.ucsb.edu/ws/index.php?pid = 36761&st = &st1.

———. "Statement on Signing the Bill to Increase the Federal Debt Ceiling." September 29, 1987. Accessed January 5, 2010. http://www.presidency.ucsb.edu/ws/index.php?pid = 33467&st = &st1.

———. "Statement on Signing the Federal Triangle Development Act." August 22, 1987. Accessed January 5, 2010. http://www.presidency.ucsb.edu/ws/index.php?pid = 34731&st = &st1.

Reedy, George. *Lyndon Johnson: A Memoir*. New York: Andrews and McMeel, 1982.

"Remarks by Senator Edward M. Kennedy." John F. Kennedy Presidential Library and Museum, May 21, 2001. Accessed January 26, 2010. http://www.jfklibrary.org/Education+and+Public+Programs/Profile+in+Courage+Award/Award+Recipients/Gerald+Ford/Remarks+by+Senator+Edward+M.+Kennedy.htm.

Rockman, Bert, and Richard Waterman. *Presidential Leadership: The Vortex of Power*. New York: Oxford University Press, 2007.

Roeberds, Stephen C. "Sex, Money and Deceit: Incumbent Scandals in U.S. House and Senate Elections, 1974–1990." PhD diss., University of Missouri–St. Louis, 1997.

Ronald Reagan Presidential Library. "Chronology of Ronald Reagan's Presidency, 1981–89." Accessed March 1, 2012. http://www.reagan.utexas.edu/archives/reference/preschrono.html.

Roper, Jon. *The American Presidents: Heroic Leadership from Kennedy to Clinton.* New York: Routledge, 2000.

Rosenberg, Morton. "Presidential Claims of Executive Privilege: History, Law, Practice, and Recent Developments." In *CRS Report for Congress*, CRS-37. Washington, DC: Congressional Research Service, 1998.

Rozell, Mark. *Executive Privilege: The Dilemma of Secrecy and Democratic Accountability.* Baltimore: Johns Hopkins University Press, 1994.

Schulman, Bruce J. *Lyndon Johnson and American Liberalism: A Brief Biography with Documents.* New York: Bedford/St. Martins, 1995.

Schultz, Jeffrey. *Presidential Scandals.* Washington, DC: CQ Press, 2000.

Scigliano, Robert. "The President's 'Prerogative Power.'" In *Inventing the American Presidency*, edited by Thomas Cronin, 236–258. Lawrence: University Press of Kansas, 1989.

Shapiro, Robert Y., Martha Joynt Kumar, and Lawrence R. Jacobs, eds. *Presidential Power: Forging the Presidency for the Twenty-first Century.* New York: Columbia University Press, 2000.

Simonton, Dean Keith. *Why Presidents Succeed: A Psychology of Leadership.* New Haven, CT: Yale University Press, 1987.

Sinclair, Barbara. "The President as Legislative Leader." In *The Clinton Legacy*, edited by Colin Campbell and Bert A. Rockman, 70–95. New York: Chatham House, 2000.

Skowronek, Stephen. *Presidential Leadership in Political Time: Reprise and Reappraisal.* Lawrence: University Press of Kansas, 2008.

Smith, Craig Allen. "Bill Clinton in Rhetorical Crisis: The Six Stages of Scandal and Impeachment." In *Images, Scandal, and Communication Strategies of the Clinton Presidency*, edited by Robert E. Denton, Jr. and Rachel L. Holloway, 173–193. Westport, CT: Praeger, 2003.

Smith, James T. "The Institutionalization of Politics by Scandal and the Effect on the American View of Government." PhD diss., University of Nebraska, 2002.

Sorenson, Dale. "The Language of a Cold Warrior: A Content Analysis of Harry Truman's Public Statements." *Social Science History* 3 (Winter 1979): 172.

Sperlich, Peter. "Bargaining and Overload: An Essay on *Presidential Power*." In *Perspectives on the Presidency*, edited by Aaron Wildavsky, 406–430. Boston: Little Brown, 1975.

Spitzer, Robert. "Presidential Prerogative Power: The Case of the Bush Administration and Legislative Power." *PS: Political Science and Politics* 24 (March 1991): 38–42.

———. *The Presidential Veto*. Albany: SUNY Press, 1988.

Taft, William Howard. *Our Chief Magistrate and His Powers*. New York: Columbia University Press, 1916.

Tatalovich, Raymond, and Thomas S. Engeman. *The Presidency and Political Science*. Baltimore: Johns Hopkins University Press, 2003.

Tempas, Kathleen Dunn. *The Veto-Free Presidency: George W. Bush (2001–Present)*. Brookings Governance Studies #4 (July 2006). Washington, DC: Brookings Institution, 2006.

Thomas, George. "As Far as Republican Principles Will Admit: Presidential Prerogative and Constitutional Government." *Presidential Studies Quarterly* 30 (September 2000): 534–552.

Thompson, John B. *Political Scandal: Power and Visibility in the Media Age*. Cambridge: Polity Press, 2000.

Trager, Oliver, ed. *The Iran-Contra Arms Scandal: Foreign Policy Disaster*. New York: Facts on File, 1988.

Truman, Harry. "Address Before the National Association for the Advancement of Colored People." June 29, 1947. Accessed January 3, 2011. http://www.presidency.ucsb.edu/ws/index.php?pid = 12686& st = &st1 = .

———. "The President's News Conference." August 5, 1948. Accessed January 3, 2011. http://www.presidency.ucsb.edu/ws/index.php?pid = 12973&st = &st1 = .

———. "Special Message to the Congress on Greece and Turkey." March 12, 1947. Accessed January 3, 2011. http://www.presidency.ucsb.edu/ws/index.php?pid = 12846&st = &st1 = .

Unger, Irwin, and Debi Unger. *LBJ: A Life*. New York: John Wiley & Sons, 1999.

U.S. Department of State. "Report of the Accountability Review Boards: Bombings of the US Embassies in Nairobi, Kenya and Dar es Salaam, Tanzania on August 7, 1998." Accessed January 23, 2010. http://www.state.gov/www/regions/africa/board_overview.html.

"US Senate to Reconsider Immigration Reform Next Week." *VOA News*, June 23, 2007. Accessed February 25, 2011. http://www.voanews.com/english/news/a-13-2007-06-23-voa21-66560197.html.

Waldman, Michael. *POTUS Speaks: Finding the Words that Defined the Clinton Presidency*. New York: Simon & Schuster, 2000.

Wallison, Peter J. *Ronald Reagan: The Power of Conviction and the Success of His Presidency*. Boulder, CO: Westview, 2003.

Warshaw, Shirley Anne. *Presidential Profiles: The Clinton Years*. New York: Facts on File, 2004.

Wegge, David G. "Neustadt's *Presidential Power*: The Test of Time and Empirical Research on the Presidency." *Presidential Studies Quarterly* 11 (Summer 1981): 342–347.

Werth, Barry. *31 Days*. New York: Doubleday, 2006.

Wildavsky, Aaron. "The Two Presidencies." *Society* 4 (December 1966): 7–14.

Woods, Randall B. *LBJ: Architect of American Ambition*. New York: Free Press, 2006.

Woodward, Bob. *The War Within: A Secret White House History, 2006–2008*. New York: Simon & Schuster, 2008.

Woodward, Bob, and Carl Bernstein. "GOP Security Aide Among Five Arrested in Bugging Affair." *Washington Post*, June 19, 1972. Accessed June 23, 2012. http://www.washingtonpost.com/wp-srv/national/longterm/watergate/articles/061972-1.htm.

INDEX

ABOUT THE AUTHORS

Ryan J. Barilleaux is Paul Rejai Professor of Political Science at Miami University, Oxford, Ohio. He holds an MA and PhD from the University of Texas at Austin and a BA (summa cum laude) from the University of Southwestern Louisiana. Dr. Barilleaux is the author or editor of nine previous books, including *The Post-Modern Presidency*, *Power and Prudence: The Presidency of George H.W. Bush*, and *The Unitary Executive and the Modern Presidency*, as well as over thirty articles and book chapters on the presidency and other aspects of politics. He was chair of the Department of Political Science at Miami University from 2001 to 2009 and was also an aide in the United States Senate.

Jewerl Maxwell is Associate Dean of the Center for Lifelong Learning and an assistant professor of political science at Cedarville University. He holds an MA and PhD from Miami University, and a BA (summa cum laude) in history, political science, and public affairs from Muskingum University. Dr. Maxwell teaches courses in the American presidency and constitutional law. His previous research focused on the use of executive orders and civil rights policy.

CPSIA information can be obtained at www.ICGtesting.com
Printed in the USA
BVOW012214240912

301259BV00001B/1/P